Social Problems in the UK

Social Problems in the UK: An Introduction contextualises the most pressing social problems of our times drawing upon the disciplines of sociology, social policy, education studies and health studies. This much-needed textbook brings together a comprehensive range of expertise in the applied social sciences to discuss the social myths and moral panics that surround many popular debates. This is an accessible text that carefully guides students through the methodology of social construction and related theories to introduce key topics in the areas of:

- 'Race' and ethnicity
- The future of work
- Poverty and homelessness
- Inequalities in education
- Health, public health and mental health
- Ageing and the 'third age'

This completely revised and up-to-date second edition covers the most urgent social issues facing the UK today, including an analysis of the Black Lives Matter movement, the COVID-19 health crisis and the new 'gig' economy. The second edition maintains the accessible style and easy-to-read format of the first edition, integrated with *Key Points* and *Further Reading* elements to further aid student learning. Situated firmly in the new post-pandemic, post-Brexit world, this text contains new chapters on all the most pressing questions raised in the media and in public debates. It will help readers understand the background and broader context of the UK's key social problems.

Stuart Isaacs is a senior lecturer in the social sciences at the University of West London. He is the contributing editor of *European Social Problems* (2017) and *Social Problems in the UK: An Introduction* (2015). He is also co-author of *Contemporary Political Theorists in Context* (2009) and *Political Theorists in Context* (2004), as well as the sole author of *The Politics and Philosophy of Michael Oakeshott* (2006), all published by Routledge. His research interests are in political and social theory.

Social Problems in the UK

An Introduction

Second Edition

Edited by Stuart Isaacs

Routledge
Taylor & Francis Group

LONDON AND NEW YORK

Second edition published 2021
by Routledge
2 Park Square, Milton Park, Abingdon, Oxon, OX14 4RN

and by Routledge
52 Vanderbilt Avenue, New York, NY 10017

Routledge is an imprint of the Taylor & Francis Group, an informa business

© 2021 selection and editorial matter, Stuart Isaacs; individual chapters, the contributors

The right of Stuart Isaacs to be identified as the author of the editorial material, and of the authors for their individual chapters, has been asserted in accordance with sections 77 and 78 of the Copyright, Designs and Patents Act 1988.

First edition published by Routledge 2015

British Library Cataloguing-in-Publication Data
A catalogue record for this book is available from the British Library

Library of Congress Cataloging-in-Publication Data
A catalog record has been requested for this book

ISBN: 978-0-367-40431-4 (hbk)
ISBN: 978-0-367-40432-1 (pbk)
ISBN: 978-0-429-35612-4 (ebk)

Typeset in Scala
by Apex CoVantage, LLC

Contents

Illustrations

Tables

Figures

Contributors

Sandra Abegglen is an education researcher at the University of Calgary, Canada. She is co-editor of *Understanding Education and Economics: Key Debates and Critical Perspectives* (2020) and *Global University, Local Issues* (2020). Her research interests are in the areas of education, peer-to-peer learning, mentoring, identity, visual narratives and qualitative research methods.

David Blundell worked as a primary school teacher and then taught education students at South Bank and North London universities. David established community sport clubs with young people in Hackney before joining London Metropolitan University as Principal Lecturer in the School of Social Sciences in 2006. He has recently retired but remains active in the field.

Jessie Bustillos is Senior Lecturer in Education Studies at London Metropolitan University. She currently focuses on the intersections between sociological theory, educational and social policy and contemporary issues in education. She is co-editor of *Understanding Education and Economics: Key Debates and Critical Perspectives* and co-author of *Universal Basic Income*, both published by Routledge. She has also written on social problems, gender studies, new media and youth cultures online. She is interested in feminist theory and looking at the theoretical, philosophical and sociological intersections between education, culture and new technologies.

Anne Foley is an academic liaison librarian and has worked with students and staff in the Faculty of Applied Social Sciences and Humanities at London Metropolitan University for several years. Her research interests are in the areas of information literacy, digital literacy, problem-based learning and learning transfer.

Norman Ginsburg has been Professor of Social Policy (Emeritus since 2018) at London Metropolitan University since 1996. He has researched and published across a range of topics, including housing, urban regeneration, racism, migration, globalisation, political economy of welfare and cross-national social policy analysis. He has been a member of the editorial collective of the journal *Critical Social Policy* since it started in 1980.

William Lez Henry was born in the London borough of Lewisham of Jamaican parentage and is a professor in the School of Human and Social Sciences at the University of West London. He is also known as the British reggae deejay Lezlee Lyrix. He is a writer, poet and community activist who is renowned as a first-rate public speaker and has lectured nationally and internationally and been featured in numerous documentaries and current affairs television and radio programmes.

Brian McDonough is Course Leader of Sociology at Solent University and teaches a number of sociological topics, including social inequalities and applied sociology in the community. His research interests include work, expertise and the use of information and communication technologies in the workplace. He is a co-author of *Universal Basic Income* (2020, Routledge), sole author of *Flying Aeroplanes and Other Sociological Tales* (2020, Routledge) and has written various book chapters and articles on precarious work and unemployment in Europe.

Jane Thomas is Senior Lecturer in Public Health at the University of Brighton. Her research interests include workplace health, health service privatisation and public control of the determinants of health.

Sean Tunney is a Principal Lecturer in Journalism at the University of Roehampton. His research interests include health communications, business journalism and the politics of media policy making in the UK.

Salim Vohra is a Senior Lecturer in Public Health at the University of West London. He founded the public health consultancy Public Health by Design and was Director of the Centre for Health Impact Assessment at the Institute of Occupational Medicine between 2007 and 2013. Salim is an expert in the applied science of Health Impact Assessment (HIA) and an internationally recognised HIA consultant, researcher and teacher.

chapter 1

Introduction to the second edition

Stuart Isaacs

It has been five years since the first edition of this text was written. Many of the issues discussed in that first introductory text persist, such as poverty, homelessness, youth gangs and organised crime. You might think that it would be surprising if these social problems were 'solved', and you would be right. As we set out in the first edition of the book, we investigated social problems not so much to rid society of them (although this would have been wonderful) but simply to understand them better. Rather than discovering the hidden alchemy that might transform social ills, the aim of a textbook like this is merely to highlight some of society's key contemporary social issues so that we might not make uninformed statements about the problems themselves. Our current prime minister in the UK, Boris Johnson, is very fond of quoting Latin phrases. One such expression he has used on more than one occasion, to the slight bewilderment of the interviewer, is a well-known maxim for classical scholars, *ignoratio elenchi*, meaning arguing to the wrong point. Now you might not think of Mr. Johnson as a great social scientist, and he may not think of himself as one either, but the fact is that this is a great phrase for understanding what we are doing, not only in understanding social problems but also in general as social scientists. In exploring some of the most pressing social issues our society faces, we should not be so arrogant as to think that we can completely solve them. What we are trying to do is to make sure that the basis of our understanding of the problem is as reasonable and based on as much evidence as possible. That is, it is founded on solid social research, qualitative and quantitative methods, theory and reasoned argument.

The purpose of this second edition of *Social Problems in the UK: An Introduction* is then to continue to help students think about the character of contemporary social problems in Britain and, most importantly, to engage you in thinking about how you begin to approach their study as social scientists. Whether you are studying sociology, criminology, education studies, youth studies or whatever, this book is designed to provoke you and make you reflect on the appropriate methodological manner to explore a range of social phenomena. In addition, even though our aim might be one of tentative exploration and building the foundations of knowledge and method, it does not mean that we must do this without a framework of constructive critique. The approach that you will find in this textbook feeds into broader perspectives about social inequalities and social justice. The very choice of subjects and the emphasis of the subjects chosen insist on this. Many of the social issues here cannot be ring-fenced away from pressing political and ideological arguments. One of the features of a social problems approach to social inequalities and social injustice that students enjoy the most is that it engages them in passionate debates. Debates about things that matter, like the Black Lives Matter movement, that are happening now and that will affect your lives. This text is no dry academic book, we hope. It will fill you with the desire to follow up with further research and maybe even propel you into activism around social concerns that impact you or those around you.

Social Problems in the UK: An Introduction, 2nd edition maintains the style and pedagogic approach laid out in the first text. A key motivation for this book continues to be to bring teaching to the page. That is, to be an accessible study aid to students that introduces them to applying a methodological perspective to familiar issues. You will find within these pages a great deal of pedagogic content. Rather than relating reams of quantitative material in relation to each of the social problems, accessible narratives, coursework questions and further readings are used to direct the student to sources that will help them keep up to date. At the end of each chapter, there are key points to help students understand the main issues and aid revision.

The book opens in Chapter 2 with a general methodological and theoretical chapter on understanding and defining social problems. This chapter introduces students to the 'common-sense' view, the social construction approach, and related sociological theories. Practical examples are given whenever possible. This is an on-going feature of the book: to tie theory and practice to guide students towards the applied character of this type of study. The overall purpose of this chapter on definitions and approaches is to try to convey to the student the importance of using methodological and theoretical tools, in an accessible manner.

Stuart Isaacs

Chapter 3 highlights one of the most urgent social problems facing the UK today. The content focuses on the historical reasons that lie behind the Black Lives Matter (BLM) movement. Although the media and public conversation tend to focus on the immediate, it is the role of the social scientist to delve further in order to give context to contemporary issues. This is exactly what Professor William Lez Henry does in this chapter. Here, the internationally renowned author situates the BLM moment in relation to colonialism and its long-lasting legacy. He illustrates why African chattel slavery is distinct to other forms of subjugation and why its affects are still with us today. The chapter provides a fascinating insight and intellectual rigor to many of the day-to-day arguments we hear in the media and all around us.

Chapter 4 concerns issues situated around the topic of health. With the international pandemic still upon us as I write, this is, of course, a timely subject area. However, as the co-authors illustrate, issues around health and the dividing lines that these social problems bring are always with us. This chapter starts by asking the question 'What do we mean by health?' The authors provide a range of definitions and measures of health that have been widely used. They then go on to think about health in a rather surprising manner: as a business. Recognising that health is an important business in the UK is an important part of understanding the types of social problems associated with it. This is because it will affect the level of health service funding it attracts from government as well as from the private sector. As might be expected in a textbook of this type, these social aspects of health are further explored. Poverty, poor housing conditions and a range of social factors, including social class, gender and ethnicity, can all impact our health. Arguably the broadest social issue of all is also given time for discussion in this chapter: climate change. How climate change should be dealt with in the context of health is an intriguing and difficult challenge that the authors discuss in some detail. All in all, this chapter throws up some surprising debates about how we think of health and public health in our society and everyday lives.

Chapter 5 follows up some of the issues previously raised related to health. However, Professor Norman Ginsburg's chapter on ageing also brings with it a number of other important discussions beyond social care and ill health. For example, there are many problematic aspects of the ideas of both retirement and a prescribed 'retirement age'. It links to many issues about paid and unpaid work found later in this textbook (see later in this chapter), as well as the deservingness or otherwise of being able to retire on a decent pension. Professor Ginsburg argues that the current situation of retired people seems to solidify and strengthen inequalities of 'race', class and gender in the labour market and across society as a whole. In addition, another dimension of the discourse around ageing as a social problem looked at here is in terms of intergenerational injustice. It is sometime suggested that older people, having benefited from secure employment and the welfare state in the post-war decades, are now kicking the ladder behind them, leaving younger people to face a much more precarious job market and a meaner welfare state. Retired people enjoy 'third age' consumerism at the expense of the generations behind them. This argument implies that there should be a redistribution of resources from older people to those of 'working age'. On this issue, Professor Ginsburg maintains that in actuality this picture of old age and the conflict between the generations is not only over-simplified but can also be potentially harmful for us all.

At the other end of the age spectrum, in Chapter 6, Jessie Bustillos and Sandra Abegglen undertake an inquiry into inequalities in education. They attempt to disentangle some of the many issues in the realms of gender, 'race' and social class in education. The chapter explores some of the growing patterns of inequality that have characterised schooling in the UK. This is broken down into three main sections. First, a section in which gender equity issues in schools are outlined and interrogated. The authors look at feminist concerns and ask whether or not we are now in a post-feminist educational era. Second, issues of 'race' and education are discussed in relation to the work of 'critical race theorists' Gillborn and Youdell. Finally, the work of recently retired, internationally renowned Professor Stephen Ball will be drawn upon to illustrate a range of issues around social class and educational opportunity.

The qualitative and quantitative research that is evidenced in the previous chapter is strengthened by this largely theoretical enterprise from Dr. David Blundell. In Chapter 7, on childhood and education, Blundell starts by stating that 'No social group figures as consistently or frequently in the discussion of social problems as do children'. In this way the author points to one of the main ways in which the social construction approach helps us to take one step back from common-sense arguments. Blundell insightfully pieces together how it is that 'the child' is constituted in various ways by us: as parents, teachers and members of civil society. As he points out, these constructions of childhood are part of a historical legacy that constitutes powerful ideological assumptions which underlie many current education policies. Blundell explores the impact this has on young people themselves as well as the wider policy implications. He argues that children are overly burdened as a source of hope in the search for solutions to many social problems. It is in the system of education and the institutions of schooling that many issues of social concern are presumed to be 'solvable'. This includes not only educational achievement but also the future of the UK's economic success, health problems, issues relating to social cohesion and crime. Fundamentally, then, this chapter explores where our ideas about children and childhood come from and why childhood and education have become so closely identified as means to solve society's 'ills'.

Stuart Isaacs

McDonough's chapter, Chapter 8 on work, is probably the most revised chapter of all those that remain from the first edition of this book. This says a great deal about the way that the character and experience of work has changed. Of course, part of this is due to the response to COVID-19, but by no means do all these changes relate only to the pandemic. Issues such as the widening of the 'gig' economy and a greater precariousness of job security are part of longer-term trends, as McDonough points out. So, too, are some of the solutions to the social problems associated with the lack of work and income relatively new. In particular, the concept of a universal basic income, in which everyone from a certain age receives a payment from the state to live on, is discussed here. Although this is not a very new idea, its legitimacy is. Whereas once this notion was seen to be at the margins of 'real politics', increasingly, there are pilot studies across the globe and in the UK experimenting with this seemingly radical notion. This issue and other contemporary ideas about how to solve unemployment and a lack of a regular income are explored in this fascinating chapter.

In keeping with the rest of the book, Chapter 9 examines the social construction of poverty. Isaacs argues that debates about poverty often demonise the poor themselves, blaming them for their own circumstances, as well as sometimes wider economic and social welfare failings. The chapter moves on to analyse New Labour's social exclusion policies and apply to the later coalition and Conservative governments. Following this, a case study is undertaken around a discussion of homelessness and its relationship to issues of poverty. Isaacs maintains that, rather than being a social problem for the few, homelessness is a fundamental social issue that affects the whole of society.

The book ends appropriately, in Chapter 10, with Foley's important review of how to research social problems. Foley has worked as an academic librarian in the social sciences for a number of years. She understands the difficulties students face in this respect, particularly first-year students new to undergraduate study. Students often struggle simply because they are not aware of the resources available or how to use them. Here, Foley carefully sets out how students can use their library's tools to locate and then evaluate what materials they need. This is done here with examples that draw from the type of social sciences literature that students will need to engage with. Common problems addressed in this chapter include the confusion that often arises about journals and journal articles, citing and referencing sources, plagiarism and how to transfer the skills learned when researching one area to researching another. It is hoped that teaching staff may also find this chapter useful as a ready-made resource to guide their students when they are searching for material.

chapter 2

Understanding and defining social problems

Stuart Isaacs

2.1 Introduction

To engage with social problems is to decide to think about issues that affect millions of people. Most of us have already had some kind of experience with these issues. This might be from a distance: for example, seeing a rough sleeper on the street. Or it could be more personal, as someone who has been homeless. Social problems are, unfortunately, part of all our problems. To illustrate this, we can start by understanding their relationship to other types of problems: namely, individual, economic and political problems.

When you wake up not wanting to go to school or college or work, this may be because you are hungover or want to avoid someone or simply because you're feeling drained. This is a problem for you, but it is not a social problem. Not unless what you were going to do was of national importance!

Individual difficulties to do with personal trauma, psychological conditions, relationship problems, financial troubles and other such private concerns are not in themselves social problems. But they could be, if looked at from a broader, more generalised social context. Psychological issues would normally fall outside the remit of social problems. But if any of the personal problems listed here were in some way tied to poverty,

Stuart Isaacs

homelessness, social exclusion, racism, sexism, homophobia, unemployment, lack of educational achievement and so on, then they could be brought into an analysis of social problems.

Overall, we can maintain that social problems may be differentiated from individual problems, except where they form part of a collective issue.

Social problems ought also to be distinguished from economic problems. There is a commonplace view that all political and social issues are reducible to questions of resources and money. If this were the case, then all we would have to do to alleviate illness or crime would be to find the right economic model to use for the National Health Service (NHS) or the police force. But this would be a rather ahistorical understanding and one that lacked sociological knowledge. Most social problems have existed for some time. They have a history to them. A range of government policies have usually already been tried, giving rise to a complex array of bureaucratic and organisational structures. For example, policies regarding immigration are tied to a long history of immigration acts that span the twentieth century and into our own age. This complex set of laws has spawned central and local government agencies, incorporating UK visas and immigration and the border force through to small refugee help centers. Economic models alone cannot help us analyse how these organisations work, how policy is implemented within them and their own histories. The organisations and agencies that address social problems through policy making and implementation cannot be analysed from a purely economic point of view. Nor can economic models help us understand the social attitudes that have already grown around these issues. Since the first wave of post-war migrants came to the UK, a varied range of social attitudes towards immigration can be observed. These attitudes span inclusive and sympathetic discourses through to outright hostility and racism. Economics may well be a part of some of these attitudes, such as the argument that immigrants are a burden on the welfare system. But economic ideas alone cannot help us interpret these opinions, assumptions or actions. Furthermore, the success or otherwise of integrationist policies or the work of organisations helping new immigrants is not solely reliant on what resources they have. It will be a matter of policy strategies, wider social circumstances and acceptability, as well as how each individual project is implemented on the ground.

Economic issues, such as the unequal distribution of wealth, may well be part of a discussion of social problems. But social problems are by no means determined by economics alone.

When it comes to distinguishing social problems from political problems, this is a much more difficult task. If we think, for the moment, of political issues as only those that government is concerned with, then a distinction is straightforward. Some social problems may be publicly debated as on-going issues, such as drug abuse. However, they may not necessarily impress themselves upon government to act, even where public debate is clearly evident. In this sense, if we are thinking of politics as only what government does, social problems may be distinguished from political problems.

There is, however, only a very minimal definition of politics underlying this argument. To reduce politics to merely central or local government activity would be to de-politicise the very idea. Politics is conventionally defined as involving the participation of citizens in debates about public issues. Ideology, power relations, conflict and the struggle over rights are one side of this public dialogue. Compromise, tolerance and responsibility are the other side. Politics is about debating rights and wrongs, justice and injustice, the good life and the bad. In this sense, exploring social problems is, arguably, one of the most politicised areas of debate in the social sciences as it involves making judgements about social rights and social wrongs.

Social problems may be distinguished from political problems in that government might not always be involved in acting on an issue that is publicly debated. But social problems are inherently political in that they are debates about the kind of society that we believe is just.

2.2 The private sphere and the public sphere

Like all concepts in the social sciences, there are no transparent or fixed boundaries to what may or may not be a social problem. We have already seen that although individual, economic and political problems may be distinguished from a social problem, we cannot entirely discount them from our definition. This is not to say that there are no parameters at all. There are. But they are not simply given or self-evident. There is no national authority that determines that this or that is a social problem, and everyone must agree. If there were, it would make studying the subject much easier! What we must do in the absence of an absolute authority is make a case: construct a reasonable definition and argument.

For Mills, the main task of social research was to investigate how our personal troubles are often tied to wider social problems. Through the collection of empirical material and by applying social theory, the role of the social scientist was to uncover the broader, collective social factors that underlay individual problems. See his famous book, *The Sociological Imagination* (1959), for these ideas.

To make a case we have a whole history of debate about concepts in the social sciences to help us. We do not have to start from scratch. Thankfully, many great minds have taken it upon themselves to do a lot

Stuart Isaacs

of the work for us. C. Wright Mills, one of the most well-known social thinkers of the twentieth century, famously made a distinction between 'personal troubles' and 'public interest' to define a social concern. For our purposes we can take this as meaning that to be a social problem, an issue must move from being private to public.

These two categories of our practical lives are often understood as the 'private sphere' and the 'public sphere'. Traditionally, in liberal democracies like the UK, the private sphere is where the state leaves us alone. It is where we interact with our families and choose our friends. It may also be where we pursue a hobby or interest or passion. Romantic love is arguably the most intense of our experiences in the private sphere when we are most completely wrapped up in just one other individual and ourselves. Hannah Arendt (1958: 242) has argued that we are in our most private state when we are in love. If we have a lovers' tiff, no one else is interested, and it affects very few people. (Although, as we shall see, scale does not necessarily help us define a social problem.)

On the other hand, the public sphere is where we are known by strangers, students in the class, shopkeepers, parents at our child's school, in political or community organisations. Most commonly we are in the public sphere when we are doing our job, and this is often the most widely known aspect of our identities.

When a concern is discussed in the public sphere, it becomes located in the broad territory where we find social problems. These might be issues that are timely and capture the public imagination for a short period. What are sometimes called 'moral panics' occasionally break out, for example, over the behaviour of teenagers and young people. Or they might be social problems which are on-going from generation to generation, such as debates about poverty.

2.3 How do social problems emerge?

Social problems are, then, issues that arise in the public sphere and become the site for general debate. The obvious next question is 'How do these issues emerge?'

The first thing to dismiss is that social problems become a public concern because of the *scale* of the problem: that is, because a large number of people might be directly affected. If they did, we would not be concerned with drug addicts or asylum seekers or many other relatively small groups of people. Rough sleepers, for example, account for only a fraction of the overall number of people who are homeless. In 2011 the homeless campaigning organisation and charity Crisis estimated that 2,181 people were sleeping rough during a single night in England. Yet a huge amount of government resources, paid and voluntary workers and charity organisations are involved in trying to alleviate the problem of rough sleeping. This group are also often the focal point for media reporting, documentaries and discussion. If you look at videos about homelessness on YouTube, almost all of them cover rough sleepers, rather than the millions of people who are not sleeping rough but are still homeless.

If it is not scale that gives rise to a social problem, then what is it?

Social problems come and go for a variety of immediate, contemporary reasons: as a result of government policy, because of a newsworthy event or due to a noticeable social change. There is no end to the number of reasons a particular issue becomes a debate in the public sphere, and there will always be an incalculable number of them at the same time.

On the whole, there will never be just one single reason why a social problem emerges; a number of factors tend to come together to highlight a problem. No one cause is ever at play. Rather like a major accident, there is never one factor that leads to the incident but a whole host of causes that happen to collide at a particular moment. Poverty, for example, might become a high-profile issue not because it has ever gone away, but because it is highlighted by prominent public figures. These figures may have been speaking on the issue for years, but their voices are heard because there may be an economic downturn. This might coincide with new statistical evidence or a widely publicised report of increased poverty, as well as a growing perception that life is simply harder. Watching human-interest stories on the TV about struggling families might add to this. All these factors – publicity, wider political or economic circumstances, people's perceptions and media coverage – might collide to establish the prominence of a particular social problem.

The immediate reasons a social problem emerges may not have anything to do with it being new or having returned. Like death and taxes, most social problems are always with us, or at least with us for a very long time. There will be immediate causes such as the ones given here that we can identify to help us understand this. However, the fact that social problems persist over time means that we can associate their emergence not just with immediate causes but with our social structures.

In the social sciences, social structures are understood as the fundamental organisational features of our society. Society is made up of social institutions that create social structures; if it were not, then there could not be a 'society', as such. The social institutions and social structures that are most identified are the family, the education system, the type of socio-economic stratification, cultural practices, the state and the legal system. These are the bedrock of our social realm. They consist of repeated patterns of organisation and behaviour that make society identifiable. If we

Stuart Isaacs

think of social problems in relation to social structures (rather than as a collection of discrete individual behaviours), then we can come to appreciate that social problems emerge because they are part of the on-going examination of the most important social institutions that make up our social world.

If we take what might appear as a relatively new social problem, that of anti-social behaviour, and look at it in this way, we find that although the language surrounding anti-social behaviour is new, the issue is not. The term *anti-social behaviour* really only became widely used to denote a type of harassment against individuals in the 1990s. This culminated in the first legislation to prevent it in 1998, the centrepiece being the notorious Anti-Social Behaviour Orders or ASBOs. On the surface of it, anti-social behaviour became a public concern because it was associated with a new form of persistent, aggravated attacks on individuals. In other words, it was quite frightening because it highlighted how vulnerable we were as individuals or defenceless families. But if we think about the issue in relation to social structures, we can argue that it emerged as a social problem because it also fed into various fears about the changing character of the family. A great deal of the debate surrounding anti-social behaviour was associated with the state of the family. Public concern was as much about anti-social behaviour being a symptom of family breakdown, too many single-parent families, lack of family guidance or childhood poverty as about the individual incidents themselves.

The point here is that social problems emerge because they appear to carry a threat to the stability of our social institutions and structures. Underlying public concern with anti-social behaviour is a fundamental anxiety about the threat to what is perceived as a normal model of the family. Competing arguments about anti-social behaviour tend to have at their core differing ideas about the desirable make-up of contemporary family life.

We can maintain from this discussion that social problems emerge from a variety of different immediate and contemporary causes which bring them to public attention. But they do so only because, underlying these particular timely events, social problems are part of the ever-present social dialogue about the character of our most important social structures.

2.4 Threat and perception

In a limited investigation, such as in your college essay, it may not be possible to trace every social problem back to its historical construction in fine detail. Nor to address every aspect of the relationship between social structures and social problems. However, both these features are important and should be recognised in any analysis, great or small.

Another feature that should also be ever present is an investigation into the extent to which the social problem is perceived as a threat. This ought to be undertaken in terms of any immediate and explicit threat, as well as one that may be implicit in its relationship to social structures. At stake here is not whether the problem is 'real', as such, but how it might be taken as potentially harmful to social stability or social values or norms.

There is no need to enter into a philosophical debate about whether the problem really exists. If social problems were about scale, we might be able to do this. Then we could use a purely quantitative measure – using statistics and factual data – to say whether it was real in this empirical sense. Yet even this would be difficult as there would be differences of opinion about what number of people an issue had to affect before it became 'real'.

Fortunately, we do not need to get into such complex debates. Social problems are defined by our perception of them and the degree to which they are understood as a threat in different ways by different social groups.

Facts and figures may inform us about the extent of a social problem, but they are not sufficient to create a convincing case of what issues are the most urgent.

Statistics may, for example, inform us how many people are unemployed and how this might compare to the previous year or decade. The collection of factual information might tell us that a great many of the unemployed are young people, are from a particular minority ethnic group or are physically impaired. But the figures alone cannot tell us *why* this is the case. They require interpretation and sociological explanations.

Sociological research involves trying to understand people's perceptions and assumptions, not only from measurable data but by drawing from a normative position and a selected theoretical framework. When we look at unemployment, we want to know not only how many and who but also if the trends relate to, say, inequalities or social injustice. Is high unemployment among certain minority ethnic groups due to racism? Are so many young people unemployed because of government policy? Is there enough support for disabled people in the workplace?

These are questions that can be addressed only through social research and investigation using a methodology, theory and quantitative and qualitative methods.

Of course, perceptions of a social problem will differ. Social scientists collate these views and come up with perspectives which they attribute to different social groups. These perspectives are knowingly generalised and 'ideal'. This means that social scientists understand that it is impossible to transfer the opinions expressed by discrete individuals in their practical lives and package them up into neat little parcels of absolutely accurate views. As soon as you start to take society as an object of study, you change it. The inevitable act of generalising individual opinions into

Stuart Isaacs

social attitudes turns what is concrete in our experience into something abstract. Sociological concepts cannot capture the infinite refinements of every individual's thoughts. However, in order to be able to say something worthwhile, it is possible, through good quantitative and qualitative research, to bring together a convincing, coherent argument that reflects, in a general way, the observed opinions held by specific social groups. When social scientists construct perspectives on social problems, they mainly do so not under the misguided belief that they are 'real', in the sense that they completely and transparently transmit the views held by individuals in practical experience, but that they are constructs or 'ideal types'. These are models, used for the purposes of comparison and analysis and to help us make sense of the observed discourses in practical experience.

Weber (1864–1920) is one of the so-called founding fathers of sociology. His notion of ideal types is important to grasp in order to understand what it is we are doing when we investigate a social problem. Weber argued that social scientists gather related social phenomena under one heading. This makes possible generalised, meaningful statements about the world. So it is that when we talk of 'capitalism', everyone understands its general traits, that it is based around a market economy. Weber argued that ideal types were not only useful for important concepts like capitalism but could also be used to understand and interpret emotions and behaviour. It is in all these ways that we use them to investigate social problems. Using social research, we construct generalised categories of social attitudes and attribute them to particular social groups, themselves 'ideal types'. So it is that we might try to argue that there is a conservative perspective on law and order and a liberal one. The attributes of these perspectives would be set out and examples given of the social groups that might represent these views. In this way, what we have to say on crime comes from observed reality but is formed into an artificial, coherent whole for purposes of analysis.

The job of the social scientist is, then, not to record exactly what every individual thinks but to construct an argument that holds together as accurately as possible for particular 'idealised' social groups. It needs to be theoretically consistent and reflect the social views expressed in quantitative and qualitative research.

In the reading that you will undertake for your classes in social problems, you will find that academic authors will present you with various ways of constructing the social problem, using different ideal types abstracted from practical experience. It will be up to you to read these accounts, to understand their arguments and to contrast them. Don't expect these to link together easily. It will be up to you to make the connections. This will be, at the centre, your own analysis of the social problem.

2.5 Methodology

It has been maintained that an enquiry into social problems is not an exact match to the experiences we have of them in our practical lives. Rather, we identify social problems by bringing together general traits of that social experience to construct ideal types. These are categories of social groups and social attitudes that, it can be argued, are significant models that bring together consistent patterns of belief, behaviour and emotions. By establishing these, we can then analyse the way that a social problem is perceived as a threat in different ways by different people.

This method does not rely on scale alone or on other empirical measures to denote a social problem. Nor do we have to get into philosophical debates about the reality or otherwise of the problem. If an argument can be made, this is sufficient for us to identify a social problem and to investigate it.

This open-ended way of defining social problems is an approach that can be associated with a particular methodology, that of social construction, which is discussed next.

In the social sciences, we use a methodology in order to justify the way that we abstract from social experience in order to explain it. A methodology is an overarching way by which to understand a topic. It enables us to analyse everyday circumstances from another point of view: that of the social scientist. There wouldn't be much point in studying at university if we were merely going to replicate everything that we experienced in practical life. Just as barristers have to have points of law at their fingertips to argue a case or a doctor the basics of human biology to make a diagnosis, a social scientist has to have a range of methodologies (and theories) to make sense of the world. This is not to 'cure' society of its social ills, as a doctor might with a patient. Neither is it to find a definitive conclusion or solution, as a court might when a person is found guilty or innocent of a crime. As social scientists, we use methodologies to try to clear some of the mental fog from our everyday thinking, to bring coherence to what appears in experience: what is normally tied to assumptions, emotions, prejudices, kindly thoughts, stereotypes, common-sense generalisations and other unreflective opinions.

When a natural scientist uses water in an experiment, they do not understand it as something to drink. For them it is hydrogen oxide (H_2O), a chemical compound. It is a familiar substance viewed from a different point of view. Similarly, as social scientists, we take the experiences and social groups that are familiar to us but use a different language to make sense of them. If you expected to transplant all the opinions and ideas you already have about society into an essay, you would have the wrong idea of what studying sociology, social policy, criminology and the social sciences

Stuart Isaacs

is all about. Just like any other form of study, looking at social problems should make you stop and think. By coming to university, you create a halting station in your experience, a place where there is a chance to reflect. These topics, of drugs and crime, lone parents, poverty, homelessness, migration, unemployment and so on may be familiar to you. But you are coming to study them in an unfamiliar manner, to learn how to enquire into them through the discipline of the social sciences. While thinking of familiar issues in this way may not replace your existing views, it may refine them or cause you to rethink in a more rigorous, reflective, thought-through way.

Although we might make a comparison between the social sciences and the natural sciences, we can go only so far. As stated earlier, when we discuss social problems, we are making judgements about what is right and wrong. It is impossible, and not even desirable, to try to be totally objective in what we do. We are studying ourselves and the lives of others. We all come loaded with ideas about the social world. We make normative judgements all the time. Judgements about what we feel are the most important principles upon which to base our actions.

A methodology such as social construction helps us use a coherent and reflective method of investigation. At the same time, it allows us to express normative arguments. Debates about social problems can be political, ideological and ethical. But there must be a legitimate way to reach these conclusions. In this sense, for you as students, your conclusions are not the most important part of your work. More important is to make sure that you can illustrate that you understand how to think as a social scientist: how to use methodologies and apply them. As you will see later, you will also need to deploy theory, as well as the right content, to indicate that you know how to use the whole of the 'language' appropriate to investigating social problems.

2.6 Social construction

The methodology that is most suited to an analysis of social problems is that of social construction. This is because it captures most about what we have already said in our search for the meaning of the term *social problem*. Social problems are fluid, not fixed, even though usually tied to historical debates and fundamental aspects of our social institutions and structures. At its heart, social construction maintains that knowledge of the world is a result of the interaction of individuals with their social environment. That environment is made up of family, school, peers, popular culture and sub-cultures, religious belief or non-belief, state institutions and the law. This interaction can be shown to construct a consistency of collective attitudes that is stable enough to translate into perspectives on social problems using qualitative as well as quantitative material.

In this way social problems are constructed in different ways depending on the social position of the groups articulating them. For an asylum seeker given leave to remain in the UK, immigration is certainly a problem. It means dealing with a strange culture, possibly hostility and racism and more than likely dirty, dangerous and difficult jobs. For those we might describe as conservative on immigration, who would like to see strong immigration controls, asylum seekers may be a social problem because they do not easily integrate into the existing culture, because they are perceived as a drain on the welfare system or because they over-extend the population. In different ways these groups, 'asylum seekers' and 'conservatives', construct the problem of immigration very differently. In order to attribute a position to 'asylum seekers' and 'conservatives' in the first place, we would have to precede the arguments we wished to associate with them by drawing them out as appropriate social models or ideal types. We would need to bring together quantitative and qualitative information to express what we meant by asylum seekers. This ought to be fairly straightforward as a great deal of debate has taken place about this particular group.

Fortunately for you, as students, you (usually) don't have to do the primary research yourselves on this or any of the social problems you will come across. The content of your essays will be based on relating the research already undertaken by academics and, in some, cases campaigning groups, charities, media commentators and policy makers. You will take material from academic sources (textbooks, journals), government statements and policy, media reporting and relevant websites.

Although it may seem daunting to use a methodology to study social problems, it is not as difficult as it may at first seem. In the lecture programs and classes that you will have at university, your tutors will highlight the important social groups and the varied social constructions that exist around them. For you as an undergraduate, your job is to bring together this existing material. Remember, you do not have to do the actual constructing yourself! Rather, you need be able to show that you comprehend the underlying methodology and theories at play when analysing social problems, as well as wade through the particular content appropriate to your topic.

2.7 Theory

Each topic you will come across will also involve theory. If, as we have acknowledged, we artificially construct social types ('the working-class', 'asylum seekers', 'a conservative perspective') for the purposes of analysis, we then have to have a way of talking about them which is meaningful.

Stuart Isaacs

This is the 'theory paradox': the categories we work with are subjective ones established through argument that may involve normative and politicised judgements. But we also use quantitative and qualitative research to try to be as objective as possible to have legitimate and significant things to say about contemporary British social problems. We work through this subjective-objective dichotomy by deploying theory. Theory is the conduit for legitimating what we have to say in terms of our subjective arguments and our evidence-based social research.

There are many theories that academics use to unpick the categories constructed from the empirical and qualitative evidence. For example, we may approach the issue of poverty by using a theory of social exclusion, a theory of welfare dependency, a feminist theory, a neoliberal theory, a theory of the underclass and so it may go on. In the reading that you undertake, you will find a whole range of such theories that authors use. In your own work, you can decide which of these theories or collections of them you find persuasive. You do not have to come up with your own theories – not unless you are thinking of starting a PhD!

The theory that you use will always be secondhand. At an undergraduate level of study, it is enough to try to get to grips with other people's theories and to try to nurture your own ability to compare and contrast them. This is the stuff of analysis that so often confuses students. When you compare and contrast various authors' theories, this is analysis. Pointing out conflicting theories is good analysis. You do not necessarily have to say which theories are 'best'. As stated earlier, it is the process of reasoning through arguments, not your conclusions, which is most important at this stage.

2.8 Social research: an example

In order to illustrate further the kind of methods, theories and forms of analysis that you will come across in your studies of social problems, what follows is a brief summary of one particular highly focused piece of social research. This research concerns higher education and minority ethnic students. It is the sort of material you might be guided to read, for example, on the social problem of inequalities relating to some minority ethnic groups and education.

The interview sample group consisted of 30 men and 35 women. There was a wide range of ethnicities: 16 were Jewish, 8 described themselves as Black-British and 7 as mixed race; there were 4 Chinese and a range from different African, West Indian and Asian families. Interviews were also conducted with parents, and a questionnaire was answered by a further 502 students.

From gathering all this research material, the authors argued that there were two ideal types of higher education students among ethnic minority groups in London. These were contingent choosers and embedded choosers. These two categories of students represented, in a general way, the main sets of reasons why minority ethnic students chose particular universities. The authors acknowledged that these were hypothetical divisions, not representing an exact fit of any single individual, but 'a step away from reality' (Ball et al. 2002: 217). However, they maintained that the construction of the problem in this way laid the groundwork for more detailed analysis.

For the contingent choosers, finance was a big issue, and choices were made without much information about or awareness of differences on offer. Because of a lack of a family tradition in higher education, parental support for choices was weak and at a distance. Contingent choosers did see the ethnic mix of the university as a factor in their decision.

For the embedded choosers, finance was not an issue, and choices were based around extensive and diverse sources of information. Parents were heavily involved in the decision making, and there was an embedded cultural practice in the family as to how the choice would be made. The choice of university was based around long-term goals and aspirations. The ethnic mix of the university played almost no part in their decision.

Overall the study found that there was not a white/ethnic minority divide in choosing a university. Even when given as a factor for their choice, ethnic mix was only one variable among many. In fact, the study found that social class and educational achievement were more important factors for student choices. In other words, contingent choosers tended to be from working-class backgrounds (those from families with little or no higher education experience), and ethnic mix was part of a rather vague and unfocused set of criteria that students used. This contrasted with the more middle-class embedded choosers (with a family history of higher education), who were singularly focused on the university's status and how their choice might impact their future careers.

The importance of this study for us is not so much the conclusions of the authors but that it is a very good example of the type of social research you will be reading when you study social problems. From this example we hope that you can see the way in which social scientists construct arguments based on their objective social research and form subjective judgements in the way that they put this research together: in this example, arguing that social class is key.

The research that the authors present also has embedded into it a number of the methodological features we have already discussed. The authors explicitly use 'ideal types' as a way of constructing their two social groups. These 'ideal types' are grounded on sound, quantitative and qualitative research. It will not always be the case in the academic texts that you come across that this will be so explicit, even if it is what is happening. But in this

Stuart Isaacs

study, we can clearly see that a particular social construction of minority ethnic students is taking place. Embedded and contingent choosers are ways of bringing together a range of individuals who come from diverse backgrounds. These categories are based on an accentuation of features that can be legitimately argued to bring them together as sharing collective attitudes.

In this study there are also aspects relating to social institutions and social structures. The conclusion of the research is that family background and social class are more important than ethnicity in relation to choice of university. In this respect, even amongst the contingent choosers, ethnic mix is only one among many factors. This, the authors argued, was a reflection of a working-class background that did not have the necessary knowledge (what is sometimes called 'cultural capital') to understand which factors might be the most important to consider when choosing a university. As we have seen, social class and the family can be considered part of the fabric upon which our society is built. Part, that is, of our social structures and institutions that give rise to social problems when they are challenged.

Finally, theories of 'race' and racism might be said to underlie this issue. This is not an explicit discussion in the research but can be extrapolated as a matter of analysis. Although the study concludes that ethnic mix is not a prominent issue for most students, many of those interviewed stated that they did want a more diverse university, and that was why they were attracted to London. Extrapolating from these comments, it could be argued that further investigation is needed to elicit whether or not this desire for diversity was attached to any kind of perceived threat of racism.

2.9 Newsworthiness

If an area of study is topical, as most of the social problems you come across will be, you may find that during the course of your studies, it will be reported in the media. This is one of the advantages of studying social problems. They are contemporary issues, and you can expect that new material which you can use will arise in at least some of your areas of study. This may be government reports or reports from campaigning organisations, pressure groups or the police authorities. New policy might also be talked about or implemented around your social problem. Or perhaps a new incident occurs: a vicious knife crime, a rise in unemployment among young adults, greater homelessness or some other newsworthy account that triggers a public debate. Although this media reporting may be beneficial to you in providing you with up-to-date material for your coursework, there are also some pitfalls to watch out for with respect to the newsworthiness of social problems.

We must be very careful when looking at the media. We have to be particularly careful about media determinism: that is, stating 'the media says' and assuming that what is read, listened to or watched totally shapes what people think. Given the multimedia environment in which we live, where information is available from a whole range of visual, printed and internet sources, this is a point of view that cannot easily be sustained. If you were doing a media studies course, you would very soon be alerted to the difficulty of translating media opinions into actual effects on attitudes and behaviour (Curran & Seaton 2003: Pt. 4, Ch. 20).

Not least of all this is because each one of us has a distinct social experience. So if you read a newspaper article that implies most lone parents are committing fraud on the benefit system but you have been brought up by a hard-working single mum, you are unlikely to believe this type of reporting.

In some cases, newsworthiness may be an important factor in making an issue a social problem. Famously, the documentary *Cathy Come Home* was viewed by millions of TV viewers in the 1960s. This single programme is credited with having had the enormous effect of raising people's awareness of homelessness. However, the reliability of media presentations of factual information is variable. The way that statistics, government policy or a particular event is reported may not be entirely accurate. A social policy, for example, will tend to be highlighted for what is most sensational or headline grabbing. But this might not be the most important part of that particular policy as far as welfare research is concerned.

It is important to be aware that debates started because they are newsworthy always need to be examined in more detail. Take the case of one social problem that has been debated in the UK over the last few years: the issue of so-called binge drinking among young people. TV programmes have been produced about this, pages of newspaper copy devoted to the revelations and medical experts brought in to discuss the implications for the future health problems of a generation. Yet all the credible research indicates that while the health- and socially related problems of alcohol may be a concern among the under-24s, it is a problem that is more than ten times greater for the affluent and those over 55 (Alcohol Harm Map 2012). Yet there are no sensationalist fly-on-the-wall documentaries made about middle-aged, middle-income drinkers having a bottle or two of wine every evening with their dinner. It wouldn't make for very exciting TV. Yet this is a better image of where these problems lie than the falling-over, puking young people who appear on our small screens.

2.10 Summary

In this chapter we have defined and understood social problems in three main ways: from the point of view of the discipline of social science; from

Stuart Isaacs

the point of view of you, the student; and from the point of view of other social actors.

The understanding of social problems set out here from the point of view of the discipline of social science is that there is no fixed or absolute way of defining the term. When a sociologist or criminologist wants to identify a social problem, they have to do so by arguing their case. This case has to be based on primary research, either their own or that of other academics. The social research will normally involve some statistics or data (quantitative analysis) and some form of collating social attitudes (qualitative analysis). Even though this kind of rigorous academic technique is employed, there is no pretence that the endeavour is without subjective judgements. The reason university lecturers are drawn to research social problems is that they have a social concern; they care passionately about social issues. This may not always reveal itself in the way they write, as the discipline requires a highly tuned technical knowledge and ability. However, even if the writing can sometimes seem dull, academics will always bring something of themselves into their work. Political, social and ethical judgements will be made to state an argument about the social problem that is identified. These arguments have to be sustained in the methodology that they use and the coherence of the theories which they draw upon. Competing arguments have to be engaged with. The whole purpose of the scholarly exploration is to try to genuinely engage with the social evidence, to think through its many different aspects and ultimately construct a point of view. However, the goal is not to 'solve' the problem. This is not something that academics (or anyone) can realistically achieve. All that those working from this disciplinary approach can hope for is to add their voice to public debate.

For you as a student, your job is to read and try to understand the methodologies, theories and social research of social scientists as they apply to various social problems. Through the lecture and seminar programme at your university, you should come to understand that there is a body of literature, written in another language – that of social science – that you need to learn. The topics you come across may be ones that you are familiar with, but the way that you will need to come to think about them will have to be altered if you are to succeed. This is not an easy task. It is not just the descriptive detail of particular topics that a student needs to grapple with; you also have to acquire the tools of the social scientist's trade in order to explain and analyse them. You need to indicate in your coursework that you understand that social problems can be constructed in different ways and that there are competing perspectives but also that there may be similarities that can be identified. And all this in an essay that is usually only around 1,500 to 2,000 words long!

As well as the academic analysis, statements about social problems come from other social actors: politicians, various media, pressure groups,

understanding and defining social problems

campaigning organisations, charities, interested public figures, think-tanks and so on. All these voices may legitimately feature as part of your research. Of all these other sources of commentary, policy content and media coverage will almost always be a part of any analysis. How government policy, past and present, has responded to a social problem will be an important component, and as it is generally newsworthy, there will also tend to be media coverage of social problems. These accounts, from government in terms of policy making or the media in terms of reporting, may not be situated on the same ground as academic concerns. For example, whereas politicians and the popular press might generally emphasise standards in education debates, academics might argue that inequalities and underlying differences in educational achievement are more important. The social construction of the problem by other social actors will generally not be based on such rigorous research material as that used by scholars. Rather, ideology, opinion, prejudice and personal experience will inform these points of view.

 Key points

Social problems are distinct and yet tied to other types of problems

Social problems are a particular way of understanding the social issues that emerge in public life. They may be distinguished from individual problems, which are largely a matter for the private sphere. However, private matters can become public concerns if a collective threat is perceived. Social problems may also be distinguished from economic issues. Economic models and theories cannot explain the historical and sociological reasons for social problems. However, significant economic change can be part of the reason for the emergence of a social problem, such as poverty. Social problems are not necessarily associated with government intervention. But discussing social problems does involve making political judgements about the kind of society we believe is just.

Social problems are contemporary and culturally embedded

Social problems come and go as public discussion shifts. These changes may be tied to what is currently going on in British society, cultural shifts such as greater ethnic diversity or the rise of insecurity

Stuart Isaacs

in the workplace. However, social problems almost always have a history to them. They are connected in some way to on-going debates about key social structures and institutions.

Threat and perception

Identifying social problems cannot be done using a purely empirical measure. The scale of the problem is no indication of its public importance. This means that the significance of a particular social problem becomes a matter of argument and debate. The most convincing arguments are based on social research, in which the assumptions of the author are made explicit.

Social construction

This is the methodological perspective that is most conducive to the study of social problems. Social scientists abstract collective identities from practical experience. To these identities (be they 'asylum seekers', 'lone parents', 'liberals', 'contingent choosers' or whatever) they ascribe particular social attitudes. This is done in order to make meaningful statements about the social world. However, social scientists undertake this task using a clear methodology and theoretical framework. Other social actors (politicians, media commentators, pressure group representatives and so on) tend to do so in a less self-reflective and analytical mode.

The role of social science

As students of criminology, social policy, sociology or any of the social sciences, our task is to try to identify the assumptions built into the discourses surrounding social problems: that is, to attempt to explain the way that the meanings and definitions implied in the language used about certain social groups are loaded with assumptions and to try to construct more rigorous explanations of social problems using the tools of social science. In short, to turn an unexamined social problem into an examined one.

 Coursework questions

How can we define a social problem?
In what ways does social construction help us analyse social problems?
What normative judgements are made when identifying a social problem?

References

Alcohol Harm Map. (2012) 'Age concern'. www.alcoholconcern.org.uk/campaign/alcohol-harm-map

Arendt, H. (1958) *The Human Condition*. Chicago: University of Chicago Press.

Ball, S. J., Reay, D. and David, M. (2003) ' "Ethnic choosing": Minority ethnic students, social class and higher education choice'. *Race Ethnicity and Education* 5(4): 333–357, in *Education Policy and Social Class: The Selected Works of Stephen J. Ball*, London: Routledge, 2002.

Curran, J. and Seaton, J. (2003) *Power Without Responsibility* (6th ed.). London: Routledge.

Mills, C. W. (1959) *The Sociological Imagination*. London: Oxford University Press.

 Further reading

There are very few books that cover the issues discussed in this section; hence, the need for this textbook! There are a great many American texts on social problems. Very few employ an approach that would be compatible to the way the subject is taught in British universities. For example, Kornblum, W. and Julian, J. (2016) *Social Problems*. Boston, MA: Pearson, now in its 15th edition, is heavily situated in an American tradition which is not very helpful for UK social problems. So be aware!

One recent book in the field, although not about the UK, would be great in a comparative analysis. This is the wonderfully interesting text:

Mis, L. (2019) *The Social Problems of the Visegrad Group Countries*. Trnava: University of Tyrnaviensis.

Stuart Isaacs

chapter 3

Black Lives Matter, decolonisation and the legacy of African enslavement

William Lez Henry

3.1 Introduction

> Slavery was not genocide; otherwise, there wouldn't be so many damn blacks in Africa or in Britain, would there? An awful lot of them survived. 'You are not culturally black Africans. You would die in seconds if you were dumped back in black Africa because you wouldn't know how to cope'.
>
> (David Starkey 2 July 2020)

> Replace "slavery" for "the holocaust" and "damn blacks" for "damn Jews" and you'd quite rightly never be allowed in the public eye ever again.
>
> (Twitter response 2 July 2020)

The chapter will argue that to fully appreciate the global groundswell of cross-social, racial, cultural, class and political support for the Black

Lives Matter (BLM) movement in the aftermath of the very public murder of 46-year-old George Floyd by officers from the Minneapolis Police Department in Minnesota, USA, the historical nature of black oppression needs to be considered. This is because many of the conversations that dominate the mainstream news media, particularly in the UK context as in the case of Starkey earlier, at the beginning of this chapter, do not acknowledge the history of racial violence and racial abuse against Europe's perceived others. Moreover, as the second extract explains, he would not dare to make such a public statement with regards to the Jewish Holocaust, the Shoah, and part the argument here is to explain why this is so. However, Starkey has been sacked from one post and quit another for this overly racist outburst, yet the point remains that the horrific, genocidal experience of the Shoah is globally publicly acknowledged, and even in the face of the most extreme 'Holocaust denial', that history is there to readily refute such claims. That is not the case with what happened to peoples of African ancestry at the hands of racist Europeans, their colonial masters, before, during and after the Berlin Conference 1884–1885, where Africa was subsequently carved up like a cake and distributed to various European countries. From this we have what

> has become known as the first genocide of the 20th century: tens of thousands of men, women and children shot, starved, and tortured to death by German troops as they put down rebellious tribes in what is now Namibia. For more than a century the atrocities have been largely forgotten in Europe, and often in much of Africa too.
> (https://www.theguardian.com/world/2016/dec/25/ germany-moves-to-atone-for-forgotten-genocide-in-namibia)

The point is that Starkey can boldly claim that what Africans experienced was not genocidal in such an irreverent way because the way the history African chattel enslavement is represented is that of Africa being the 'white man's burden'. That is why Starkey can state that blacks in the diaspora are not 'culturally African and would not survive in black Africa'. His comments only make sense in the context of the portrayal of Africa as the 'dark continent', locating it firmly under the banner of the European 'New World' civilisation project. Patterson speaks to this revisionist take on history when he suggests the following:

> The ease with which it is to shift from the meaning of 'master' as 'man having control or authority' to that of 'a teacher or one qualified to teach' reflects the ease with which it is possible to shift from our conception of the slave plantation as a brutal system of exploitation and

William Lez Henry

human degradation to a pastoral college for the edification of poor savages eager to learn the superior arts of the civilized 'master'.

(Patterson cited in Henry 2007: 80)

Consequently, it is the history of people of African ancestry who were, as will be explained later, Europe's 'chattel slaves' who currently represent the black diaspora that will be given consideration here. However, the suggestion is not that racism should be considered as the only social marker of difference that merits analysis; an intersectional approach to the overall black experience in the West would expose the folly of such a position. Rather, for the sake of brevity, it is necessary to make the focus of this discussion known from the outset as the terms black Asian and minority ethnic (BAME) and people of colour are conflations that obscure the vagaries within the lived experiences of African/black oppression in white societies. For this reason, the racialisation process that gave birth to a dominant aesthetic that arguably underpins this notion of 'whiteness' will be considered in the context of how it assists in the 'moulding and shaping of black reality' (Henry 2007). The argument will contend that addressing the historical circumstances that created the black/African 'other' as an inferior to a white/European 'self' is necessary to a contemporary understanding of black reality and the decolonising process. Moreover, to place the BLM movement in context, the history of black oppression in the West will be used as a platform for debating alternative models for creating a more equitable society, thereby challenging Starkey's myopic view that 'You cannot decolonise the curriculum because you, Black Lives Matter, are wholly and entirely a product of white colonisation' (David Starkey 2 July 2020).

3.2 Slavery or chattel enslavement?

Occasionally, it is mistakenly held that Europeans enslaved Africans for racist reasons. European planters and miners enslaved Africans for economic reasons so that their labour power could be exploited. Indeed, it would have been impossible to open up the New World and to use it as a constant generator of wealth had it not been for African labour (Rodney 1972: 88).

The reason the term *chattel enslavement* is used here to explain the systematic dehumanisation and barbaric treatment meted out to peoples of African ancestry during this historical moment is that it was a unique arrangement born of economic exploitation and European racism. Rodney makes known the process the enslaved African went through to become the absolute 'property' of the European master, and a rudimentary understanding of the word *chattel*, as 'moveable property' or 'cargo', is central to this discussion. It is important to frame this discussion in this way because, far too often, there is a tendency to equate what happened to enslaved Africans with other instances of historical slavery or forms of unfreedom. What this does is present an unfair and unjust comparison that obscures the reality of these historical occurrences when simply relying on such descriptors as the 'Transatlantic Slave Trade' or the 'Triangular Trade'. Now, whilst there is value in these descriptions, they do not readily lend themselves to a greater historical or sociological understanding of what truly happened to Africans and their descendants at the hands of racist Europeans, from the fifteenth to nineteenth centuries proper and, arguably, up to the present moment.

Similarities exist within all forms of slavery, peonage, serfdom or general unfreedom, such as being subjugated to the will of another and receiving draconian punishment at the whims and wishes of the master. Yet to place BLM, the death of George Floyd and the taking of countless black lives at the hands of the state in the USA, the UK or any other white-dominated society, this incomplete picture needs to be corrected. There are commonalities that can only be explained by excavating aspects of the history of chattel enslavement that make known the stark differences in the treatment of African women, men and children to fully understand the critical moment we find ourselves in. Indeed, Zoellner (2020: 55) speaks to the differences in other forms of slavery or unfreedom that were known in West and Central Africa at the time and finds nothing to equate with what racist Europeans did to African people. He suggests that 'Captured humans – or those who had been born into the role of slaves – were treated as small-scale field laborers, fishermen, gold miners, or household servants or hunters', which makes for a qualitatively different experience. That is why Starkey's suggestion that 'what of course that brings you up to confronting is of course slavery was not the equivalent of the Holocaust' is questionable when this is considered in a proper historical context.

The idea of 'property' or 'cargo' as an absolute form of 'legal' ownership during chattel enslavement was permanent, not temporary or negotiable after a period, as was often the case in other forms of slavery. Thus, this 'arrangement' differed from anything that occurred before, during or since this point in human history, exemplified in the 'three-fifths compromise', which was introduced by James Wilson and Roger Sherman on 11 June 1787. This 'compromise' was unique as it meant that enslaved Africans in the USA were legally regarded as 'three-fifths of a person', and no other members of the human family have ever been reduced to a mathematical equation. Similarly, in other forms of slavery, the pregnant slave would have ownership of their child whilst in the 'employ' of the master and would therefore have parental control over the newborn. Yet, according to Patterson, the enslaved Africans were subject to 'natal alienation', which meant the unborn child belonged to the master and therefore could

William Lez Henry

be sold, traded or swapped in much the same way as those born into this system of human commodification. Add to this that Africans, taken from various parts of mostly West and Central Africa, went through a process of 'culture stripping', in which their names were replaced with European ones, they were forbidden to speak their indigenous languages, and they were branded to determine who their owner or trader was.

It was even suggested that the negro 'has no values and culture to guard and protect', which means the negro [African] either had a culture and 'forgot it' or did not have a culture in the first place. The latter can be dismissed relatively easily as 'a European who is deceived about who he is merely succeeds in deceiving non-Europeans' (Ani 1994: 322). However, Glazer's definition is interesting when we consider that many early social scientists were of the belief that the slaves' indigenous cultures were all but destroyed during chattel enslavement. A perspective that runs parallel to Starkey's claim about 'not culturally black Africans' 'because Africa and "Africaness" were negatively valued, it was often assumed that no vestiges of his original culture could be left after the African was forcibly transported to the New World' (Davis & Simon 1983: 26). What is obviously missing here is an explanation of the legal codes that forbade Africans from openly practicing or celebrating their indigenous cultural ways of being, which is quite different from not having recognisable cultures. Unsurprisingly, then, the legacy of slave 'institutions' is embedded within the 'social forms and perceptions of New World peoples' (Mintz 1989: 62), but this embeddedness is 'hidden', as are the codes that determined the structural placement of the enslaved Africans in Europe's New World.

Crucially for us to consider here, then, is the blurring of the distinction between legal and non-legal codes that were used between the fifteenth and nineteenth centuries to subjugate enslaved Africans and their progeny in Europe's New World economies. These codes for governing the capture, transportation, sale and movement of the enslaved were in many instances overly complicated and deliberately vague, thereby allowing for the widest interpretation to justify more or less any treatment the master deemed appropriate to ensure the total subjugation of their enslaved chattels. Consequently, unimaginable tortures were visited upon the rebellious ones through what was known as the 'seasoning' process, and Thomas Thistlewood, a notoriously cruel Jamaican plantation owner, created a punishment called 'Derby's Lunch' (Zoellner 2020: 20). This was named after an incident in which the enslaved were formed in a circle, and Derby was held down in the middle whilst another chattel, under fear of punishment or death, was forced to defecate in his open mouth. After this, the mouth was firmly wired shut. This was endured for hours, and Zoellner suggests that such punishment was 'unremarkable', and therefore commonplace on slave-making and slave-breaking islands like Jamaica. Another documented and therefore widely known aspect of said 'seasoning' process was when a pregnant woman would be hung upside down from a tree, in the middle of a circle of the enslaved, and the master would have her stomach cut open so that the unborn child fell to the ground and was then stomped to death. Explanations have been offered to suggest that this instilled the greatest amount of fear in those who witnessed such atrocities, but the common feature was the enslaved were the master's property to do with as he wished, including the 'intentional wounding', maiming and killing of the enslaved.

In line with Foucault's take on 'sovereign power' and 'spectacular punishment', which in a sociological sense are ultimate weapons of deterrence and instilling deference, the master had the absolute power and authority over the enslaved and could determine their right to life or their right to death. Simply put, the master, in a legal sense, determined how they should live and, in many cases, the length of time they would live, so their only relationship with their master was that of total domination and brutal subjugation. The point is that to fully appreciate the contemporary incidents of the murders of black people at the hands of the state, in the USA and UK contexts in particular, they need to be foregrounded in this history of racial oppression. For instance, as suggested previously, the nebulous legal codes were up for interpretation, so, whilst the killing of an enslaved person was frowned upon, slaves could be killed for resistance to the wishes of the master. Thus, for a perceived or real failure to perform their tasks adequately, being caught reading or being found to have the ability to read and write, the enslaved were liable to lose their lives. The death sentence was invariably delivered to the enslaved who tried to escape, but in cases in which they were deemed 'too useful' to be killed, they would generally be 'hobbled'. This is when the Achilles tendons were severed so that they had to 'shuffle' or hobble about the planation, unable to run away.

With the advent of racial sciences like eugenics during the nineteenth century, the act of running away was regarded as a sign of mental illness. Pseudoscientists like the physician Samuel Cartwright provided a rational explanation for what was deemed to be an irrational and pathological desire to 'escape from freedom', which he named 'drapetomania'. Notice the onus is not on the enslaved escaping from subhuman bondage or servitude, but rather the incomprehension that they would seek life away from the 'freedom' of the plantation. Hence the word *drapetomania*, derived from the Greek, translates as *drapetes* (to escape) and *mania* (a diseased mind). Thus, black pathology was scientifically justified and socially embedded within the white psyche. Unsurprisingly, then, in the rare case when the death of a slave was deemed to be excessive or illegal, the owner would receive, at worst, a monetary fine of a negligible amount because the inhuman treatment of the enslaved was institutionalised and normalised. Thus,

William Lez Henry

it is the 'hidden' and socially obscured historical legacies that need to be acknowledged in any discussion of the pernicious nature of white racism, which continues to negatively impact global black communities to this day. More so, when we seek to comprehend white supremacist thought and action and its central role in maintaining and reinforcing 'white privilege' in myriad ways, to appreciate the contemporary fallout from what we have considered thus far because:

> Black Lives Matter is an ideological and political intervention in a world where Black lives are systematically and intentionally targeted for demise. It is an affirmation of Black folks' contributions to this society, our humanity, and our resilience in the face of deadly oppression.
> (www.BLM.com. 2016)

3.3 Whiteness, heritage and devaluing humanity

Students were told that they must learn 'our heritage' before going on to study 'other' cultural traditions. Conflict erupted, however, when a significant number students and faculty questioned the 'we' who were defining 'our' heritage as a shelf of books written in another time (before World War I) and in another place (Ancient Athens and Western Europe). How could a self-appointed academic aristocracy in the United States wrap itself in a cultural heritage that included no authors from the Americas, not to mention any women or persons of non-European origin? (Rosaldo 1989: X)

Rosaldo, in the previous questioning of 'we' and 'our', contextualises what is at stake in any debate on the notion of BLM, because there are 'hidden' conventions that speak to the reality of a system that is divided on racial lines. Sometimes, as is the case here, these divisions become subsumed under the idea of a publicly celebrated and annually commemorated ideal of 'heritage', which one is naturally enwrapped in via birth or citizenship. Yet for the unbelonging blacks, the focal point of this piece, who never quite get this celebratory feeling that this represents 'our cultural heritage', there is an awareness of this being another attempt at championing the multiculturalist project. The point is that the mere suggestion that 'All lives matter', as a counter to BLM, logically assumes a recognition of the sanctity of all forms of human life on the planet and does little for the decolonisation of thought. This stance actually works to the contrary, for when placed under critical scrutiny, the reality is that far too many black lives clearly do not matter. More so when we think about notions of British heritage in the context of blacks who were born in Britain, post HMT *Empire Windrush*, the ship that carried Caribbean migrants from the colonies and docked at Tilbury, Essex, on 22 June 1948. In fact, before the passengers aboard the ship had disembarked, their heritage and legal status were being questioned by sections within the Labour government that 'invited' them in the first place but wanted to turn them away. Indeed, the colonial secretary at the time, one Arthur Creech Jones, suggested that 'these people have British passports and they must be allowed to land' and 'they would not last one winter in England anyway, so there was nothing to worry about'. This was due to concerns regarding what is known as the UK 'colour bar', which was not an official form of segregation like the 'Jim Crow' laws in the USA, which, in many cases, brutally enforced racial segregation through beatings, lynching and hangings, but was a known local tactic used by whites to exclude black 'others' in the wider public arena. For example, whilst it is commonly known about the Montgomery bus boycotts, headed by Rosa Parks in the USA in 1955, the Bristol bus boycott took place in 1963 and was led by Paul Stephenson. This boycott was a result of the 'colour bar', under which the Bristol Omnibus Company refused to employ black or Asian bus crews, which subsequently shed light upon other areas of systematic exclusion from employment to the housing needs of racialised others.

The point is that by celebrating your 'otherness' without addressing the historical circumstances that created that 'other' as an inferior in the wider public arena, you run the risk of becoming embroiled in a fruitless tautological endeavour, such as debating whether 'all lives matter'. For instance, how can the framing of the BLM movement make sense, in a UK context, without making a direct correlation with the current 'Windrush scandal'? A name that is derived from the fallout of the Conservative government's 'Hostile Environment' policy that, since 2012, in many cases illegally, targeted generations of those who came from the colonies as 'subjects' of the British Empire. Including the word *subjects* in this way speaks to the reality that the 'Windrush generation' were de facto citizens in name only, as the reality was quite different, proven in the successful and on-going challenges to the government's tactic. As a result, the promotion of 'All Lives Matter' can be regarded as an attempt to decentre black voices and thus steer the argument away from the particular to the general. For instance, when the Radio 5 Live presenter Danny Baker sent an offensive tweet with a couple walking hand in hand with a monkey, he stated he 'didn't know' it was Prince Harry's wife, Meghan Markle, 'who had given birth', yet many of his BBC friends and colleagues rallied behind him, even after he admitted it was an 'error of judgement' and just a 'bit of banter'. Even more telling was that he received a standing ovation at the first public event he did after he was sacked by the BBC, which is why this is an example of 'racism with intent' (Guess 2006). Similarly, a banner was flown behind an aeroplane, stating 'white lives matter – Burnley', before a British Premier League match

William Lez Henry

on 22 June 2020, between Manchester City, which has several black first-team players, and Burnley at the Etihad Stadium in Manchester. Indeed the 'white lives matter' theme was witnessed on the T-shirts of right-wing marchers in London on 13 June 2020, who sought to 'protect' aspects of white culture and British heritage they perceived to be under threat from BLM protesters. However:

> Trying to communicate this to you is tricky. Because of this very system, you haven't been exposed to this sociocultural divide. You haven't had to witness first-hand the different forms it takes. You literally do not see the disparity in how your racial group is treated compared with others. You might not have noticed, for instance, the inherent biases of news media, such as the language used in coverage of different racial groups. You may be saying to yourself, 'I don't agree with the idea that the government treats racial groups differently'. But the thing is, you are absolutely, categorically wrong.
>
> (Damiani 2017)

Damiani's 'you might not have noticed' speaks to how the black 'other' is often rendered invisible in the white psyche because the dominant white society uses its resources, like the mainstream media, to shift the parameters for said debate. It does so by maintaining the distance between their dominant position and the subjugated 'reality' of the racially oppressed, conveniently abstracting perceived differences whilst measuring them against a white norm. One way to consider this is through the notion of 'inequitable situations', such as the known anti-black biases in mainstream representation and 'epistemic violence', which Spivak argues denies the 'subaltern' an active public voice by rendering them 'voiceless'. This is a useful way to problematise the idea of 'discrete' races that can be observed and categorised and are central to promoting cultural diversity: social inclusion as multiculturalism. Moreover, this notion of cultural diversity can, rather ironically, be promoted as 'universally' acceptable because it does little to dispense with the quaint, exotic or even bizarre notion of the inferior 'other', who is deemed to be culturally different in myriad ways. The thinking here speaks to the way in which the black other in the UK is often reduced to popular cultural artefacts like 'rasta colours', 'jerk chicken', 'hard food', 'fufu' or 'jollof rice', all representative of a form of 'commodity fetishism'. Or, as in the case of the BLM protests in Bristol when the statue of the former slave owner Edward Colson was pulled down and dumped in the river, Home Secretary Priti Patel called the protesters a 'mob' and said that the act was unjustified and 'utterly disgraceful'. The fact is that, rightly or wrongly, the removal of the statue represented a teachable moment as many were not aware of its existence, nor what it ultimately represented in the context of the decolonisation process. This point was obviously lost on Starkey, who:

> When asked what he would say to BLM activists who want to 'decolonise the curriculum' during the controversial interview on Tuesday, Dr Starkey replied: 'You cannot decolonise the curriculum because you, Black Lives Matter, are wholly and entirely a product of white colonisation'.
>
> (David Starkey 2 July 2020)

Starkey further endorses the point that was raised about the 'culture-stripping process' that Africans went through during the plantation era, which, simply put, means they have no viable, alternative histories to learn from a decolonised curriculum as they do not exist. This viewpoint conveniently fits into the idea that Africans have never contributed anything of note to the storehouse of human knowledge, in line with Enlightenment philosopher Immanuel Kant's 'this fellow was quite black . . . a clear indication that what he said was stupid' (Eze 1997). However, racialised otherness can be openly celebrated and tolerated during ephemeral moments when public visibility is high, such as during the October Black History Month celebrations. Yet such celebrations cannot deal with the 'real' issue of how 'race' and its highly stratified nature are an ever-present, but nebulous, aspect of our contemporary social reality. For once the month is over, the issues are shelved for a calendar year, during which the wider public will be once again 'exposed to this sociocultural divide', the effects of which are inescapable to most of the black populace, who experience this divide in all areas of human activity on a daily basis. Hence, the sense of 'distance' between the 'races' that was formulated and perpetuated by 'scientific' discourse, as previously discussed, presently manifests as a 'veneer of inclusion' (Hunter 2011) in various ways premised on a black/white dichotomy. Thus:

> When discussing inter-racial relations, we speak of 'non-white' people. We will refer to people all over the world as 'white' and 'non-white'. Notice that that particular choice of words gives precedence to 'white people' by making them a center – a standard – to which 'non-white' bears a negative relation. Notice the different connotation when we say 'colored' and 'non-colored', or 'black' and 'non-black'. Our thinking is so foggy on this issue that we describe our complexions as if they are qualities strewn along a yard-stick, the opposite ends of which are painted black and white respectively – black being the negative end.
>
> (Cleaver 1990: 15)

The suggestion is that to appreciate the profundity of the dichotomous relationship between people that dominates public reasoning on matters

William Lez Henry

of human worth – 'Black Lives Matter', 'All Lives Matter' or even 'White Lives Matter' – the grey areas in between need consideration as they will shed light on why we ended up with these categories in the first place. Consequently, the 'particular choice of words gives precedence to "white people" by making them a center – a standard', which manifest as the 'grey' areas that contain the uncomfortable truths that many blacks and whites are not ready to discuss openly and honestly. However, these are quite often the areas that deal with the transcendental codes that underpin black worldviews, acting as viable counters to white domination across a range of contexts.

In this type of analysis, where an understanding of the effects of 'systemic' or 'institutionalised' racism is crucial to the outcome, there must then be a focus on the historical particularities of the communities in question 'for there is nothing simple about being black in British society' (John 2006: 279). John's suggestion is that we need an explanatory framework, from which we can dismiss matters of coincidence or the 'unwitting' actions of individual racists and ascertain how certain beliefs have so much currency in contemporary British society. Otherwise, we run the risk of reproducing the same line of argument that ignores the voices of those who are the black 'insider-outsider', read as the main recipients of discriminatory practices, because 'people are trapped in history and history is trapped in people' (Baldwin 2017). Thus 'race' is synonymous with being an 'acceptable Briton' (white) and is linked, historically, to the threat of the 'unacceptable' non-Briton (black) 'other', who 'we', the dominant 'white self', have successfully managed to control and exclude from certain central positions of power. What is crucial to consider here is the pragmatic manner in which this notion of being an 'acceptable Briton' excludes those blacks who were born in Britain yet refuse to define themselves as British due to their subject position within a society that privileges being white.

Perhaps of equal importance is that this notion of 'white privilege' is nebulous, in the sense that not all white people are privileged, and aspects of class and regional disparities speak to and adequately demonstrate this social fact. However, all white people can and often do benefit from the systemic and epistemic injustices that maintain it. Systemic in the sense that there are institutionalised processes that have a traceable history, which is why we have an anti-racist movement in the UK that has challenged said injustices. The work of Stuart Hall is useful here as he shifted the focus of sociological enquiry from class to culture and ideology as crucial to our understanding of post-war immigration from the Commonwealth. Therefore, Hall suggests that to understand contestations around identity and belonging, in this case how blackness and whiteness are essentially mutually exclusive categories when measured against Britishness, one must appreciate their embeddedness within our society. One explanation for this is that whiteness can be equated with Englishness as Britishness; thus, if you are white, you are English, and if you are English, you are a British citizen by racial birthright. Black-ness, however, cannot be confused with whiteness in this sense because it speaks to phenotypical differences, regardless of where you were born as a member of a subject race, so you can never be truly British. The point is that the sole emphasis on anti-racism in many ways can reduce all the concerns that the black communities face in the UK to a singular battle with racism, which, as has been suggested, means they become a 'problem' or a 'victim'. This means that in racialised discourse, which can perhaps be assisted by a right-wing populist agenda, black people are reduced to criminality and other forms of social deviance. Similarly, with a narrow emphasis on an anti-racist discourse, the focus can be reduced to victimhood, which serves those who claim movements like BLM are merely the product of disgruntled citizens with the proverbial 'chip on their shoulder' playing 'identity politics'.

3.4 Black life as the 'insider-outsider'

Systemic white ignorance makes denials of complicity seem justified, and this, in turn, protects white moral innocence on the one hand and shields unjust systems from being interrogated on the other. As long as white complicity is not acknowledged, I explain, the status quo remains beyond challenge (Applebaum 2010: 7)

Applebaum makes known that 'denials of complicity' are used to justify claims of 'moral innocence', yet it is her take on 'shielding' that is of real interest here because this speaks to a consciousness of what would be the right thing to do but a lack, perhaps, of the 'moral courage' to do it. The suggestion is that 'whiteness' as an aspect of systemic oppression can be observed through an anti-racist lens, to acknowledge, for instance, the on-going treatment of the Windrush generations, who are the main victims of the Conservatives' 'Hostile Environment'. This is where claims around nationality, legislation and immigration control become ways to ensure that the unfair treatment to black British citizens is 'justified' as it is sanctioned by the state and, therefore, cannot be racist. Consequently, the home secretary, Priti Patel, can claim that the unfair treatment of the Windrush generations is premised upon 'institutionalised ignorance', not racism: a statement that mirrors other such explanatory descriptors like 'unwitting', 'unconscious', or 'unintentional' biases that that are conveni-ently rolled out to avoid the real, historical points of discussion. By doing so, the power differential in the relations between so-called blacks and whites will remain hidden, and the 'decentred' African/black person will remain confused. Awraj (2008) suggests this is a form of 'caucasionization' and posits:

> The term 'caucasianization of blacks' is very likely to be dismissed as absurd and nonsensical by those who are caucasianized (and, perhaps, even by caucasianizers), simply because the term is sufficiently provocative as to make such awareness painful, exposing as it does the fact that blacks have succumbed to the subtle, dignity-stripping mind colonization process of the white man.
>
> (Awraj 2008: 1)

The rationale behind Awraj's thinking is to provide blacks with a platform for debating alternative models of social, economic and political discourse, from their own cultural and epistemological standpoint, by recognising the commonality of their condition. In this way, giving consideration to the process of 'caucasionization' through mediums such as the politics of identity and difference sheds light on the aspects of the struggle for black social justice that are 'hidden' from the wider public gaze. However, the danger here is that whilst blacks have a theoretical model out of which they can articulate and even valorise their differences, its influence on 'race' and racialised thinking in the wider public arena could be counter-productive. That is why Awraj is cautionary when he suggests that the notion of 'caucasionization' will likely be dismissed as 'absurd' because 'white studies has become an industry' (Ignatiev 1997). Therefore, any challenge to a white aesthetic such as 'caucasionization' will be confronted by 'a form of ghoulish separateness – a form of segregation which exists simultaneously with cosmopolitanism' (Harris 1993: 38). On this issue of the cosmopolitan, Hall argued that what was required in the UK context was a more relevant take on strategies around anti-racism, and this he called a 'politics of representation': a type of political viewpoint which, at its core, challenges the damaging and ubiquitous racial stereotypes that presented the 'caucasionized' 'other', as an exemplar of how to 'fit' in the wider public arena. This meant challenging the mainstream media depictions of black life and the racial stereotypes they invested heavily in, particularly from the 1960s through the 1980s. For instance, TV shows like *Till Death Do Us Part*, which aired on the BBC network at primetime from 1965 through 1980 and starred Warren Mitchel as Alf Garnett, Dandy Nichols as Elsie Garnett and Una Stubbs as their married daughter, Rita Rawlins. The show was overtly racist in its language and depiction of people of African and Asian ancestry in particular, regularly referring to them as 'coons', spades' and 'pakis', and the writer, Johnny Speight, often stated that he was being ironic and that the point of the show was to out bigots through satire. In fact, Warren Mitchell stated that:

> You can't help it if people are idiots. I had a bloke come up to me one day and say 'I love that show of yours, Alf, especially when you have a go at the coons'. I said, 'Actually we're having a go at bastards like you'. Whoever comedy writers, actors and comedians have in as their target audience is not the point. The point is, who is laughing?
>
> (Cited in Nathan 2015)

What is interesting about this viewpoint is the fact that it is not new and has been discussed within black communities for years, due to the obvious but crucially 'hidden' power dimension that gives them their social and racial currency. Moreover, this 'hidden' aspect of racialised discourse lends itself to the maintenance of white power/privilege, which becomes apparent when, for instance, in the context of contemporary British society, all that made Britain 'Great', as in the Empire, is being eroded daily. The suggestion is that 'the mirage of great power status is a comfort blanket to cling to in an uncertain world, but the truth is Britain's voice has stopped being a roar' (Conversation 2015). It is the 'struggle for acceptance' that is of interest here because a failure to accept its diminished global status has led to many ordinary white Britons flexing their racial muscles on a local level through an investment in white privilege, consciously or unconsciously. This is evidenced in the Home Office report that confirmed what many blacks were experiencing on a street level: a 41 percent increase in racial or religious attacks in post-Brexit Britain. Many white commentators in the mainstream media suggest this increase threatens to 'split our society in two', comfortably forgetting that these forms of racial abuse have histories that contextualise this impending schism.

The specificity of the historical experiences of the African/black communities, whose forefathers and foremothers were regarded as property and cargo and treated as chattels, must be given primacy in conversations around societal schisms. Hence, whilst in the realms of academia, it is accepted that there is no 'scientific' evidence to support any notion of an inherent superiority or inferiority premised on phenotypic difference between the so-called races, this does not translate to the lived experiences of ordinary people. For example, Ware argues that such perspectives 'derive their meanings from the historical memory produced by centuries of slavery and colonization' (Ware 1996: 81). That which the current prime minister, Boris Johnson, endorsed in his notorious comments in *The Spectator* in 2002 about the Queen's need for 'flag waving picaninies' to reinforce ideas of the Commonwealth when she visits her former colonies. He also suggested that 'we' (the British) should 'scramble for Africa, but this time don't

William Lez Henry

feel any guilt', whereby Johnson makes known that the 'institutionalisation' of myriad forms of racial violence has a history of black/African subjugation at its core. More importantly, when considering the notion of 'racism with intent', by stating 'don't feel any guilt' about the re-scrambling for Africa, PM Johnson is no doubt aware of what happened in the Congo under King Leopold II of Belgium. From 1885 to 1908, he ruled Congo Free State and turned it into his own private plantation: a country that is 76 times larger than Belgium. So, unlike the other European powers who received African territories in the name of their countries, the Congo was solely owned by him. They became one of the biggest exporters of rubber, but when the quota was not met by the subjugated people, he had them mutilated and killed. Although he never set foot there, he committed one of the worst genocides in human history with estimates that between 10 and 15 million African men, women and children were slaughtered during his 23-year reign.

The point is that whilst it seems fine for Europeans in positions of power like Starkey and PM Johnson to extol the virtues of empire and colonialism, peoples of African ancestry are encouraged to be historically amnesic because, 'the white man has already implanted numerous historical myths in the minds of black peoples; those have to be uprooted' (Rodney 1972: 51). One way to deploy Rodney's 'uprooting' process is by realising that a major concern of the black recipients of white domination is rooted in the process of marginalisation, wherein they become the 'insider-outsider' in places like the UK.

3.5 Summary

Those who are naturally different, obviously based on phenotype, cannot in this present moment be considered as truly belonging in societies where 'race' becomes a politicised weapon in a separatist discourse promulgated by white racists. This discourse finds its efficacy in discussions that fail to give due consideration to the history of African chattel enslavement that speaks to the 'dignity-stripping mind colonization process' that Awraj suggests is caucasionisation. This is because the way the BLM argument is framed within the wider public arena ensures that the 'subtle' nature of racism's negative process masks its pernicious nature. In this way, by conveniently abstracting perceived racial differences, whatever they may be, and subsuming them under a human rights, 'All Lives Matter'–type agenda, the particularities of the BLM movement will be lost. Consequently, what this means is that these broad definitions of what races are and, more importantly, what race means become obscured by the nuanced nature of the racialisation process. For instance, satire and irony do have their place in the social as they are what underpin the comedic; however, when that element is lost and the ironic and satiric become weaponised, the black recipients as the butt of these 'jokes' experience the hurt, psychologically and physically, as was the case with the 'royal monkey' mentioned earlier.

The suggestion is that if the mind suffering from the legacy of chattel enslavement is externally controlled, then the actions driven by that mind cannot be analysed by solely looking within. Moreover, any pursuit of an equitable society that valorises the value of black lives but is divorced from the history of chattel enslavement will never achieve social justice. This is where the common denominator, phenotypic difference, has a healthy disregard for the most obvious physical differences or variations within the dominant racial categories, ensuring 'the good fortune of those who rule, and the misery of those who are ruled' (Kuper 1974: 67). Thus, the only remedy for this is to decolonise society by including the known histories and contributions that will serve as a counterbalance to the way we are taught about peoples of African ancestry. This does not mean destroying canons of knowledge or even removing statues of white racists or litera-ture; rather, it means locating them in a more truthful and, therefore, edi-fying context, and then perhaps, one day, there will be no need for a BLM movement as the picture will be far more complete.

 Key points

BLM

It is important to place the Black Lives Matter movement in the con-text of the history of black oppression in the West. To do so gives us a clearer understanding of the way forward not only with debates about 'race' but as a platform for debating alternative models for creating a more equitable society.

Chattel enslavement

The use of the term *chattel enslavement* is important to explain the systematic de-humanisation and barbaric treatment of peoples of African ancestry. It was a unique arrangement born of economic exploitation and European racism. Its embeddedness in the very fab-ric of economic, social, cultural and political life in the West has had profound and long-term consequences.

The black 'other' is often rendered invisible in the white psyche because the dominant white society uses its resources, like the mainstream media, to normalise 'whiteness' and set blackness as marginal or 'other'. We see this in debates about sport, crime and education. We refer to this as institutionalised and structural racism.

William Lez Henry

Coursework questions

1 Provide an explanation of what the BLM movement seeks to achieve.
2 Consider some of the critiques of the movement in the UK and USA contexts.
3 Explain what is meant by systemic or institutionalised racism with examples to assist a group discussion.
4 What are the key features of the legacy of decolonisation?

References

Ani, M. (1994) *Yurugu: An African-Centred Critique of European Cultural Thought and Behaviour*. Trenton, NJ: Africa World Press, Inc.

Applebaum, B. (2010) *Being White, Being Good: White Complicity, White Moral Responsibility, and Social Justice Pedagogy*. Lanham, MD: Lexington Books.

Awraj, S. (2008) 'Overcoming caucasianization and dehumanization'. https://lovefreedomorquestionwhoyouare.com/wp-content/uploads/2014/05/Overcoming-Caucasianization-and-Dehumanization.pdf

Baldwin, J. (2017) *Notes of a Native Son (Penguin Modern Classics)*. London: Penguin Classics.

Cleaver, E. (1990) 'As crinkly as yours'. In Dundes, A. (ed.), *Mother Wit from the Laughing Barrel*. Jackson and London: University of Mississippi Press.

'Britain still thinks it's a great power but it isn't'. (2015, December 2) *The Conversation*. http://theconversation.com/britain-still-thinks-its-a-great-power-but-it-isnt-50641

Damiani, J. (2017) 'Every time you say "all lives matter" you are being an accidental racist'. www.huffpost.com/entry/every-time-you-say-all-li_1_b_11004780

Davis, S. and Simon, P. (eds.) (1983) *Reggae International*. London: Thames and Hudson.

Eze, C. E. (1997) *Race and the Enlightenment: A Reader*. London: Wiley-Blackwell.

Guess, T. (2006) 'The social construction of whiteness: Racism by intent, by consequence'. *Critical Sociology* 32 (4): 649–673.

Harris, L. (1993) *Racism, the City and the State*. Edited by M. Cross and M. Kieth. London: Routledge.

Henry, W. 'Lez'. (2007) *Whiteness Made Simple: Stepping into the GREY Zone*. London: Learning by Choice Publications.

Hunter, M. L. (2011, June) 'Buying racial capital: Skin-bleaching and cosmetic surgery in a globalized world'. *The Journal of Pan African Studies* 4 (4).

John, G. (2006) *Taking a Stand: Gus John Speaks on Education, Race, Social Action and Social Unrest*. Manchester: Gus John Partnership.

Kuper, L. (1974) *Race Class and Power*. London: G. Duckworth & Co. Ltd.

Mintz, S. W. (1989) *Caribbean Transformations*. New York: Columbia University Press.

Nathan, J. (2015) 'I fear more would have laughed with Alf Garnett than at him'. www.thejc.com

Rodney, W. (1972) *How Europe Underdeveloped Africa*. London: Bogle-L'Ouverture Publications.

Rosaldo, R. (1989) *Culture and Truth: The Remaking of Social Analysis*. London: Routledge.

Ware, V. (1996) 'Defining forces: "Race", gender and memories of empire'. In Chambers, I. and Curti, L. (eds.), *The Postcolonial Question: Common Skies, Divided Horizons*. London: Routledge.

Zoellner, T. (2020) *Island on Fire: The Revolt That Ended Slavery in the British Empire*. London: Harvard University Press.

 Further reading

Fanon, F. (1986) *Black Skin, White Masks*. London: Pluto Press Ltd.

Gabriel, D. (ed.) (2020) *Transforming the Ivory Tower Models for Gender Equality and Social Justice*. London: University College of London Press.

Hall, R. (2012) 'The Bleaching Syndrome: Western civilisation vis-à-vis inferiorized people of color'. In Hall, R. (ed.), *The Melanin Millennium: Skin Color as the 21st Century International Discourse*. East Lansing, MI: Springer.

Henry, W. A. (2012) 'Shades of consciousness: From Jamaica to the UK'. In Hall, R. (ed.), *The Melanin Millennium: Skin Color as the 21st Century International Discourse*. East Lansing, MI: Springer.

Ignatiev, N. (1997) 'The point is not to interpret whiteness but to abolish it'. *Race Traitor Journal of the New Abolitionism*. http://www.campusactivism. org/server-new/uploads/abolishthepoint.pdf

Leary, J. D. (2005) *Post Traumatic Slave Syndrome: America's Legacy of Enduring Injury and Healing*. Milwaukee, WI: Uptown Press.

Monrose, K. (2019) *Black Men in Britain: An Ethnographic Portrait of the Post-Windrush Generation*. London: Routledge.

Rigby, P. (1996) *African Images*. Oxford: Berg.

Ware, V. and Back, L. (2002) *Out of Whiteness: Color, Politics and Culture*. Chicago: University of Chicago Press.

William Lez Henry

chapter 4

Health, public health and health inequalities

Jane Thomas, Salim Vohra and Sean Tunney

4.1 Introduction

This chapter starts by asking the question 'What do we mean by health?' People are fascinated by health. It certainly sells news in all its formats, and the number of people using the internet to find out about health problems has increased dramatically in the last few years. There are other dimensions to health also reported in the media. Health is increasingly seen as a business in parts of the UK, particularly in England. The level of health service funding is contentious. And the factors that influence our health are key topics for discussion. The COVID-19 global emergency puts an additional spotlight on health. The crisis highlights the links between politics, health and the economy.

After looking at public health, well-being and tools for analysis, the chapter continues by considering what determines health. This is complex. It requires investment in research studies to provide evidence that can help us understand whether, for example, damp housing causes health problems. Or is it just the mould in damp housing? Evidence is often inconclusive, which sparks further debate and research. But to consider these questions as important probably requires some commitment to, and care for, others. We will also look at ethical issues in this chapter.

Throughout the chapter, we specifically draw out questions on health-related problems for debate (Thomas, 2018). Climate change, for instance, is of an all-encompassing significance. The debates around this topic are on how climate change should be dealt with and who will be the winners and losers. Academic arguments need to marshal evidence. It is important for students to look at questions from different angles and to use a variety of theories to analyse social processes.

The chapter ends with some success stories. Many of the UK's responses to health problems have been successful and creative. Again, we need to critique and ask how and why we have managed to see improvements, such as falling smoking rates, declining TB incidence and increasing levels of cycling, for example.

4.2 What do we mean by health?

People can mean different things when they say they're 'feeling healthy'. For some, health is the absence of disease, whereas others define health as a more positive feeling of well-being. These differences are reflected in divergent definitions of health and mental health provided by different authors and agencies. Even the World Health Organization (WHO) uses various definitions. The most famous of these is that 'health is a state of complete physical, mental and social well-being and not merely the absence of disease or infirmity'. Notwithstanding the WHO's positive definition of health, we start by assessing ill health in the UK.

Measuring health

Some of the most reliable sources of information on the health of a country are basic data on births and age at death. These data are generally undisputed, and studying them can provide powerful evidence of social problems affecting some groups more than others. As the economist John Maynard Keynes said when promoting government intervention to combat unemployment: 'In the long run we are all dead'. But government policy influences which groups, statistically, have a longer run.

Demographics is the study of populations' characteristics, such as the number of 20-to-30-year-olds in the population or place of birth. Epidemiology looks at diseases and health problems across populations – from accidents at work to viruses like COVID-19 and hepatitis – and indicates how many people in the population are affected by these issues, that is, their prevalence, and their causes.

In the UK, some health problems have been improving over the last ten years, such as dementia among the elderly. We can apply epidemiological and demographic analysis to this issue. The epidemiology indicates

Jane Thomas, Salim Vohra and Sean Tunney

that the number of people with dementia per 100,000 of the population has fallen. This may be due to healthier lifestyles, increased education and improved preventive care for conditions such as heart disease. However, because of the changing demographics of the UK population, there are now more people aged 65 and over, so the number of individuals living with dementia has increased significantly.

Epidemiologists' analysis of mortality data takes into account different populations' age profiles via a formula called 'standardisation'. This enables comparisons between, for example, the nations of the UK and other countries. Epidemiologists also investigate associations between diseases like COVID-19 and factors such as poverty, class, ethnic group, air pollution and obesity.

After World War II, the main causes of death in the UK became cancer and cardiovascular disease, which are 'non-communicable diseases' (NCDs). Within the kingdom, there is variation. Heart disease rates in Scotland are particularly high, and higher again in the most deprived areas of Scotland. Some cancers have shown poorer one-year and five-year post-diagnosis survival rates in comparison to other European countries and the USA. Therefore, UK services aim to address this by speeding up diagnostics, reducing waiting times and investing in increased treatment capacity. Additionally, staff have run campaigns to improve public recognition of cancer symptoms and encourage specific population groups to seek a medical opinion. This 'social marketing' needs to be carefully targeted at the most 'at-risk' groups. Single men over 50 working in lower-paid jobs, for instance, may be less likely to go to a doctor if they find a lump.

Some NCDs, like cardiovascular disease, may be prevented by lifestyle changes, such as healthy eating, promoted in Northern Ireland and the three nations of Great Britain. NCDs are increasing globally, alongside continuing malnutrition and high infant mortality in low-income countries. Yet, for other health issues, 'pandemic' conditions can arise, meaning most countries are affected and there is a world-wide epidemic, as happened with COVID-19. Human immunodeficiency virus (HIV) is typically considered to be a pandemic because it has spread globally. Global public health initiatives are necessary to protect health across countries, in part because, as the adage goes, 'bugs don't respect borders'.

4.3 Public health

The American Charles-Edward Winslow coined a well-known definition of public health in the 1920s. This has been adapted to become the following: 'Public health is the science and art of promoting health, preventing disease and prolonging life through the organised efforts of society'. Public health focuses on: (i) health improvement and prevention, (ii) protecting health and (iii) developing health services. Prevention of health problems takes place at different stages. Primary prevention is stopping problems happening in the first place – for example, stopping mesothelioma lung disease by checking for, and where necessary safely removing, all asbestos in buildings. Secondary prevention is about stopping health problems from progressing and reducing recurrence – for example, helping children with asthma exercise more. This is how Laura Trott became a British Olympic medal-winner: by cycling to improve her childhood asthma. Tertiary prevention helps people with conditions that cannot be improved to become more comfortable.

Health problems can take a long time to 'gestate' following 'insults' like regular exposure to air pollution. For example, if we look at the health of current students in 30 years' time, we can refer to longitudinal studies and predict that those with sedentary lifestyles who smoke or drink above the recommended units are statistically more likely to develop health problems. On the other hand, for some issues such as the impact of e-cigarettes on lung disease, there has not been so much time to gather evidence. Therefore, Public Health England has instigated annual evidence updates. The 2020 review suggests smokers explore help to quit, including e-cigarettes.

Ironically, most primary prevention does not take place in primary care. Primary care is delivered by family doctors, or GPs, practice nurses and community staff. It is the first point of contact with the health system. High-quality primary care is key to secondary prevention and in supporting those with long-term conditions, such as arthritis and diabetes. Primary prevention is more likely to take place in shops, schools and workplaces, for instance. Lee and Freudenberg (2020) argue for changes in commercial activities to prevent NCDs.

Public health agencies in the UK identify priorities for action on health problems. The issue of antibiotic resistance is high on the agenda. The UK population is quite dependent on antibiotics, which are used to treat millions of infections arising from surgery and trauma, as well as pneumonia and other bacterial illnesses. Inappropriate use causes resistance in the bugs. Campaigns to inform the public of the difference between a virus and a bacterial infection are part of the solution, along with tougher controls on prescribing among both doctors and vets. Sequencing the whole genome of a pathogenic organism provides further data to target antibiotics.

As an indication of the wide scope of public health, Brexit, as well as its health impact, has also been a focus. At the time of publication, the effect of the UK's withdrawal from the European Union on the health of UK residents and their health services is unclear. The UK-wide Faculty of Public Health (FPH) has produced a briefing report on post-Brexit trade, based on a 'Do No Harm' campaign, and literature on 'healthy' trade agreements – these are trade agreements that might promote clean production

Jane Thomas, Salim Vohra and Sean Tunney

techniques or workers' rights, for instance. Years of declining health and social care services, and the desire to put more money into the NHS were reasons given by some for voting to leave the EU. The concern of the FPH is that public protections and standards will be watered down as negotiators bargain and give way in order to gain access to markets.

4.4 Beyond health, to happiness

Public health's broad remit, including politics and economics, extends what we might consider typically to be health concerns. In recent years, economists themselves have focused attention on measuring the happiness and well-being of the population. This movement has been based on a critique of assessing a country's success by gross domestic product (GDP), or economic growth. GDP can include all sorts of industries of dubious 'worth', such as those selling tobacco. The Office for National Statistics (ONS) collects happiness data through surveys. This has shown some interesting results, with an overall increase in happiness immediately after the Brexit vote. However, the increase was only evident in England, not in Northern Ireland, Scotland or Wales. And, of course, correlation does not necessarily mean causal connection.

Alongside the development of the happiness index, researchers have tried to identify ways for people to promote their own well-being. Government scientists on the Foresight Programme have identified 'five ways to well-being' as connect, be active, take notice, keep learning and give. The 'five ways' have been promoted by various NHS bodies and charities. Indeed, this approach was the foundation for much of the mental health promotion advice during the COVID-19 lockdown. However, there has been a debate on the robustness of the evidence base for this advice, with the chief medical officer for England stating in 2014 that public health departments should not allocate funds on this basis as there was insufficient evidence of its effectiveness. This is not to say that further scientific research will not be conducted to back up claims for the 'five ways'. Also, some charities, such as Mind, have added a 'sixth way to well-being'. This is 'care for the planet . . . look after your community and the world'. This provides further substance for debate.

4.5 Public health tools and models

Public health is resplendent with debates on evidence: from the adverse effects of drinking alcohol when pregnant and the dangers of the measles, mumps, rubella (MMR) vaccine – which were dangerously overstated – to the health risks of living under pylons or the ingestion of microplastics, and the ethics of 'universal measures', such as water fluoridation.

Building on epidemiological analysis, other public health 'tools' are used to investigate population health. Risk assessments, for example, investigate the likelihood of problems arising and multiply this by the harm caused if a problem or event does happen. This highlights a further issue: that is, guidance and policy needs to be implemented. According to the UK's Health and Safety Executive (HSE), employers should conduct risk assessments on workplace stress. However, the Trade Union Congress (TUC) has labelled current non-compliance with this guideline shockingly high and a distressing failure. Another example of risk assessment implementation failure was the government's inability to ensure cost-effective supplies of personal protective equipment (PPE) for front-line workers during the COVID-19 crisis (Marmot et al. 2020b).

Health impact assessments are another tool used in the UK to analyse population health issues. Here, the impact on health of building a new road, for example, is assessed. Nevertheless, as with the example of employers not doing risk assessments, there has been criticism of the lack of health impact assessments on the UK government's post-2010 austerity measures.

Along with other academic disciplines, public health uses a set of theories and models to help understand processes. Theories generally describe and explain how activities work. A theory should be applicable to, and tested within, different settings. A model is a representation that also helps to explain processes, or how things work. Beattie's model of health promotion assists in categorising activities to improve health. He creates four boxes by drawing a vertical line headed with 'authoritative' and with 'negotiated' at the base, then intersects this with a horizontal line labelled 'individual' on the left and 'collective' on the right (Beattie 2002).

Taking, for example, the problem of increasing obesity – the top right-hand box in Beattie's model is 'legislative action' to address health problems, such as a sugar tax. Below this, 'community development' takes a less-structured approach. An example could be charities promoting walks among people using a local GP surgery. The bottom-left quadrant is 'personal counselling'. This might be one-to-one advice on how to quit smoking without putting on weight. Finally, the top-left quadrant, 'health persuasion', might involve running a social media campaign promoting 'dry January' and suggesting the benefits of cutting out drinking alcohol to lose weight.

4.6 The wider determinants of health

Health problems are not just associated with issues such as access to medicines. The wider determinants of health are socio-economic issues, such as education, housing, transport, income and employment. Trends, such

Jane Thomas, Salim Vohra and Sean Tunney

as dramatic increases in the number of adults in private rented accommodation or living with parents, mirrored by an explosion in rentiers, impact on population health. At an individual level, genetics also plays a role in determining health. Although, it has been argued that genetic differences between different ethnic groups have been over-exaggerated in explanations of poorer health among groups such as British Asian men or Black women. Professor James Nazroo (2003) suggests that statistically higher rates of poverty in these populations can explain differences in health, while racial discrimination affects inequality.

The impact of different factors on health is of great interest to researchers, with new findings emerging regularly. One famous study was conducted on civil servants. Professor Sir Michael Marmot looked at the health of these staff at different pay grades. He found that at each step up in grade, even when controlling for smoking and drinking, health improved. This finding was counterintuitive to thinking at the time, which associated stress at work with higher grades. Further work since the 1970s has sought to understand and address the gap in health between the best-off and the less well-off. In 2010, the Marmot Review team published a report called *Fair Society – Healthy Lives*. In it, the following actions were called for:

Give every child the best start in life.
Enable all children, young people and adults to maximise their capabilities and have control over their lives.
Create fair employment and good work for all.
Ensure a healthy standard of living for all.
Create and develop healthy and sustainable places and communities.
Strengthen the role and impact of ill-health prevention.

These actions aim to reduce the 'health gap' between the better-off and those with below-average incomes. Generally, those in the poorest groups in the UK are dying around ten years before the best-off. The impact on pensions claimed is obvious. Yet not only are the less well-off dying earlier; they also tend to experience disability, such as chronic lung disease, earlier in life and for more years. Health services and councils therefore aim to 'add years to life and life to years'. Doing this is, of course, challenging. Julian Tudor Hart, a GP in Wales, suggested the 'inverse care law', whereby those most in need of services, support or protection are those least likely to receive these. The Marmot report's recommendations are about issues that local councils of different political make-up across the UK can help to influence. And central government, likewise, has a crucial role. A 2020 update of the Marmot report has shown the impact of Conservative government policy. Wealth inequality increased faster in the UK than in any other OECD country between 2010 and 2016, apart from the USA. The richest 1 percent of the population had 20 percent of the wealth in the UK in 2016, compared with 16 percent in 2010 (Marmot et al. 2020a).

The link between lower incomes and poorer health is well established. At the same time, groundbreaking research on how wealth is becoming ever more concentrated in fewer hands has been published by Thomas Piketty (2020). He uses Jane Austen's novel *Pride and Prejudice* (1813) as one of his teaching tools. (Given Piketty is a political economist known for his long books, it is a coincidence that the novelist made the front of the Bank of England £10 note in 2017 with a beguiling quote from a character in the book whose family fortune was 'acquired by trade': 'I declare after all there is no enjoyment like reading!'.) Piketty traces inequality through the extremes of the slave trade (abolished in Britain from 1833), Austen's era, and the industrial revolution, which kicked off with Scottish engineer James Watt's 1776 steam engine. Now, with early twenty-first-century capitalism, he finds the rich are getting successively richer again. Piketty argues one way of dealing with this is by central government increasing progressive, not regressive, personal and corporate taxes.

Nevertheless, across the UK, corporation tax, needed for local authority and central services, has been cut, from 42 percent in the 1970s. The UK rate levied on profitable companies is now below all Western Europe's major states, at 19 percent in 2020. And some private health-care providers in England have been criticised for failing to pay tax, such as tycoon Richard Branson's Virgin Care, registered in the British Virgin Islands. The Tax Justice Network estimates that money for the salaries of 34 million nurses is lost to tax abuse and evasion every year (www.taxjustice.net). Even government ministers, such as pro-Brexit Jacob Rees-Mogg, have used overseas tax havens, thus depriving the UK government of funds to pay wages.

Ethics plays an important part in how we interpret information about the health gap, as well as in how much we feel society should invest in supporting groups with poorer health. Prisoners' health, for example, is generally particularly poor. Yet the Prison Reform Trust struggles to gain public sympathy for actions to help prisoners develop skills. Although some commentators regard imprisonment as often being a symptom of failed mental health services and poverty. And the high rates of mental health problems among prisoners do suggest that prevention of incarceration could be helped by better primary and secondary prevention of mental illness. Added to this, for most, prison is not a life sentence and, therefore, supporting prisoners to develop skills may improve their health outside prison, and help them to stay outside.

Jane Thomas, Salim Vohra and Sean Tunney

Ethical issues are often categorised into four principles (Beauchamp and Childress, 2013). In this chapter, we have discussed issues pertinent to each:

Autonomy – this refers to health professionals respecting the rights of patients to control their care. And, in public health, it links to the control communities have over factors affecting their health.

Beneficence – this means that health staff should do all they can to benefit patients and the public.

Non-maleficence – this is the principle of 'first do no harm' (hence the name of the FPH's Brexit work, referred to earlier).

Justice – finally, this is an important issue that drives people to seek evidence to uphold their beliefs. A wide income distribution is one area that some see as unjust.

In academic research and writing, a distinction is made between 'normative' issues, in which researchers reach conclusions about what is right and wrong, and more 'value-free', objective or descriptive work. It is important to recognise where writing moves into normative terrains.

4.7 Climate change and health

In the previous section, we talked about the determinants of health, from income to education. Climate change is another key determinant of health; it is referred to as the greatest threat to human health. Weather patterns have been changing as a result of increasing atmospheric carbon dioxide produced by fossil fuels. Sir David King, as Chief Scientific Advisor to the UK government, told a public health conference on climate change in 2017: 'Climate change is the biggest challenge that our civilisation has ever had to face up to'. The health impact of climate change ranges from increased illness and trauma from floods and wildfires through to economic disruption, increases in food prices and homelessness. The UK is susceptible to all these impacts, although lower-lying countries are experiencing more problems earlier. Nevertheless, flooding in Wales and England in 2020 was unprecedented and the risk of the Thames breaching in London, for instance, is predicted to be increasing, with potentially life-threatening consequences.

The UK has a major role in influencing responses to climate change. It is a contributor to the most important global body that produces evidence for states to base policy on – the Intergovernmental Panel on Climate Change (IPCC). The IPCC, whose website is constantly updated (www.ipcc.ch/), is open to all countries of the United Nations and currently has 195 members. Global action is decided via the UN Climate Conference – the United Nations Framework Convention on Climate Change.

The World Health Organization reports on the health impact of climate change. It has said that anticipated additional deaths per year as a result of climate change stand at 250,000, up to the year 2050. In addition, the WHO notes billions of dollars of costs resulting from the negative consequences of climate change. Added to this, it points to the health benefits of reducing carbon production: 'Reducing emissions of greenhouse gases through better transport, food and energy-use choices can result in improved health, particularly through reduced air pollution' (WHO Climate Change and Health Key Facts, 2018; also see updates in *The Lancet*).

In the UK, governments have struggled to produce effective policy. Recently, investment in green technology, such as heat pumps, has actually fallen. The House of Commons Library provides briefing papers on policy issues for all political parties. They wrote a review of the government's 2018 25-year plan for the environment (www.parliament.uk/commons-library). Reaction from political parties is reported in the review. The Scottish National Party, for instance, claimed that the plan is already being delivered in Scotland and contains nothing new.

Nevertheless, to help the environment, public health agencies recommend 'active travel', for example, walking to work; accessible green and blue spaces, such as parks and rivers; well-insulated and affordable homes; and sustainable nutrition, which is also healthier. The NHS in England itself contains a small unit – the NHS Sustainability Unit – devoted to supporting the health service in cutting its carbon emissions. This is quite logical given the future health impact of climate change.

The British Medical Association has pointed out that 'decisions are made every day in the UK . . . on policy, legislation and regulation' relating to climate change. And the association actively encourages action by individuals to influence the policy process. Citizens' engagement with organised politics is needed to steer improvements. Recent policy changes include the tax on plastic bags (www.bma.org.uk/collective-voice/policy-and-research/public-and-population-health/climate-change). However, influencing policy is not easy, for a variety of reasons. Firstly, as Naomi Klein, who is by background a journalist, points out, climate science can intimidate non-scientists. Luckily for us, she overcame her fears and produced an accessible book on climate change (Klein 2015). In the UK, organisations such as the Wellcome Trust also aim to demystify medical science and the health impact of climate change so that the wider public can participate in debates.

Nevertheless, there are other difficulties in influencing policy to reduce the carbon dioxide emissions that are overheating the planet. Power and control over decision making are important to analyse. Cambridge

Jane Thomas, Salim Vohra and Sean Tunney

professor Stephen Lukes writes about elites and rulers keeping important issues off the public agenda (1974). The 'un-politics' of air pollution, poverty and climate change describes the lack of debate and action on these topics. So, Klein (2015) points out owners and shareholders profit, in the short-term, from continuing along a path of reckless, high-carbon growth, and she documents the stifling of debate. Increasing wealth inequalities make tackling climate change more difficult as the super-rich buy more political power and burn more carbon.

Concerns over employment can prevent citizens from raising objections to health-harming pollution. These 'jobs versus pollution' issues cause splits and tension within organisations representing workers, such as the GMB union, with more than 600,000 members. The union previously supported the expansion of Heathrow Airport saying it would create thousands of new jobs. On the other hand, more political arms of the Labour movement in the UK, including the Labour Party, have opposed Heathrow expansion, due to its environmental impact. They argue that, in the longer term, more jobs would be created by flying less and developing new technologies. These issues need to be debated by students and the public in order to empower and encourage participation in deciding the fate of the planet. Students studying social science and health subjects can contribute to and inform the debate through their critical thinking and appraisal of evidence.

The power of elites in influencing debate in the UK is not always difficult to identify. London's *Evening Standard* newspaper is a good example. It is part-owned by wealthy friends of Boris Johnson and its editor-in-chief has been George Osborne, former Conservative Party chancellor. It is supported by advertising, and, in a normal working day, around 800,000 paper copies have been distributed free to commuters. Private ownership and links with advertising are two reasons for students and researchers to think critically when using mass media as sources.

Another reason for the importance of more public involvement and democratic political control over elite power is that so many issues impact on health. A series of highly controversial decisions with health consequences have been taken in recent years by politicians. Our first example concerns Labour politician Peter Mandelson, who was secretary of state for trade and industry. Before the 2008 global recession, he rejected the idea of an explicit 'industrial strategy' and was wedded to a rolling back of elements of democratic planning within the economy. He supported a campaign to remove the Labour Party's famous Clause 4, which explicitly referred to public, as opposed to market, control over production, distribution and exchange. However, when global markets crashed in 2008, as a reflationary measure, he oversaw a car scrappage scheme. This, in tandem with tax incentives, ramped up the number of diesel cars on the UK's roads. The pollutants from diesel cars have now been assessed as causing thousands of additional deaths per year. The extent of diesel pollutants was compounded by Volkswagen's manipulation of emissions tests on their cars. Ironically, the traditionally more pro-market Conservative government has now attempted to develop an industrial strategy for the UK, published in 2017.

The carte blanche that was given by the Conservative-Liberal Democrat government of 2010 to 2015 to Health Minister Andrew Lansley has also been seen as historically controversial, affecting health services in England. With a view to increasing privatisation, he set about a major upheaval of NHS structures. (Here again, Scotland and Wales have taken another path. They have reintroduced free prescriptions, for instance, which, it has been argued, re-establishes the idea that the NHS should be free at the point of delivery.) The distraction of expensive and ongoing reorganisations, it is claimed, has had an opportunity cost. These unnecessary reorganisations have taken attention away from dealing with big issues, such as climate change and pandemic planning.

Finally, the building by Chinese and French state companies of a new nuclear power station on British land in Somerset is a highly debatable health-related decision that will last for millennia. The democratic and planning process that enabled signing off Hinkley Point C are themselves health issues. Klein (2015) lists a range of arguments against nuclear power development, including that investment in renewables already has the potential to provide for the country's needs.

Thus, we can see that a wide range of difficult debates exists in public policy that impact on health. While Lukes and Piketty highlight the interests of those intent on taking information out of the public domain, students and researchers can aim to draw out and debate data.

Two of the most important health-related political issues in UK politics to argue over are as follows:

- economic growth versus action to address climate change and
- home building versus food security, environmental preservation and action on climate change.

These issues require research and public oversight. Some solutions aim to reduce the 'either-or', 'zero-sum', nature of the problem by arguing for investment in green technology and clearing 'brown-field' sites for dwellings. But at the moment these solutions are not the ones being picked for the UK. There are also ethical issues involved here, and people's answers can depend on how much we care for others, including future generations. As we are currently living through the largest extinction of species in 65 million years – with insect and bird populations in the UK plummeting – all

Jane Thomas, Salim Vohra and Sean Tunney

academic disciplines can be relevant to understanding humanity's best solutions to these problems. The UN's 'sustainable development goals' show the potential benefits of coordinated action.

4.8 Responses to health-related social problems

As we have seen, climate change and other wider issues are important determinants of health. But health can also be improved by society through services, social arrangements and changing attitudes.

Primary care services, discussed earlier, have a significant impact on health, and these are the NHS services where most can be done to reduce inequalities in health. High-quality primary care is important in promoting breastfeeding, the early diagnosis of cancers and in regular check-ups for people with long-term conditions, such as type-2 diabetes or depression, for instance.

You can find out about the health of the population in your local area by reading the latest annual public health report for your council. This is over-seen by the director of public health. Elected councillors also receive rep-resentations from constituents about health issues. Here again, as Tudor Hart posited, the best educated are the most likely to contact their elected representatives with problems and suggestions.

Social services such as those for children and adults with disabilities are generally overseen by councils. There are around 13.3 million disabled people in the UK, almost one in five of the population, around 17 percent of whom were born with their disability (www.dlf.org.uk). Disabilities among dependent children and adults impact on families, especially where social services support is weakened. The cost of bringing up a disabled child is estimated to be three times greater than a non-disabled child, and, at the same time, the average income of families with disabled children is around a quarter lower than the average. Thus, support for these fami-lies is important in ensuring that the health of all family members is not adversely affected.

Apart from anomalies such as dentistry, the NHS, unlike means-tested social care, is 'free at the point of delivery' and funded through general taxation. This is a social solution that pools risk and of which the UK population is generally proud. However, Scotland and Wales have increas-ingly resisted international and neoliberal pressure to privatise healthcare, whereas in England more services are run by private for-profit companies and hedge funds, the latter being capital investment funds that switch money between different companies. And businesses such as Virgin Care, at the time of writing, sometimes employ nurses, doctors and other staff to provide these state-funded services.

Decisions on who gets hospital care in the UK are based on clinical need and not individual ability to pay. Cosmetic procedures that individuals can feel make a difference to their quality of life and job prospects, such as the 'correction of abnormally protruding ears', alignment of breasts of different sizes, removal of skin flaps caused by weight loss and tattoo removal, are not currently funded by the NHS. NICE, the National Institute for Health and Care Excellence, provides evidence reviews and recommendations on what medicines and procedures are funded.

People with mental health problems can face difficulties accessing services. Mental health problems are wide ranging, from depression and anxiety through to complex personality disorders and severe and enduring psychosis. French theorist Michel Foucault discusses different regimes of supervising and controlling those with mental health problems. Before any treatments were available, Foucault describes people with symptoms being put onto boats and sailed off. Nowadays, stigma against people with mental health problems can prevent individuals and families from seeking help. But campaigns led by famous people like Stephen Fry and groups such as 'Time to Change' have had considerable success in reducing stigma in the UK and improving knowledge of, and attitudes towards, those with mental health problems, as evidenced by public surveys.

A further important health problem, which does not divide politicians down party lines, concerns assisted dying for those with terminal illnesses. The UK parliament debated and rejected assisted suicide in 2015. While some US states such as California, as well as Canada, the Netherlands, Belgium and Switzerland did adopt legislation at the turn of the millennium. Around 4 percent of deaths in the Netherlands are now of this nature. The reasons given are to stop pain and to end dependency.

Aside from a focus on health and social care services, a major area that affects health is employment, while unemployment has a deleterious effect on health. As most of the adult population in the UK is in work, employers are able to influence population health by providing measures such as adaptations to support those with disabilities to stay in work, secure contracts, improving low pay, flexible working and paternity leave, which can help family bonding and reduce stress. Due to competition between companies, these rights are normally set at a national level by governments.

Workplace stress can be caused by anti-social shift patterns as well as low control over work combined with high workloads. These stresses tend to affect lower-paid workers more. Mental health problems are also caused by workplace bullying, racism and homophobia, for instance. Staff can raise concerns, often with union support, over conditions and pay.

Also, the #MeToo scandals have shown how so-called gagging clauses, settlement and non-disclosure agreements (NDAs) can operate. These are legal documents signed by thousands of workers threatened with job loss within local and central government, and in the private sector in the UK. They can stop workers speaking out about employers. Since, if individuals don't sign, they can be left without a reference needed to get another job. Film producer Harvey Weinstein's former assistant, Zelda Perkins, for example, described to the UK Parliamentary Committee for Women and Equalities in 2018 the extreme stress caused by employers wielding these legal instruments.

Partly as a result of women struggling with long working hours and competing demands, increasingly many countries are seeing falling birth rates. South Korea has the world's lowest birth rate. But delayed childbirth and obesity in the UK are factors leading to demand for in vitro fertilisation (IVF). On the flip side, while falling, the UK also still has comparatively high teenage pregnancy rates, indicating poor sex education, inaccessible services and low ambition among young women in lower-income areas. UNICEF has also produced a damning report of children's lives in the UK, with lower trust between children than in any other Western nation (2017).

Employment rights and the freedom to 'organise in the workplace' have been won and lost over many decades. Edwin Chadwick, a Victorian reformer who initiated many public policies supportive of health, was partly motivated by wanting to 'avert the Chartists', who were campaigning to bring in more workers' and citizens' rights, around the 1840s. He, for instance, instigated the opening of parks at times when Chartists had been planning marches, as a distraction. More recently, trade union activity has been associated with a lowering of income inequality, which, as we discussed earlier, is a contributor to inequalities in health. However, 'in-work poverty' has increased.

The Joseph Rowntree Foundation (www.jrf.org.uk) monitors in-work poverty and offers recommendations for the Scottish and UK governments on how to address poverty in their budgets. Nevertheless, many of the goods and services we use come from across the globe – where did your clothes, household goods and electronic devices come from? And what was the 'carbon footprint', or how much carbon dioxide was put into the atmosphere, as a result of this delivery? The conditions of employment can be even lower in countries exporting to the UK and often go unreported and hidden from sight.

While agencies like Public Health Wales and responsible employers run campaigns to improve health, marketing by some industries can undo this work. Sports sponsorship by sugary drinks manufacturers like Coca-Cola had a high profile during the 2012 London Olympics, and the tobacco and alcohol industries find circuitous routes to wield influence (Cave & Rowell 2015). Nevertheless, there has been some further regulation: public health advocates have been successful in controlling cigarette advertising in the UK, for example.

4.9 Summary

Health is a subject that is infused with an extraordinary number of political and ethical questions. From state spending on tattoo removal through to taxing sugary drinks, democratic decisions on how unequal we want wealth to be are central to the health inequalities debates. Key questions for the coming decade are around adjudication between forms of economic growth and work to address climate change. After the COVID-19 lockdown, from a public health perspective, what Piketty documents as trends in growing income inequality, the use of tax havens and the exploitation of the media by elements of 'the 1%', need to be challenged. Theories from the social sciences can help us with analysing these questions. Utilising diverse theories such as elite, pluralist, Marxist and feminist theories provides different perspectives and supports the development of new solutions to these persistent problems. Epidemiological, demographic and biochemical studies also have an important role. There is plenty of research to be done on addressing the UK's health problems.

 Key points

Defining health highlights that different people may have different conceptions of what it means to be healthy

The World Health Organization has a significant influence on conceptions of health within countries such as the UK, with its definitions seen as a 'gold standard'. The extent to which different activities impact on prevention of health problems varies. And the effect of services on different groups is a focus in health policy research.

Public health looks at health from a population perspective

Debates in public health centre on the relative health impact of wide-ranging factors, from damp and overcrowded housing to parenting classes. Evidence, in the form of large-scale statistical analysis, expensive randomised control trials and other scientific research can affect health policies, such as on the introduction of a sugar tax. Questions to be asked include: Is there a strong evidence base for this shift? Will policy implementation increase or decrease inequalities in health? Debates and hypothesis testing, informed by existing evidence, are needed to illuminate different perspectives.

Jane Thomas, Salim Vohra and Sean Tunney

Ethical and political perspectives can sway how health problems are addressed

Different countries within the UK have taken divergent positions on how health services are delivered. Perhaps people in Wales and Scotland are more likely to be opposed to profit seeking in health care provision. Or have devolved political institutions listened to citizens more and thus blocked privatisation? Either way, differences have emerged in how health problems are addressed. Similarly, international comparative studies show a variation in how health and social care problems are being dealt with.

Inequalities in health between different income groups show a gap of around ten years

To improve the health of the population as a whole, we need to improve the health of the less well-off. Not only do these groups die younger, but they also experience disabilities associated with old age at younger ages. These findings have social justice implications as well as financial costs for health services, families and employers.

Climate change is an unprecedented problem for all nations

The health problems of climate change range from issues such as increases in depression and anxiety associated with flooding, through to job losses in fishing. Coupled with these immediate human health-related costs is the mass extinction of plant and animal species. Action to address climate change is taking place in a political and economic context that is generally hostile to regulation and social solutions. In addition, we can feel bamboozled by the science and the enormity of the problems involved, thus ending up 'burying our heads in the sand'. But this is the purpose of education – to develop powers of reasoning and analysis, and debating skills, in order to enter into, and lead, the discussion on solutions.

 Coursework questions

What factors should be considered when deciding whether to build dwellings on farmland and green spaces?
Can a notion of happiness be used to plan national policy?

To what extent is health an issue of individual responsibility?

Should the age at which the state pension is claimed differ by social class?

What are the pros and cons of nuclear power?

References

Beattie, A. (2002) 'Knowledge and control in health promotion: a test case for social policy and social theory'. In Bury, M., Calnan, M. and Gabe, J. (eds.), *The Sociology of the Health Service*. London: Routledge, pp. 162–202.

Beauchamp, T. and Childress, J. (2013) *Principles of Biomedical Ethics*. Oxford: Oxford University Press.

Cave, T. and Rowell, A. (2015) *A Quiet Word*. London: Penguin.

Klein, N. (2015) *This Changes Everything*. London: Penguin.

Lee, K. and Freudenberg, N. (2020) 'Addressing the commercial determinants of health begins with clearer definition and measurement'. *Global Health Promotion* 27(2): 3–5.

Lukes, S. (1974) *Power: A Radical View*. London: Macmillan Press.

Marmot, M., Allen, J., Boyce, T., Goldblatt, P. and Morrison, J. (2020a) *Health Equity in England: The Marmot Review 10 Years On*. London: Institute of Health Equity.

Marmot, M., Allen, J., Goldblatt., Herd, E. and Morrison, J. (2020b) *Build Back Fairer: The COVID-19 Marmot Review*. London: Institute of Health Equity.

Nazroo, J. (2003) 'The structuring of ethnic inequalities in health: Economic position, racial discrimination, and racism'. https://ajph.aphapublications.org/doi/full/10.2105/AJPH.93.2.277

Piketty, T. (2020) *Capital and Ideology*. Cambridge, MA: The Belknap Press of Harvard University Press.

Thomas, J. (2018) 'Pedagogy in motion: Drafting resolutions holding debates'. www.uwl.ac.uk/sites/default/files/Departments/Research/Vistas/Web/PDF/publication_series/uwl_new_vistas_0401_thomas.df

 ## Further reading

Naidoo, J. and Wills, J. (2016) *Foundations for Health Promotion* (4th ed.). London: Elsevier.

Jane Thomas, Salim Vohra and Sean Tunney

chapter 5

Ageing

Norman Ginsburg

5.1 Introduction

Ageing in itself is by no means a social problem. The fact that people are living longer than ever before, globally and in the UK, is a huge bonus for humanity, reflecting (until recently at least) rising living standards and household incomes for most people, as well as improved public health measures and health-care provision.

It is important at the outset to consider briefly the category 'older people'. In the UK it has become commonplace to consider 'older people' as those aged 65 and over, and this usage is adopted in this chapter. This convention appears to have come about because, in 1925, 65 was set as the age at which individuals contributing to National Insurance could claim the basic state pension. For women, this state pension age (SPA) was reduced to 60 in 1940, but since 2010, it has been increased rapidly and controversially – in 2018 it reached parity with men at 65. The government has been increasing the SPA incrementally from 2019. There is no national 'retirement age' as such, despite its widespread equation with the SPA. So 'old age' has for almost a century been officially constructed as beginning at 65, which, despite its arbitrariness in terms of individual life experiences, has the virtue of simplicity.

The population of the UK is getting older. In 1976 the proportion aged 65 and over was 14.2 percent; in 2016 it was 18.0 percent, and by 2046 it is projected to be 24.7 percent (ONS 2017a: Table 1). However, if older people are in paid work, doing unpaid care or other voluntary work or enjoying retirement as consumers, then, on the face of it, ageing is just a demographic phenomenon, with older people contributing to the economy and society like other adults. Yet there are many problematic aspects of the situation of older people in the contemporary UK, which are explored here, focusing in turn on income and health inequalities, social care needs and provisions, disability and intergenerational conflict.

5.2 Retirement and paid work

The notion of retirement from paid work with a decent pension is still widely considered to be something which all older people deserve, something which has been 'earnt' and paid for by pension contributions. It is or used to be seen as a social right, which originated after the Second World War with the enactment of the universal state pension. This is sometimes referred to as 'the welfare state model' of retirement. So, in the second half of the twentieth century, 'the idea of "retirement" was an essential part of the narrative driving the reconstruction of ageing [to become] a social institution' (Phillipson 2013: 73). For most older men, leaving paid employment has become something of a rite of passage to a new stage of life – a third age between working adulthood and a fourth age of disability and decline.

The welfare state model has never been fully realised in the UK because many adults have never had three or four decades of formal (i.e. protected by National Insurance) full-time paid employment, while the basic state pension has never achieved a decent retirement income for all. Retirement on a decent pension was also very much a gendered concept, based on the 'male breadwinner' division of labour in the family, in which it was assumed that women would derive income in old age from their partner's pension. It is only in more recent decades that many more women have earned retirement pensions in their own right.

Although the idea of a universal right to retirement with a pension remains hegemonic, it collides head on with some of the fundamentals of a capitalist society (e.g. that able-bodied adults are obliged to take up paid employment or run their own business in exchange for the means to live: 'the work ethic'). This really implies that older people should work 'until they drop'. In this model, retirement is only achievable through access to private pensions, either directly purchased or organised as a perk by employers as a workplace pension. With the rise of neoliberalism in the UK since the early 1980s, this pre-1945 individualistic model has come back to prominence as governments raise 'the retirement age' and prevent employers from arbitrarily retiring older workers. The neoliberal model of retirement is nevertheless held back by the cost of private and workplace pensions; the last two decades have witnessed widespread reductions in the generosity of workplace pensions and a decline in coverage.

The problematic aspects of the neoliberal model are self-evident in that it leaves responsibility for incomes and pensions in old age to individuals and their employers, inevitably risky and under resourced for many. But what are the problematic aspects of the welfare state model? First, the notion of a universal retirement age is inflexible, not in tune with the realities of individuals' working and non-working lives. Workers have sometimes been forced (or incentivised) into or chosen early retirement; others would choose not to retire until ill health or disability forced them to; others needed to stay in paid employment to maintain an adequate income. The realities of 'choice' here are complex. Secondly, enforced retirement by an employer at any age is likely to involve age discrimination. In 2011 the UK government passed legislation to prevent employers forcibly retiring workers on an age basis 'unless they had a legally justifiable reason for doing so' (Phillipson et al. 2016: 192). So far, only a few employers have sought such legal justification, so mandatory retirement has disappeared for the time being. A third problematic aspect is simply the shortage of decent jobs, so it can be argued with some legitimacy that older people in well-paid and pensioned employment should make way for younger people who may otherwise be crowded out of jobs by their seniors. Finally, for governments driven by an ideology of austerity, there is the problem of the cost of state pensions, which appears to justify increases in the pension eligibility age.

Universal retirement with a state pension remains in very many respects a wonderful achievement of the workers' movement in the twentieth century, but it is increasingly vulnerable to neoliberalism and to being too rigid in a context of growing insecurity and/or choices about when working life might end. One indicator of the scale of the shift away from a standard retirement age is that in 1961, 91 percent of men aged 60 through 64 were in or available for paid employment, while only 25 percent of men aged 65 and over were in or available for paid employment. The 1960s saw the peak of the standard welfare state model. By 1995 the employment rate for men aged 60 through 64 had fallen to 45 percent, and for men aged 65 through 69, it was 12.8 percent. Since the 1990s, however, employment rates have risen for men in both age groups to 56.4 and 24.2 percent, respectively, in 2014 (Phillipson et al. 2016: Table 1). In the UK, there have been two phases of male retirement. The period from the 1960s to the 1990s, the era of deindustrialisation, saw a mass of early forced retirements for skilled and semi-skilled men; since the 90s, higher proportions of older men have remained in paid employment, mostly staying in their jobs rather than finding new ones. For older women, the data on paid employment are somewhat different. Employment rates for women aged 60 through 64 increased steadily from 17.6 percent in 1985 to 40.1 percent in 2014, and for those aged 65 through 69 from 6.3 percent in 1985 to 17.1 percent in 2014. So there has been something of a dramatic shift towards older women finding paid employment, from quite low proportions in the 1980s to levels approaching those for men by 2014. So it seems that, in the earlier era, governments and employers sought to remove older people, mostly men, from the workforce while, more recently, governments have sought to 'prolong working life'. Neither aim is necessarily in the best interests of the older people affected: generally the less wealthy and less privileged in the labour market.

This is reflected in perhaps the most strikingly problematic aspect of the retirement/paid work issue – the inequalities in the take up of retirement. There are substantial differences according to household income in the proportion of those retiring before the state pension age (SPA): 27 percent of the lowest 40 percent of the income distribution retire before the SPA, compared with 49 percent of those in the top 20 percent. As Thomson (2018: 12) puts it

> those who are most likely to be in lower paid, poor quality work that will lead to longer-term health problems are also the people who have to work for longer from financial necessity, as well as being most at risk of falling out of work involuntarily.

So, perhaps perversely, it is older people with low incomes with a lower healthy life expectancy who are most likely to extend their working lives.

Thus, retirement is gradually being taken away from many of those who perhaps most need it: people with relatively low incomes, little or no wealth and lower healthy life expectancy. A more blatant example of the Matthew principle – to them that hath, more shall be given – is hard to imagine. With rising retirement ages for the less well-off, they will increasingly 'subsidise the better off by dying' before they can claim the state pension so that 'wealthier people become [greater] beneficiaries of what remains of the welfare state' (Hill 2017a).

Another related aspect of ageing as a serious social problem is the substantial number of older people whose basic needs are not being adequately met. This involves a lot of suffering for individuals, and it is a 'social' problem because of its scale. It is 'social' because it is a waste of human resources, sometimes leading to costly and preventable crises which use scarce resources, whether from family, health-care or social care budgets. The dimensions of the problem are many and various, including, of course, inadequate income, illness, disability, loneliness – these experiences are obviously not confined to older people, but they are more often combined in old age. Hence, we now consider the social problem of inadequate income in later life.

5.3 Inadequate income

A 2015 AgeUK survey found that 26 percent of adults aged over 50 were either 'just about getting by' or 'finding it difficult' in terms of managing

Norman Ginsburg

on their income. Of those surveyed, 29 percent said 'they were living comfortably', which rather bluntly encapsulates the basic class inequality among older people (AgeUK 2018: 17). State pensions have become a flat-rate 'safety net' provision in the UK, adopted as explicit policy from the 1980s; private and workplace pensions only provide substantial income for the affluent. So the State Pension provides 80 to 90 percent of income for people in the lowest two-fifths of the income distribution (AgeUK 2017: 2). Largely as a consequence of inadequate pensions, almost two million (16 percent) pensioners in the UK live below the official 'headline low income measure'. In other words, they experience income poverty with incomes below 60 percent of the median household income after housing costs (HBAI 2017). Pensioners over 80 are at significantly greater risk of income poverty than those under 80, reflecting historically less access to private and workplace pensions and less paid employment among those over 80. This is obviously perverse in relation to the likelihood of greater care and fuel needs for this group.

It seems invidious and simplistic to compare the needs of elder households in income poverty with those of non-pensioners in income poverty. Certainly the proportion of pensioners in poverty on this measure has fallen in recent decades from an astonishing peak of 40 percent in the late 1980s to 16 percent in 2016, but many are living just above the line, and many have income pressures which are greater in later life (e.g. for fuel). One indicator of the inadequacy of pensions in the UK is that substantial numbers are eligible for income-tested support in the form of the Pension Credit and Housing Benefit. In May 2017, 2.2 million pensioners (17 percent of the total) were claiming Pension Credit, but an officially estimated 38 percent of those eligible did not claim it, missing out on an average of £42 a week. This suggests that, overall, 29 percent of pensioners are eligible, demonstrating the inadequacy of the state pension. Similar proportions of eligibility and non–take up apply to the Housing Benefit, so it has been estimated that a total of £3.5 billion of these two benefits went unclaimed by pensioners in 2014–2015 (AgeUK 2018: 18). This is a major failing of the safety net element of the welfare state, obviously contributing directly to unmet need, deprivation and ill health among people in old age.

Research Findings 1

Hill et al. (2011: 63) carried out 25 in-depth interviews with older people in the East Midlands. Their personal testimonies show 'the extent of the sheer hard work required in order to get by and just how constraining living on a low income can be. Having little money means little opportunity for spontaneity and affects people's freedom and independence'. Some of the respondents 'had to economise on fulfilling basic needs, for example by only heating their homes for part of the day'. 'If you are only just keeping your head above water, it is hard to deal with unexpected or additional expenses. Someone who has planned their regular expenses carefully may find it hard, for example, to foot the bill for house or car repairs, to visit a sick relative at the other end of the country, or to replace a broken appliance'. 'The findings show how a combination of having poor health and mobility, and living in more isolated areas without accessible and affordable transport or social networks, can make some older people more disadvantaged than others'.

Another problematic aspect of low incomes in old age is gender difference. Two-thirds of claimants of Pension Credit, the income-tested supplement to inadequate state pensions, were women in 2017. In 2015 'the average weekly amount of State Pension received by women was 79% that of the average for men; on average women received £114.48 per week, compared to £144.64 for men' (Thurley et al. 2015: 3). In addition, 'women are less likely to be in receipt of a private pension and their private pension wealth is lower than that of men at all ages – particularly among the over 65s'. Gender inequality in incomes in old age is deeply entrenched, reflecting continuity in the structured economic disadvantages of women in British society.

Ethnic differences are also a problematic aspect of low income in old age. In the early 2010s, it was officially estimated that 14 percent of white pensioners lived in relative income poverty, compared with 27 percent of Asian/Asian British and 30 percent of black/African/Caribbean/black British pensioners (ONS/DWP 2017: Table 6.5db). In the early 2010s, the mean gross income of pensioner households was £492 per week for white British people, compared with £423 for Asian people and £350 for black people (Vlachantoni et al. 2017: 1029). Further research provides evidence that 'ethnicity remains a strong determinant of one's pension protection prospects through being in paid work, being an employee and working for an employer who offers a pension scheme' (Vlachantoni et al. 2015: 801). White British men are particularly privileged in getting access to workplace pensions. These disparities are the outcome of a complex set of processes linked to factors such as migration experience, low pay, employment patterns and under-protected small businesspeople. They certainly indicate persistent and substantial racialisation of low income in old age.

Norman Ginsburg

5.4 Income and wealth inequalities

Another problematic facet of later life in the UK is the striking income and wealth inequalities among older people.

> Half of those aged 55–64 had wealth of over £400,000 in 2008–10 and nearly a tenth more than £1.3 million . . . but a tenth had total assets of all kinds of £27,000 or less to see them through retirement, apart from the state pension and/or benefits. This ratio between those near the top and those near the bottom of nearly fifty to one gives a measure of how great inequality is, even within the same age group.
>
> (Hills 2017: 155)

The amount of wealth held in private pensions in payment is also strongly gendered. Median private pension wealth (for pensions in payment) for women was £85,900 in 2014 through 2016, compared to £195,400 for men (ONS 2018: Table 15). Such enormous disparities, of course, reflect women's adverse status in employment and remuneration, as well as strong historical traces of women's dependence on partners' pensions.

For some, the real problem of ageing is constructed in terms that suggest that succeeding generations and employers cannot afford the costs of pensions and benefits for elders. This is a serious distortion when one considers these facts of inequality. A redistribution of wealth among the over 55s would significantly improve incomes for elders struggling on state pensions and benefits, without having to burden further the under 55s. However governments persist in wealth taxation policies which increasingly and blatantly favour the better-off, including exemption of main residences from capital gains tax (£28 billion), income tax relief for employees' private pension contributions (£24 billion) and tax relief on employers National Insurance pension contributions (£17 billion) (Resolution Foundation 2018). The taxation system is constructed to protect and consolidate the wealth of the most privileged elders at the expense of the rest, particularly the least wealthy.

5.5 Health, disability and health inequalities

While it is far from problematic that more people are living into their 80s and beyond, the increasing number of older people with health and disability problems is very significant. Age UK (2017: 4) reported that

> the numbers of people aged 85+ in England increased by almost a third over the last decade. . . . By their late 80s, more than one in three people have difficulties undertaking daily living unaided. . . . [D]isability-free life expectancy at age 65 has been falling from its peak in 2010–12.

These phenomena clash head on with restraints in public spending on the NHS and social care, particularly in the era of austerity since 2010. Underfunding is compounded by insufficient preventive measures and poorly coordinated services. Hence, older people are admitted to acute care hospitals because of crises which might have been avoided had better support and care at home and in the community been available. Data is not collected nationally on this, which in itself is symptomatic of the inefficient use of resources in coordinating services. What is certain is that the numbers of older people in NHS acute beds has risen dramatically in the last five years, along with levels of 'delayed discharge' (i.e. patients staying in hospital unnecessarily because social and/or informal care is not available) (NAO 2016: 6). The National Audit Office has estimated that

> the NHS spends around £820 million a year treating older patients who no longer need to be there and who could be cared for at an annual additional cost for other parts of the health and social care system of around £180 million.

> (NAO 2016: 7–8)

In other words, the taxpayers could save £640 million annually if the delayed discharge problem was successfully addressed. Issues around mental incapacity and dementia are discussed later in this chapter.

The English Longitudinal Study of Ageing (ELSA) project has accumulated data for 2002 to 2015 on socio-economic differences in health outcomes among older people. This shows very significant class differences in healthy life expectancy and in mortality. Using four different parameters of 'class' (workplace social group, income, wealth, education), there were similar differences, but the greatest disparity was linked to wealth. Hence, for example, the healthy life expectancy differential between the top and bottom thirds of the wealth distribution, measured by 'the estimated additional years expected to live in good health at the age of 50, was around 12 years, eight years for disability-free life expectancy, and ten years for illness-free life expectancy' (Zaninotto et al. 2016: 101). In other words, the wealthiest third of the population can expect over a decade more of good health than the least wealthy third of the population. These class disparities become progressively less pronounced at ages beyond 50, partly because the higher mortality rate among the less affluent reduces their overall numbers. Compared with such class disparities, gender differences are much more modest, with women at 50 expecting to live up to three years longer in good health than men. Ethnic disparities in experiencing bad health appear to be very substantial. In survey data for 2009 through 2011, 32 percent of white British elders aged 60 to 74 reported that their health limited their typical activities, compared with 55 percent of Indian,

73 percent of Pakistani, 65 percent of Bangladeshi, 50 percent of black Caribbean and 56 percent black African heritage elders (Evandrou et al. 2016: Table 2). Even 'after controlling for income and deprivation . . . a health disadvantage remains, with Indian, Pakistani and Bangladeshi elders consistently reporting worse health than white British persons' (Evandrou et al. 2016: 661). Thus, the ethnic inequalities and injustices inscribed into British society over the post-war decades maintain strong traces into later life.

Health inequalities among older people are increasing as inequalities in wealth and income continue to diverge. As Coote (2009: 58) points out, 'if everyone enjoyed the same average good health as people in the highest socio-economic group, the costs of running the NHS could be cut significantly. . . . [S]o health inequalities are unethical, unjust, dysfunctional and wasteful'. This is particularly true for older people; reducing health inequalities and improving health status for older people on low incomes would save the taxpayers and the economy billions.

5.6 Social care

Social care for older people covers all forms of support and services which help with daily life, including informal care by friends and family, home-care services, neighbourhood day-care services, sheltered housing and residential care. It could and should include helping people overcome isolation and loneliness in later life. Here, we will focus on four problematic aspects: unmet needs, access to support and services, costs and finance and abuse of service users.

AgeUK (2014) has estimated that over a million people over 65 had unmet social care needs in England. More specifically, over 30 percent of older people who had difficulty in carrying out one or more 'activities of daily living' (ADLs: getting out of bed, washing, using the toilet, eating) did not 'receive any help from care workers or informally from family, friends or neighbours and [were] left to struggle alone' (AgeUK 2014: 1). Vlachantoni (2019: 667) suggests that the proportion may be even higher at 55 percent not receiving any support in meeting these needs. Data from the Health Survey of England suggest that older people in the most economically deprived areas are twice as likely to have unmet ADL needs as those in the least economically deprived areas (Savage 2017). The consequences of not meeting these needs is not only great individual suffering but also the likelihood of expensive crisis situations further down the line for the NHS, care services and families. Iparraguirre (2015: 4) estimates that 'meeting these needs would cost £4.2 billion per year', which is equivalent to a mere '3.8 percent of the NHS budget for England in 2015/16'. There are, of course, aspects of unmet need beyond ADLs, such as loneliness and mobility issues, which are documented in AgeUK (2018).

ageing

IpsosMORI (2017) investigated personal experiences of unmet need for care through 24 in-depth interviews. Many of the participants experienced precarious support, 'particularly unpaid support from family, friends and neighbours'; also, 'where participants were heavily reliant on support from one person this could lead to intermittent unmet need, or the possibility of serious future unmet need if that support was no longer available (IpsosMORI 2017: 64). They also reported difficulties in getting information about available services and in finding local authority support, which included 'local authorities not offering assessments, delays in providing equipment or support, or older people believing they would not be eligible for help from the local authority so not contacting them' (IpsosMORI 2017: 64).

Access to appropriate care and support for older people is unnecessarily complex and haphazard. Unlike the basic pension and the NHS, in England, there are no clear rights to services and no universal access; England relies on a mix of informal care and private services, with public funding for some services for those deemed to be in financial need.

One of the most problematic and high-profile issues is the very real fear, even amongst the comparatively affluent, of the potential impact of high care costs. According to estimates cited by Baxter and Glendinning (2014: 8–9), between 20 and 25 percent of people receiving home care and 40 to 45 percent of those in residential care homes are paying the costs privately. These proportions of self-funders are gradually increasing as means testing for local authority support becomes more stringent. In England people with assets over £23,250, including their home, receive no financial state support for residential care, so public funding is concentrated on those with very few assets. While this seems fair, it means that owner occupiers with fairly modest assets can be forced to sell their homes to fund their care. So, in paying for care, a fairly small minority of older people, around 10 percent of those aged 65 and over, 'can lose the majority of their income and assets . . . widely regarded by the public as unfair' (Dilnot 2011: 12). While it may be argued that those who can afford to pay should do so, it is manifestly unfair that 'individuals cannot protect themselves against the risk of very high care costs by pooling their risk', unlike with car or home insurance; 'this is the only major area in which everyone faces significant financial risk, but no one is able to protect themselves against it' (Dilnot 2011: 13). Andrew Dilnot, the chair of a government commission on care funding, described the current 'system' as 'the most pernicious means-test in the whole of the British welfare state' (Hill 2017b). Recent governments

Norman Ginsburg

have promised to introduce a 'cap' on costs, but at the time of writing, there is no prospect of implementation.

The 2010s witnessed an escalating crisis in publicly funded social care for older people in the UK, owing to several factors:

> Central government grant reductions to local authorities have been passed on to care providers in the form of reduced fees or below inflation increases; combined with shortages of nurses and care workers, higher regulatory standards and the introduction of the National Living Wage.
>
> (Humphries et al. 2016: 3)

Between 2005–2006 and 2013–2014, the number of older people receiving social care support from local authorities in England fell by 31 percent. Services 'such as meals on wheels and day centres . . . experienced particularly deep cuts, those most associated with prevention, support for independent living and support for informal carers' (AgeUK 2018: 26). 'No one has a full picture of what has happened to older people who are no longer entitled to publicly funded care: the human and financial costs to them and those who care for them are mounting' (Humphries et al. 2016: 3). Women are bearing the brunt of this crisis – 'the majority of those in need of care and the majority of the care workforce, paid and unpaid, are women' (WBG 2017: 1).

Another problematic aspect of social care for older people, whether publicly or privately financed, is the experience of neglect and abuse, whether in the home, in residential care or in NHS hospitals. The Equalities and Human Rights Commission (EHRC) conducted an inquiry into the abuse of elders' human rights as home-care service users. While 'half of the older people, friends and family members who gave evidence . . . expressed real satisfaction with their home care . . . the evidence revealed many instances of care that raised real concerns' (EHRC 2011: 4). Greener (2015: 142) reviewed evidence of neglect and abuse in private residential care homes, suggesting that in many cases, the work processes experienced by the staff mitigated against 'ensuring the comfort, dignity and wellbeing of the residents'. It is difficult to assess the scale of the problems, and there is clearly a huge variation in the quality of care across UK care homes. In some homes, older people are 'warehoused' with basic needs met but little else. In others, there is plenty of activity and variation in residents' daily lives. The Care Quality Commission suggests that 'only' around 2 percent of care homes are inadequate, but a BBC Radio 4 investigation suggested that there could be an average of two sexual assaults a day in care homes, mostly involving older people (BBC 2016). Inadequate funding and poor regulatory oversight are obviously major explanatory factors, but these are symptoms of a deeper problem of ageist societal attitudes which see elders as a burden. As Herring (2019: 284) observes, 'the ageist notion that older people are a "waste of space" and always complaining about things, deters victims of elder abuse from seeking help or indeed even leads them to believe that the behaviour is not abusive'.

The extent of inadequate care for and neglect of older people in NHS hospitals is also difficult to assess. In 2011 the Health Service Ombudsman published a report on ten particular cases of complaints upheld against the NHS involving lack of basic care. She concluded that she had 'yet to see convincing evidence of a widespread shift in attitudes towards older people across the NHS that will turn the [ethical] commitments in the NHS Constitution into tangible reality' (HSO 2011: 10). Such issues came to prominence in the scandal surrounding the Mid-Staffordshire Hospitals Trust. Prompted initially by pressure from bereaved relatives, it emerged that hundreds of older patients died prematurely due to neglect between 2005 and 2009. Eventually, after a public inquiry, a thorough and lengthy report on Mid-Staffs was published in 2013 (Francis 2013), which identified inadequate staffing resources and poor management as the key factors, as well as some clinical staff lacking compassion towards patients. A follow-up investigation by the medical director for England found similar issues affecting the care of older patients in 14 other hospital trusts (Keogh 2013). All this seems to indicate that the NHS has a systemic problem regarding the care of older patients. This view is certainly argued with much supporting evidence by Mandelstam (2011), a lawyer with considerable experience representing older patients and their relatives in complaints against the NHS. If, as it claims, the NHS is a 'command and control' national organisation with responsibility all the way to the very top, then the responsibility for the systemic problem lies there and not simply with local staff and management. The situation is likely to have significantly improved since Mid-Staffs, but it is far from clear to what extent and how permanently. It would also be reasonable to conclude that such problems reflect long-established ageist attitudes and stigmatisation of old age. As the World Health Organization's Declaration on the Global Prevention of Elder Abuse asserts, 'ultimately elder abuse will only be successfully prevented if a culture that nurtures intergenerational solidarity . . . is developed' (WHO 2002: 1).

5.7 Social problems of the fourth age

The title of this chapter is perhaps somewhat misleading because we are not covering the whole of the ageing process: that is, the full life cycle from birth onwards. The chapter is only discussing the later stages of the life cycle, reflecting a widespread understanding of 'ageing' as focused on people in retirement and/or over 60 or 65 years of age. Ageing, however,

Norman Ginsburg

also conjures up an image of an older person coping with mental and/or physical ill health and/or disability. These two images reflect the sociological distinction between the third and fourth stages of the life cycle, the first stage being childhood and the second 'working' adulthood. The third stage or 'third age' did not come to prominence until quite recently as retirement on a decent pension in good health became a reality for many from the 1960s onwards. The third age envisages retirees enjoying consumerism, personal growth and some freedom to shape their lives as they wish, actively responding to changes in physical and mental powers which ageing dictates. The increasing number of third agers is perhaps only a social problem in relation to matters discussed earlier, particularly the financial exclusion of a substantial number of retirees and the obligations of third agers to the generations behind them.

The 'fourth age' is the final stage in the life cycle, in which those who reach it experience debilitating changes in their physical and/or mental faculties which limit or prevent the activities enjoyed by third agers. The 'fourth age' suggests a more profound and intractable social problem, particularly as their number has increased significantly in recent decades. It is not a problem simply related to class or gender inequality, though women live longer than men and maybe experience more of the fourth age. People from lower income groups with less longevity may enter the fourth age at an earlier chronological age. The fourth age is clearly not simply a matter of chronological age; people may experience debilitating physical and/or mental impairment at any age, but people over, say, 75 are obviously more likely to do so.

Gilleard and Higgs (2017: 1682) argue that 'it is in the distinction between the fit and the frail, between those who are and are not "ageing successfully", where one of the greatest social divisions of later life is now realised'. Sociologists of ageing and social gerontologists have used parallel binary distinctions such as that between 'young-old' and 'old-old', 'fit' and 'frail' elders or 'successful' and 'unsuccessful' ageing. It is almost inevitable that notions associated with the third age like 'successful ageing' or 'active ageing' can cast a shadow over fourth agers as 'unsuccessful'. There is even an underlying implication that they may, to some extent, be to blame for their disabilities by failing to pursue a healthy, 'active' lifestyle. Hence, Latimer (2018: 847) suggests that 'bad' ageing, like poverty, is sometimes constructed as a failure of the individual to live up to 'neoliberal forms of personhood' embodied by successful third agers. The distinction between the third and fourth ages is, of course, by no means hard and fast, illustrating the limitations of using a simple binary model. Clearly, also, social science research has much more work to do in analysing the experiences of fourth agers, which go beyond the problematic constructions discussed here.

We have already discussed the growing numbers of older people needing social care, particularly among the 'old-old' living into their 80s and beyond. As we have seen, this is compounded by inadequate access to and provision of services. This is perhaps a reflection of a deeper social problem – the stigma of disability, physical and/or mental in old age, from which long-term recovery is impossible. Such stigma is linked to everyone's fears of disability and of death. Higgs and Gilleard (2015: 14) suggest that public understanding of 'real' old age is dominated by such fears, in which the fourth age is conceived as 'a location stripped of . . . the articulation of choice, autonomy, self-expression and pleasure'. They suggest that in 'the public's attitudes to what is seen as "real" old age . . . the fourth age acts as a metaphorical "black hole" of ageing' involving 'fear of passing beyond any possibility of agency, human intimacy or social exchange' Higgs and Gilleard (2015: 16). While such a perspective may go some way towards a critical understanding of the stigma and social exclusion of fourth agers, it seems problematic in several respects. First, there is no data which corroborates the assertion that a 'black hole' conception as such is predominant. Second, it appears to equate fourth agers with those suffering the most severe mental impairment; this is only a proportion of those who might be said to have left the third age behind. Third, Higgs and Gilleard put significant emphasis on admission to a care home as the criterion for entry into 'the black hole'; while this might be true of some of those with no direct contact with fourth agers, it is surely an over-generalisation. There are many fourth agers who are not in care homes, and there are many in care homes who are by no means as debilitated as 'the black hole' analogy implies.

Grenier (2012: 174) suggests that in 'recognising the fourth age as characterised solely by impairment, older people in this category become socially and culturally "othered" – both from society and within groups of older people'. She presents accounts from adults with physical impairments in late life which demonstrate active, complex and reflexive adaptation to their circumstances. The fourth age and/or the black hole implies the loss of a person's control over their lives, perhaps completely, so that their 'agency', their existence as an active human subject, disappears, at least in the eyes of carers and health-care professionals. Hence 'attention to agency as reduced or diminished in late life – and/or constructed as reduced – draws attention to the importance of analysing and addressing the power relations where increasing marginalisation and vulnerability are concerned'(Grenier and Phillipson 2013: 72). Assumptions about lack of agency are perhaps too deterministic –

the forms or expressions of agency from within the 'fourth age' may differ from those which we currently know and expect of agency at other

Norman Ginsburg

periods of the life course . . . and may also take the form of outright resistance or disruptive acts.

(Phillipson 2015: 90)

Mental or physical impairment should not necessarily compromise 'agency', though individual subjective expressions of agency in the fourth age are likely to take challenging and unfamiliar forms.

The 'black hole' analogy might perhaps be more appropriate for understanding social constructions around those experiencing more advanced dementia. Latimer (2018: 2) suggests that some 'media representations of older people with dementia are created spectacles of "othering"', in which sufferers represent a threat to the order and rationality of normal life, much in the way that people labelled mad were incarcerated in asylums, as discussed by Foucault (1965). McParland examined public responses to dementia which, conventionally at least, reflect 'a profound fear of developing a condition that appears utterly arbitrary and beyond the control of the individual or . . . medicine' and a visualisation of a future involving 'loss of self, living in poor care and being viewed as "mad"', which she labels 'dementiaism' (McParland et al. 2017: 261). This is beginning to change as relatives, carers and medical professionals increasingly understand and recognise the complex and diverse humanity within those experiencing advanced dementia. This is illustrated, for example, in the work of Nicci Gerrard, a writer and campaigner for the rights of people with dementia and their carers. Drawing on philosophers of ethics and her own experience of caring for her father, she argues that 'those with dementia have, individually and collectively, been deprived of their human dignity and respect because of our culture's increasing emphasis on autonomy, rationality and self-possession' (Gerrard 2019: 62). In other words, people with dementia too easily become dehumanised and the importance of their sociality denied. So, for example, a campaign to allow carers to stay in hospital, just as parents do with their sick children, started in 2014 and has been widely adopted in the NHS. This is a reflection of the emergence of 'dementia activism', campaigning by sufferers with carers and supporters for their human rights. Bartlett (2014) researched 'activists with dementia', finding three motivations or 'modes': 'protecting-self against decline', '(re) gaining respect', and 'creating connections with other people with dementia'.

People in later life with physical or mental impairments are not customarily constructed as belonging to the category 'people with disabilities'. The latter perhaps conjures up an image of an adult of 'working age' (i.e. in the second age). The disability rights movement (DRM), as it emerged in the second half of the twentieth century, has focused on the social rights of people of 'working age'. Public understanding of services and caring for older people with impairments has been dominated by a medical, health-care model. Certainly, people with dementia are confronting similar social barriers to other people with disabilities within and beyond the health and social care services, as documented by Thomas and Milligan (2018: Table 1). More recently social scientists and activists are making links between the DRM and dementia activism, though as Shakespeare et al. (2019: 13) point out, this is not easy: 'the usual language of disability rights is hard to apply. What would 'Dementia Pride' mean for example?'

Nevertheless, the rights of people with physical or mental impairments in later life including dementia are increasingly and usefully becoming framed within the human rights discourse, which, in the UK, means the Equality Act 2010 and the UN's Convention on the Rights of Persons with Disabilities (CRPD), which the UK ratified in 2009. This is not unproblematic for people with profound intellectual disabilities because it is rooted in individualism and self-representation, which sits uncomfortably alongside the 'complex, messy, interdependent reality of life' (Shakespeare et al. 2019: 13).

5.8 Intergenerational division

A common construction of ageing as a social problem suggests that older people are benefitting unfairly from public social expenditure on pensions, the NHS, winter fuel payments, free public transport and so on while, in many cases, enjoying generous private pensions and wealth accumulated through home ownership. The nub of the problem, according to this construction, is that succeeding generations of younger people are, in effect, being ripped off by their parents, often dubbed the baby boomers – those born roughly between 1945 and 1965. The baby boomers as consumers are routinely accused of misspending their children's inheritance. According to Bristow (2016: 578) 'since about 2006. . . the cultural script of the Baby Boomers has hardened into the (overall consensus) that this generation "took their children's future" (Willetts 2010)'. Bristow (2016) has analysed how such negative representations came to the fore in British newspapers 'to create a media discourse that is one-sidedly hostile to the Baby Boomer generation . . . exemplified by the motif of "Boomergeddon"' (Bristow 2016: 580). There is a more or less thinly veiled message which blames older people for the very real problems faced by younger generations – the failures to deliver affordable housing, decent and secure employment and improved living standards, particularly since the financial crisis in 2008. The effect, if not always the intention, is to deflect public attention away from the political and economic factors behind these manifest failings of capitalism in Britain and, instead, to pin the blame on older people or, at least, on demographic change.

Norman Ginsburg

2010: The Boomergeddon Boom

The year 2010 witnessed the adoption of austerity measures by the UK government, severely curtailing public spending on the NHS, and particularly social care services, particularly affecting older people. This coincided, perhaps not altogether accidentally, with an extraordinary explosion of public discussion on Boomergeddon, including three books and a pamphlet enthusiastically endorsing this construction – Willetts (2010), Howker and Malik (2010), Beckett (2010) and Boorman (2010) – written not by social scientists, but by journalists and a senior Conservative politician, David Willetts. The titles could not be more explicit:

The Pinch: How the Baby Boomers Took Their Children's Future – and Why They Should Give It Back

Jilted Generation: How Britain Has Bankrupted Its Youth

What Did the Baby Boomers Ever Do for Us? Why the Children of the Sixties Lived the Dream and Failed the Future

It's All Their Fault: A call to arms, a chance for those born in the 70s and 80s to respond to the chaos. We cannot stop the debt bomb but we can remove the Boomer politicians from office

Such views are found not only on the right and centre-right; they have has also been taken up by some on the left and centre-left, such as Beckett (2010) and Hutton (2010), and later by Elliott (2016).

These constructions of the ageing problem play on two features of contemporary social discourse. First, there is the question of the undermining of the unwritten generational contract underpinning the post-1945 Keynesian welfare state. This contract is 'based upon the view that today's old people helped to bring about the rising prosperity enjoyed by the non-old – and therefore the non-old should support them' (Macnicol 2015: 142). The contract has been broken because the non-old are no longer enjoying rising incomes and wealth, amid concern about the possibility that the current non-old generations are less likely to enjoy secure employment, homeownership, a decent company pension and a salubrious environment than the baby boomers. This is unquestionably deeply problematic in a society in which the intergenerational solidarities implied by the welfare state are increasingly weakened by its decline and its replacement with more individualistic private contracts associated with neoliberalism.

Second, there is the allegation that 'the baby boomers form a uniquely selfish "welfare generation"' (Macnicol 2015: 143), not just by hogging public resources but also in their private behaviour: 'The metaphor of the Baby Boomers having thrown a "party" and expecting their children to clear up "the mess" recurs in the cultural script of the Baby Boomer problem' (Bristow 2016: 581). So, in this neoconservative perspective, the health- and social-care needs of older people are linked to their lives in the 1960s and 1970s, stereotyped as an era of sexual licence, drug abuse and other 'risky behaviours'. To make matters worse, they are now engaged in spending their children's inheritance on an irresponsible consumerist binge. There is very little solid evidence to support the selfish baby boomer thesis. On the contrary, there is lots of evidence that baby boomers are increasingly supporting their children and grandchildren, and vice versa, of course.

Evandrou et al. (2018) analysed National Child Development Study data showing that around three-quarters of sons and daughters received support from their parents between leaving full-time education and the age of 42. This was mostly financial, accommodation and child-care support. Increasingly 'the safety net of the parental home is for many an invaluable form of support . . . difficult to quantify in monetary terms' (Heath 2018: 284). Possibly more significant is parental financial support in becoming a first-time home buyer; 'the proportion of first-time buyers under 30 who were reliant on family support rose from less than one-tenth in 1995 to around four-fifths in 2011' (Heath 2018: 285). So, on a considerable scale, those parents who can afford to do so are investing savings and retirement funds in financing home ownership for their children, filling some of the gap left by the failure of housing policy to deliver affordable rented housing or homeownership. Older people's support of younger generations is, of course, reciprocated; 55 percent of mid-life adult children (at age 50) were providing support to their parents, mostly with less demanding tasks such as transport, gardening and repairs; 4 percent of sons and 10 percent of daughters were providing continuous social care (Evandrou et al. 2018: 333). This data suggests that the private generational contract is very much in operation, even if its public equivalent is faltering.

The biggest distortion in the 'Boomergeddon' constructions is to homogenise all older people as affluent baby boomers. As demonstrated here, most older people in Britain are living on very modest incomes with little wealth, apart from that tied up in their own homes if they are homeowners. The economic class divide among older people (as in younger generations) is massive and widening. It is also apparent that far from being selfish, the privileged minority of older people with good pensions and savings are supporting their children financially. It is utterly misleading and divisive to suggest that the whole cohort of older people is selfishly denying resources to younger generations. This can be understood as an

Norman Ginsburg

attempt to legitimise the austerity discourse which has been and continues to be widely accepted by the political mainstream and the electorate. However, it is also reflexive of a public discourse which is hostile to the idea of the third age and even of retirement. Pickard (2019) cites a number of examples of this from leftish, liberal sources, which she describes as an 'age ideology' or 'age system', an increasingly virulent form of social stratification working alongside 'race', class and gender.

5.9 Summary

This chapter has discussed to what extent and how ageing has been constructed as a social problem in the UK in public discourse in recent decades, becoming more pronounced since the financial crisis of 2008 and the advent of 'austerity' social policies. Retirement from paid work with a pension, particularly for men, was a great achievement of the post-war welfare state but also became problematic as workers were forced into early retirement or to leave work involuntarily at retirement age as unemployment and deindustrialisation took effect, particularly in the 1980s. Pension income proved meagre for a substantial proportion of retired people, despite significant improvement in state pensions since the 1990s. Increasing income inequality in old age has produced a more pronounced division between the haves and the have-nots; the haves can choose to retire early on a decent workplace pension and enjoy a good life expectancy; the have-nots either survive on a pension just above the poverty line or continue working to maintain an income, with a much lower life expectancy. Women and minority groups are disproportionately represented among the have-nots.

It is widely understood that the increasing numbers of older people needing health care and social care has required more resources for those services; yet in the 2010s, in particular, public social spending was severely restrained, particularly for local authority social-care services. Problems around inadequately met basic needs and neglect of older people, whether in their own homes, in care homes or in the NHS, have increased significantly. Impairment in physical and mental capacities affects much-increasing numbers of older people, whose needs for care and support are often met inadequately. Many of the issues here parallel those taken up by the disability rights movement. The complexities of mental incapacity and dementia pose great challenges to the medical model and demand a more humanistic, respectful approach which goes beyond a black hole conception of the fourth age.

Notions such as 'the demographic time bomb' and 'Boomergeddon' have suggested that older people are ripping off younger generations by hogging public social spending in the form of pensions and care services.

We have countered such ageist constructions with an examination of the social dimensions of ageing in the UK, arguing that the most pressing social problems associated with ageing are linked to divisions of class, ethnicity and gender. Inadequate income, health care and social care in old age leading to unmet basic needs is not experienced by all – it is concentrated among those with a particular social class heritage, as well as among non-white ethnic groups and lone women. Looking at the whole picture, it could be argued that institutional ageism underpins the 'race', class and gender power structures.

 Key points

Retirement from paid work on a decent pension is widely regarded as a just reward for a full adult working life. However, it runs against the 'work ethic' and, in some instances, is imposed on workers against their will. It is also problematic for many women, who, until recently at least, did not enjoy full-time paid employment for their 'working life', with the consequence of lower retirement pensions and/or dependence on a partner in later life.

Retirement pension income is structured by class inequality, particularly between those with a decent workplace pension and those whose income is predominantly from the state pension schemes. A substantial number of retirees are living on incomes just above the poverty line, restricting their opportunities and often making daily life a struggle to meet basic needs. Minority ethnic groups tend to have significantly lower incomes in retirement.

Inequalities in wealth and in health outcomes are particularly significant among older people. The wealthy among them benefit from tax breaks, which, if withdrawn, could fund improved incomes for the less well-off. Comparatively higher life expectancy and better health are enjoyed by higher income groups and by white people.

Health-care and social-care services are not rationally coordinated

The NHS spends almost a £1 billion a year on 'overstaying' older patients because social care is not available. Over a million older people have unmet care needs, which are distressful and sometimes experienced in social isolation. The 2010s witnessed an escalating crisis in social-care services as austerity hit local authority budgets, as well as 'self-funders' increasingly struggling to meet private care home fees.

Norman Ginsburg

The fourth age, when older people experience mental and/or physical frailty, is sometimes portrayed as a black hole, reflecting people's fears of late ageing and the stigma of disability. The binary contrast with a third age of successful consumerism is a useful sociological device but reinforces the notion of the fourth age as 'unsuccessful'. More humane understanding of and communication with people in the fourth age, such as those with dementia, are emerging but need to go much further, supplementing and challenging the medical model and recognising the agency of fourth agers.

The notion of intergenerational conflict between retirees and young adults has come to much greater prominence in the era of austerity of the last decade. This can be used to legitimate a shift from state support to family obligation. The reality is certainly that retirees, if they can afford it, are supporting their adult children financially and by living together. Equally, working-age adults are helping their parents by providing unpaid care and support.

 ## Coursework questions

To what extent has retirement become an outdated concept which does not fit with contemporary capitalism?

Is inequality in later life a social problem, and what are its key parameters?

How useful is the 'fourth age' is understanding later life?

How significant is intergenerational conflict in understanding the problem of ageing in contemporary Britain?

References

AgeUK. (2014, August 14) 'Older people with care needs not getting crucial help'. *Briefing*. www.ageuk.org.uk

AgeUK. (2017) 'General Election 2017 briefing: A decent income'. www.ageuk.org.uk

AgeUK. (2018, January) 'Later life in the UK'. www.ageuk.org.uk

Bartlett, R. (2014) 'The emergent modes of dementia activism'. *Ageing and Society* 34(4): 623–644.

Baxter, K. and Glendinning, C. (2014) 'People who fund their own care'. *NIHR School for Social Care Research*. http://eprints.whiterose.ac.uk/83306/1/sscrSelfFundSR11.pdf

BBC. (2016) 'Sex crimes against the elderly – Are they being ignored?' www.bbc.co.uk/news/uk-37416483

Beckett, F. (2010) *What Did the Baby Boomers Ever Do for Us? Why the Children of the Sixties Lived the Dream and Failed the Future*. London: Biteback.

Boorman, N. (2010) *It's All Their Fault*. London: Harper Collins/The Friday Project Limited.

Bristow, J. (2016) 'The making of "Boomergeddon": The construction of the Baby Boomer generation as a social problem'. *British Journal of Sociology* 67(4): 575–591.

Coote, A. (2009) 'The uneven dividend: Health and wellbeing in later life'. In Cann, P. and Dean, M. (eds.), *Unequal Ageing*. Bristol: Policy Press, pp. 53–76.

Dilnot, A. (2011) *Fairer Care Funding: Report of the Commission on Funding of Care and Support*. London: Department of Health. https://webarchive.nationalarchives.gov.uk/20130221121534/www.dilnotcommission.dh.gov.uk/our-report/

EHRC. (2011) *Close to Home: An Inquiry into Older People and Human Rights in Home Care – Executive Summary*. London: Equality and Human Rights Commission. www.equalityhumanrights.com/en/publication-download/close-home-inquiry-older-people-and-human-rights-home-care-executive-summary

Elliott, L. (2016, January 6) 'Each generation should be better off than their parents? Think again'. *The Guardian*.

Evandrou, M., Falkingham, J., Feng, Z. and Vlachantoni, A. (2016) 'Ethnic inequalities in limiting health and self-reported health in later life revisited'. *Journal of Epidemiological Community Health* 70: 653–662.

Evandrou, N., Falkingham, J., Gomez-Leon, M. and Vlachantoni, A. (2018) 'Intergenerational flows of support between parents and adult children in Britain'. *Ageing and Society* 38: 321–351.

Foucault, M. (1965) *Madness and Civilization*. New York: Random House.

Francis, R. (2013) *Report of the Mid Staffordshire NHS Foundation Trust Public Inquiry*. London: Stationery Office.

Gerrard, N. (2019) *What Dementia Teaches Us About Love*. London: Allen Lane.

Gilleard, C. and Higgs, P. (2017) 'Ageing, corporeality and social divisions in later life'. *Ageing and Society* 37: 1681–1702.

Greener, J. (2015) 'Embedded neglect, entrenched abuse: Market failure and mistreatment in elderly residential care'. In Irving, Z., Fenger, M. and Hudson, J. (eds.), *Social Policy Review 27*. Bristol: Policy Press, pp. 131–149.

Grenier, A. (2012) *Transitions and the Lifecourse: Challenging the Constructions of 'Growing Old'*. Bristol: Policy Press.

Norman Ginsburg

Grenier, A. and Phillipson, C. (2013) 'Re-thinking agency in late life: Structural and interpretive approaches'. In Baars, J., Dhomen, J., Grenier, A. and Phillipson, C. (eds.), *Age, Meaning and Social Structure*. Bristol: Policy Press, pp. 55–80.

Heath, S. (2018) 'Siblings, fairness and parental support for housing in the UK'. *Housing Studies* 33(2): 284–298.

Herring, J. (2019) 'Older people and deficiencies in the formal care system'. In Westwood, S. (ed.), *Ageing, Diversity and Equality: Social Justice Perspectives*. London: Routledge, Ch. 18.

Higgs, P. and Gilleard, C. (2015) *Rethinking Old Age: Theorising the Fourth Age*. London: Palgrave.

Hill, A. (2017a, March 29) 'A world without retirement'. *The Guardian*.

Hill, A. (2017b, April 6) 'Social care reviewer condemns UK system and calls for new tax'. *The Guardian*.

Hill, K., Sutton, L. and Hirsch, D. (2011) *Living on a Low Income in Later Life*. London: AgeUK. www.ageuk.org.uk

Hills, J. (2017) *Good Times, Bad Times*. Bristol: Policy Press.

Howker, E. and Malik, S. (2010) *Jilted Generation: How Britain Has Bankrupted Its Youth*. London: Icon.

HSO. (2011) *Care and Compassion: Report of the Health Service Ombudsman on Ten Investigations into NHS Care of Older People*. London: The Stationery Office.

Humphries, R., Thorlby, R., Holder, H., Hall, P. and Charles, A. (2016) *Social Care for Older People: Home Truths*. London: The King's Fund/Nuffield Trust. www.nuffieldtrust.org.uk/research/social-care-for-older-people-home-truths

Hutton, W. (2010, August 22) 'The baby boomers and the price of personal freedom'. *The Observer*.

Iparraguirre, J. (2015) *How Much Would It Cost to Meet the Unmet Social Care Needs of Older People in England*. London: Age Concern. www.ageuk.org.uk

IpsosMORI. (2017) *Unmet Need for Care*. London: IpsosMORI. www.ipsos.com/sites/default/files/2017-07/unmet-need-for-care-full-report.pdf

Keogh, B. (2013) *Review into the Quality of Care and Treatment Provided by 14 Hospital Trusts in England*. London: NHS. www.nhs.uk/nhsengland/bruce-keogh-review/documents/outcomes/keogh-review-final-report.pdf

Latimer, J. (2018) 'Repelling neoliberal world-making? How the ageing-dementia relation is reassembling the social'. *Sociological Review* 66(4): 832–856.

Macnicol, J. (2015) *Neoliberalising Old Age*. Cambridge: Cambridge University Press.

Mandelstam, M. (2011) *How We Treat the Sick: Neglect and Abuse in Our Health Services*. London: Jessica Kingsley.

McParland, P., Kelly, F. and Jones, A. (2017) 'Dichotomising dementia: Is there another way?' *Sociology of Health and Illness* 39(2): 258–269.

NAO. (2016) *Discharging Older Patients from Hospital*. London: National Audit Office. www.nao.org.uk

ONS. (2017) 'Overview of the UK population: July 2017'. www.ons.gov.uk

ONS. (2018) 'Wealth in Great Britain Wave 5: 2014 to 2016'. Office for National Statistics. www.ons.gov.uk

ONS/DWP. (2017) 'Households below average income: 1994/95 To 2015/16'. www.gov.uk/government/statistics/households-below-average-income-199495-to-201516

Phillipson, C. (2013) *Ageing*. Cambridge: Polity Press.

Phillipson, C. (2015) 'The political economy of longevity'. *Sociological Quarterly* 56: 80–100.

Phillipson, C., Vickerstaff, S. and Lain, D. (2016) 'Achieving fuller working lives: Labour market and policy issues in the UK'. *Australian Journal of Social Issues* 51(2): 187–203.

Pickard, S. (2019) 'Age war as the new class war? Contemporary representations of intergenerational inequity'. *Journal of Social Policy* 48(2): 369–386.

Resolution Foundation. (2018, January 23) 'UK's £155bn tax relief bill. . .'. Press Release. www.resolutionfoundation.org

Savage, M. (2017, December 16) 'Social care postcode gap widens for older people'. *The Guardian*.

Shakespeare, T., Zeilig, H. and Mittler, P. (2019) 'Rights in mind: Thinking differently about dementia and disability'. *Dementia* 18(3): 1075–1088.

Thomas, C. and Milligan, C. (2018) 'Dementia, disability rights and disablism: Understanding the social position of people living with dementia'. *Disability and Society* 33(1): 115–131.

Thomson, P. (2018) 'A silver lining for the UK economy: The intergenerational case for supporting longer working lives'. *Centre for Ageing Better*. www.ageing-better.org.uk/publications/silver-lining-uk-economy

Thurley, D., Keen, R. and McGuiness, F. (2015) *Women and Pensions*. London: House of Commons Library Briefing Paper CBP07286. https://research-briefings.parliament.uk/ResearchBriefing/Summary/CBP-7286#fullreport

Vlachantoni, A. (2019) 'Unmet need for social care among older people'. *Ageing and Society* 39(4): 657–684.

Vlachantoni, A., Feng, Z., Evandrou, M. and Falkingham, J. (2015) 'Ethnicity and workplace pension membership in the UK'. *Social Policy and Administration* 49(7): 801–823.

Vlachantoni, A., Feng, Z., Evandrou, M. and Falkingham, J. (2017) 'Ethnic elders and pension protection in the UK'. *Ageing and Society* 37: 1025–1049.

WBG. (2017) *Social Care: A System in Crisis*. London: Women's Budget Group. https://wbg.org.uk/analysis/social-care-system-crisis/

WHO. (2002) *The Toronto Declaration on the Prevention of Elder Abuse.* Geneva: World Health Organization.

Willetts, D. (2010) *The Pinch: How the Baby Boomers Took Their Children's Future – And Why They Should Give It Back.* London: Atlantic Books.

Zaninotto, P., Demakakos, P., Head, J., de Oliveira, C. and Batty, D. G. (2016) 'Socio-economic differences in healthy life expectancy and mortality among older people in England'. In Banks, J., Batty, D. G., Nazroo, J. and Steptoe, A. (eds.), *The Dynamics of Ageing: Evidence from the English Longitudinal Study of Ageing 2002–15 (Wave 7)*. London: Institute for Fiscal Studies, pp. 101–122. www.ifs.org.uk/publications/8696

 Further reading

Cann, P. and Dean, M. (eds.) (2009) *Unequal Ageing: The Untold Story of Exclusion in Old Age.* Bristol: Policy Press.

Lodge, C., Carnell, E. and Coleman, M. (2016) *The New Age of Ageing: How Society Needs to Change.* Bristol: Policy Press.

Macnicol, J. (2015) *Neoliberalising Old Age.* Cambridge: Cambridge University Press.

Phillipson, C. (2013) *Ageing.* Cambridge: Polity Press.

Westwood, S. (ed.) (2019) *Ageing, Diversity and Equality: Social Justice Perspectives.* London: Routledge.

chapter 6

Issues of gender, 'race' and social class in education

Jessie Bustillos and
Sandra Abegglen

6.1 Introduction

This chapter seeks to disentangle some of the many inequality issues in the realms of gender, 'race' and social class in education. The opening discussion sets the scene by using constructivist theory to offer a critique of education and schooling as important sites where social problems and social inequalities are regularly and historically addressed through prescribed inclusion policy. It is against this rationale and premise that the chapter will move on to untie and develop some of the growing patterns of inequality that have characterised schooling in the United Kingdom for many years. Firstly, there will be a section in which gender equity issues in schools are outlined and interrogated (Skelton et al. 2006); this will be followed by a critique of the notion of post-feminist education (Ringrose 2007). Secondly, there will by explorations around issues of 'race' and education, articulated through an analysis of Gillborn and Youdell's (2000) research around the 'rationing of educational opportunity'. Thirdly, the work of Ball (2008) will be used to illustrate some issues around social class and educational opportunity. The chapter ends with an overview of how, although schooling has been characterised by particular gender, 'race' and social class inequalities, it still remains one of the key sites for attempts of social inclusion to be realised.

6.2 Schooling as a site to tackle inequalities?

When discussing and thinking about social problems, we might think about things that have gone wrong with our societies or new trends that threaten the way in which people live together in societal arrangements. In this book there are various chapters suggesting how social problems emerge, how they can be defined and how they have been addressed, and whilst there is a historical and long-standing plethora of social policy attempting to respond to social problems, no social institution is so central to the tackling of social problems as schooling has been and continues to be. This chapter is an attempt to explore some of the main issues of inequality that characterise schooling in the UK, yet it is also important to understand the ways in which schooling as a social institution is utilised to highlight and address any current social problems that a society might have identified.

This chapter, similar to the others in this book, presents arguments as to how social problems are constructed as part of a social fabric which is never static, but rather changes frequently. Some of the reasons for the changes in how social problems are identified and articulated can be said to be impacted by socio-political agendas: that is, whatever social problems we talk about often find their beginnings in political ideology and media/news attention at the time. Nevertheless, what is constant is that the system of schooling, and of education in general, are very often utilised to respond to emerging social problems. Schooling, seen from this constructionist perspective, is a socio-historical amalgam which acts as a site – both physically as a space and intellectually as an ideal – where social problems and their consequences are mitigated. Hence, it is in these environments where governments have decided to implement policies to tackle the most common social problems in society. This is discussed by Smaeyers and Depaepe (2008), who talk about the educationalisation of social problems, which transfers social responsibility to the school. An example of this might be the many days, events, assemblies or weeks dedicated to creating an awareness of road safety, healthy eating and sex education, amongst many other things, or the responsibility schools now have of running breakfast clubs and after-school clubs to help struggling families. Many of these initiatives are included in the day-to-day running of schools to address wider social problems surrounding obesity, teenage pregnancies and poverty, amongst other well-known social problems in the UK.

In the same way schooling bears a lot of the responsibility in addressing inequalities in society, it has also been discussed as being at the centre of the reproduction of social inequalities. Particularly since schools, from a sociological perspective, are used as a means to socialise pupils (formally and decidedly) into the ways of a society: that is, of course, the desired ways in which a society wants to develop and maintain itself. Giddens and Sutton (2013) discuss how Durkheim viewed education as key for transmitting social and cultural values and also for reproducing a skilled labour force. Giddens and Sutton (2013) also discuss how other theorists, such as Bowles and Gintis, point to how education, instead of levelling or resolving inequalities, might be creating further divisions or reproducing patterns of inequality. For example, black students still win fewer undergraduate places than other applicants with similar qualifications, despite long-standing efforts to support their access to and participation in higher education (Adams 2017). One of the main aims of this chapter is to open up possibilities for thinking about schools as sites that are not only created, run and regulated to tackle social inequalities and social problems but that also have historically inherited inequalities.

Against this understanding of education and schooling as a means to address and foster equality, this chapter will proceed to illustrate and discuss some of the patterns of inequality that nevertheless still exist in modern schools in terms of gender, 'race' and social class. These patterns of inequality will be explained first by dealing with key notions and, secondly, by drawing on classical educational and academic research which focuses on explaining the relational patterns between the particular inequalities and schooling.

6.3 Understanding gender and gender differences

It is important in this section to reflect on a question which underpins many of the debates around gender and schooling. Why do boys and girls tend to behave so differently in society and education as a whole? Where do these differences come from, and how do they become manifested in aspects of schooling? Across different societies, there are patterns of behaviour and expectations around gender which shape the socialisation of boys/men and girls/women. These expectations vary from place to place and from society to society; the important thing is that these notions and invisible rules work to organise and codify the behaviour of people in social situations, such as schools. These codes and notions surrounding boys and girls are not necessarily equal but might, in fact, be disempowering and restrictive. So what are some of the formations around gender that are found in our society?

We tend to think of gender as being explained through biological differences between men and women and that consequent differences in gender and sex behaviours are a result of diverting genetic properties. These ideas correspond to the view of gender as explained through biology and

Jessie Bustillos and Sandra Abegglen

evolutionary psychology, which justify our gendered behaviours on Darwinist ideas of evolution as the survival of the fittest (Birkhead 2001). However, other educational theorists have put forward ideas which openly challenge evolutionary arguments and psychology's take on gender and argue that this is a simplified and narrow view of how gender is constructed in society.

The social determinist view explains that there are plausible and important social explanations for why women and men are seen as needing to conform to certain types of behaviour in order for them to be categorised as male or female. Following these ideas, 'first-wave' feminist writers have argued how gender differences are far from being natural or innate; they are continued because of unequal treatments and social conventions around gender in society. For instance, Wollstonecraft wrote in the eighteenth century about how the exclusion of women from higher education and other parts of education – for example, particular curriculum subjects such as science and mathematics – resulted in the wider educational exclusion of women. Much later, in the 1970s and 80s, 'second-wave' feminists and activists argued how gender differences and the reinforcement of gendered 'sex-roles' (e.g. women as 'homemakers' and men as 'breadwinners') were learned through interactions with important social institutions such as schooling and the family (Skelton et al. 2006).

Importantly, the view that gender differences happen as a consequence of social forces, conventions and constructions underpins the ideas discussed in this section. Of particular interest to the ideas developed here is the view that, as one of the major social institutions, schooling – as compulsory and socially influential – is crucial for the reproduction of gender roles and gender differences in society. In what follows, we will discuss and illustrate some of the most common gender differences and inequalities that have characterised education in the UK. There will also be important commentary on some of the most influential academic works which have attempted to explore and explain these inequalities.

Understanding gender inequalities and schooling

Before World War II, systems of education in the UK were made up by some fee-paying, state-run and other church- and charity-based provisions which would be considered very 'patchy' in comparison to today's compulsory and free (at least to a certain extent) systems of schooling. Although education became compulsory for both boys and girls and solely state funded after World War II, there were still issues surrounding a gendered curriculum and unshifting gender and sex roles which affected both girls and boys. To this effect, Spencer (2005) explores in her book *Gender, Work and Education in Britain in the 1950s* how, despite positive and overall inclusionary changes to schooling, which opened up new opportunities in education and employment for girls, there was still a universal belief that women's place was in the home.

Some of these arguments are continued further by the work of David (2015: 163). who, in her analysis of the same historical period, sees education and developments in schooling as the very mechanism through which women were 'returned to the home' after they had gone out in huge numbers to work to help the war effort. This return to the home that David (2015) discusses was carried out through the continuation of a gendered curriculum which still relegated girls to an education that was not as extensive as that of boys and which was based on subjects that developed girls' quiet character and domesticity, such as needlework. The inequalities in the treatment of women were also evident when attempts were made to produce educational policy as there was an overall lack of concern in addressing the gap between boys' and girls' participation in further education. David (2015) discusses how the Crowther Report in 1959 pointed to the existence of a 'wastage of talent' since both boys and girls were not pursuing courses in further education, with 25 percent of boys in further education and only 6 percent of girls; it therefore recommended raising the school-leaving age to 16. Although the Crowther Report highlighted these pressing issues, it failed to provide solutions for the lack of education still faced by many girls and proceeded to provide recommendations for boys' continued engagement in education. The report also stated that, in the case of the education of girls, 'The prospect of courtship and marriage should rightly influence the education of the adolescent girl. . . . [H]er direct interests in dress, personal experience and in problems of human relations should be given a central place in her education' (David 2015: 170). In this way, the school's main educational concern for girls stayed with their preparation as future homemakers, mothers and wives; these ideas were accepted and continued because of the belief that boys and girls were to live very different lives, in turn reinforcing some of the gendered 'sex-roles' discussed earlier. This is an important example which shows how gender inequality in schooling is tightly connected to the ways in which we understand the role of men and women in society, as 'taken for granted' and part of a 'common-sense', which presents unequal educational opportunities for both men and women. These ideas and trends in behaviour around gender are argued to be socially constructed; produced by sets of social relations which occur in all aspects of social life; and, as we have discussed so far, embedded in systems of schooling.

Meighan and Harber (2007: 375), discussing issues of inequality of opportunity in education for boys and girls, point to 'a lack of a well developed comparative perspective of education . . . a systematic comparison with other countries (e.g. Russia, Sweden) would have presented some

Jessie Bustillos and Sandra Abegglen

disturbing information about women, education and occupations else-where' as occupations and further study in applied sciences and other subjects were considerably more populated by women. Meighan and Harber (2007) continue to explain that it was in the 1970s when there was a recognition that sex differences in education as an 'official' problem needed to be investigated. The government announced in 1973 that it planned to ask Her Majesty's Inspectorate (HMI) to conduct an inquiry to determine the extent to which difference in attitudes and school curricula continued to affect girls' and boys' life chances. This request resulted in the HMI's (1975) document titled *Curricular Differences for Boys and Girls*, which

> showed the persistence of the familial emphasis in secondary school-ing. And there is no further evidence, in policy rhetoric, or research, to suggest that by the end of the decade girls were no longer taught that their adult lives would consist of two activities, one of which would be the care of the home and children.
>
> (David 2015: 184)

All of these developments led to the creation of the Sex Discrimination Act 1975, which stipulated that neither boys nor girls should be refused access to any courses solely on grounds of their sex or the appointment of teachers (except in single-sex schools). The Equal Opportunities Commission (EOC; now the Equality and Human Rights Commission) made direct and indirect discrimination against women illegal. Although the differences in the curriculum for both boys and girls are not as glaring as they used to be, because the 1975 Sex Discrimination Act made unequal curricula illegal, there are still prevailing gender inequalities. For example, girls still show more negative attitudes towards maths (Gunderson et al. 2012) and hence display less interest in STEM (science, technology, engineering and mathematics) fields than boys, and because of this, girls also perform lower in these subjects (Shapiro & Williams 2012).

Whilst the 1970s saw considerable change around gender differences and discrimination on the basis of gender, there are persistent patterns which have continued, such as subject uptake by gender. Francis (2000) discussed in her book *Boys, Girls and Achievement: Addressing the Classroom Issues* how these patterns of inequality could be explained by problematising the dominant norms and behaviours associated to a particular femininity or masculinity. Part of Francis's argument is that within an environment of social change, which has seen the introduction of policies to balance gender inequalities in society, the classroom and its dynamics have been characterised by a continuity of traditional attitudes towards gender. Francis's work examines schooling and the classroom as an environment that reproduces society's values but also, more critically, as reproducing some of the inequalities that characterise that society.

Similarly, Valerie Walkerdine's (1988) work *The Mastery of Reason: Cognitive Development and the Production of Rationality* presents a complicated review of issues in the classroom. For Walkerdine many of the more insidious inequalities that we find in schools and in the intimacy of the classroom are as a result of stifling and unshifting attitudes to teaching and learning which are gendered and place both boys and girls in disadvantageous positions. Walkerdine looks at specific examples of boys' and girls' perceived lacks in certain subjects and also how certain subjects have become marginalised in the school curriculum. In the case of boys, Walkerdine points to how the unsuccessful paths in languages, which see them historically underperforming in subjects such as English and other modern languages, are normally explained by the suitability of boys for languages, a subject which is more associated with femininity. Similarly, girls' apparent disinterest in mathematics was constructed based on the methods used by girls to learn and perform mathematical calculations, which were seen as non-traditional. This inherent method suggested that there was a 'right method' for learning mathematics which girls struggled to comply with; teachers therefore encouraged girls not to take the higher examinations in this subject. This problem was made worse by how boys were seen to dominate classroom talk and interactions, with teachers not addressing the imbalances between boys' and girls' contributions during classes (Walkerdine 1988).

However, in recent years, there have been several stories in the media landscape which point to how boys are being failed by the educational system, and boys' underachievement has been constructed as problematic and as in direct opposition to the achievements of girls. Some examples of these headlines are 'Boys are being failed by our schools' (2006) and 'Why lack of male teachers could be the reason for boys fail in the classroom' (2012). There have been many critics of this narrative since it places boys and girls in competition with each other in the education plane, and the panic associated with boys' underachievement might suggest that boys outperforming girls is the status quo; thus, the sudden shift is constructed as a threat. This narrative of boys being outperformed by girls is also constructing girls' achievement as detrimental to the boys and also as harmful to the boys. Should we not want everyone in education to perform to the best of their ability, regardless of their gender? Why is female success constructed as harmful and as a threat to male achievement? And why is boys' underachievement placed in direct opposition to girls' achievement?

Ringrose (2007) has addressed how the construction of educational underachievement through gender binaries produces new disadvantages in the world of education. Ringrose's work explores how the 'successful

Jessie Bustillos and Sandra Abegglen

girl' discourse, co-constructed by 'girl power' cultural and social shifts in the 1990s, has led to 'divisive educational debates and policies where boys' disadvantages/successes are pitted against girls' disadvantage/success' (Ringrose 2007: 471). Ringrose raises questions about the silence in educational policy and public debate that surrounded the many years of educational exclusion and undermining experienced by girls in the UK. As with this chapter, Ringrose's work understands schooling as a crucial environment, productive of cultures and practices which in themselves reflect society's views on gender. Yet schooling is also conceived as a space in which gender binaries should be challenged and called into question. Ringrose's work also suggests that the educational focus on 'successful girls' alienates those girls who fall out of this category and, therefore, become deviant in the world of schooling. Rising numbers of girls' school exclusions might be associated with this phenomenon. More importantly, the focus on girls' and boys' achievements helps us overlook more pressing social issues to do with sexuality and gender in schools: for instance, the unequal access to STEM subjects at higher education by girls and the rise in sexual violence and sexual harassment in schools in recent years, which led to an inquiry into these issues by the Women and Equalities Committee in 2016.

As reviewed in this section, schooling is very often the space in which traditional gender inequalities have been addressed. Historically, evidence of how gender is constructed and understood can be found in key educational policies, as presented by the work of David (2015). These same differences can be traced back to classroom and school practices as explained by Walkerdine (1988). Schooling remains a site in which we both reproduce and challenge gender stereotypes and mandates. However, it is important to develop the criticality necessary to recognise where the debates lie and how to engage with them. Thinking about schooling and education as a site for locating, understanding and tackling social problems is a useful critical perspective to engage with issues of gender and inequalities. Nevertheless, it is important to also examine critically how the very responses from policy and institutions to perceived problems can be damaging, undermining or neglectful of other issues.

6.4 'Race'

Besides gender, 'race' is an important factor to consider when speaking about social inequalities. Generally speaking, 'race' is the idea that human beings can be classified into groups based on their physical appearance: their facial features, skin colour or type of hair. As history shows, the categorisation of human beings according to their physical appearance is highly problematic as it led to racist ideas about innate predispositions of different groups, attributing the most desirable features to the white

European race and arranging the other races along a continuum of progressively undesirable characteristics. This led not only to racial discriminations and racial inequalities, some of which exist to this day, but also to eugenics, the troublesome desire to improve the genetic quality of a particular population, which further embedded ideas of the superiority of some human beings to others.

However, historically, 'race' has not always been used as a distinguished feature of how humans are different from each other. Initially, 'race' was used to refer to speakers of a common language and then, later on, to denote continental or national affiliations. This means that the term has not always been used to define humans in terms of perceived physiological differences but to describe and distinguish groups of people according to their place of origin and/or their culture. However, the work of early anthropologists and physiologists – plus historical processes of exploration and conquest, which brought Europeans in contact with groups from different continents – actively promoted the idea of human difference based on appearance and, through that, fostered ideas of inherent racial privilege.

The first to actively challenge this concept of 'race' on empirical grounds was the anthropologist Franz Boas, who argued that 'race' was an invalid designation because human form and behaviour stemmed from the environment and not biological or genetic predisposition. His groundbreaking work was taken up by other (social) scientists and thus:

> By the 1970s, it had become clear that (1) most human differences were cultural; (2) what was not cultural was principally polymorphic – that is to say, found in diverse groups of people at different frequencies; (3) what was not cultural or polymorphic was principally clinical – that is to say, gradually variable over geography; and (4) what was left – the component of human diversity that was not cultural, polymorphic, or clinical – was very small.
>
> A consensus consequently developed among anthropologists and geneticists that race as the previous generation had known it – as largely discrete, geographically distinct gene pools – did not exist.
>
> (Marks 1995 cited in Marks 2007: 234)

This means that nowadays most scientists – including social scientists – agree that 'race' is a social construction. This led to the term 'race' being replaced by less ambiguous and emotionally charged terminology, which allows individuals to self-identify as belonging to a particular social group. For example, people might identify as black or white, regardless of their skin colour. Because of this, many refer now to ethnicity, the ethnic classification or affiliation, rather than 'race', when asking people to which socio-cultural group they belong.

Jessie Bustillos and Sandra Abegglen

Racialised worlds: the challenges of schools and schooling

However, although there is strong agreement amongst social scientists that 'race' is a social construct, and new language is being employed to describe group membership, racialised ideas are still pervading social life with 'real' effects on people's lives and life opportunities. For example, black and ethnic minority graduates with a first degree are more than twice as likely to be unemployed than their white peers, and those in employment earn less than their white counterparts (Trades Union Congress 2016). These closed-down life chances could be referred to as racial discrimination – 'the discrimination, unfair treatment or bias against someone or a group of people on the basis of their race' (HarperCollins 2017) – which often coincides with racist mindsets whereby individuals of one group come to perceive themselves as superior to those of another group. This, in turn, leads to racism and abusive or aggressive behaviour towards members of another 'race' or, as in this case, closed down life changes for those who belong to a particular group.

In this context, institutionalised practices can support racialised ideas; hence, schooling has an important part to play in tackling racism. Educational institutions have long been asked to promote 'race' equality. Over time, various educational policies have been implemented to ensure that schooling promotes equal opportunities for all, in particular in terms of learning outcomes. More recently, initiatives have been promoted to ensure schools adhere to the Race Relations (Amendment) Act 2000, which places a duty on public authorities to have 'due regard' to eliminate unlawful racial discrimination, promote equality of opportunity and promote good relations between people of different racial groups. Although these (educational) initiatives have good intentions, they often foster the very same issues they are trying to eliminate. This phenomenon is referred to as 'institutionalised racism', a form of racism prevalent in the practice of social and political institutions such as schools.

A study that explicitly looked at the issues of institutionalised racism in schooling was conducted by Gillborn and Youdell's (2000). The study explored how racial inequality is created and sustained in educational settings. Based on their findings, Gillborn and Youdell (2000) put forward the argument that, particularly in a neoliberal context, schools are 'rationing education', meaning they unwittingly deny pupils equal experiences and opportunities. The neoliberal context to which the authors refer involves the many policies and political pressures placed on schools, specifically the rise of competition between schools and the opening up of education as a consumer-led market, which leave schools fighting for a privileged position in publicly available league tables.

Because of the racialised ways that ability is constructed in a neoliberal context, it is black and ethnic minority students who are 'significantly over-represented in the group of pupils deemed to be without hope' (Gill-born & Youdell 2000: 200). They are implicitly discriminated because of their 'race'. The discrimination comprehends a rationing of the best resources, teaching, experiences and overall school's investment in their educational futures based on the belief that the outcomes of their educa-tional careers will be less favorable than those of others. As asserted by Gillborn and Youdell (2000: 199):

> The extraordinary demands of the A-C economy are such that both our case study schools are seeking new ways of identifying suitable cases for treatment – pupils who will show the maximum return (in terms of higher-grade passes) from receipt of additional resources of teacher time and support.

Gillborn and Youdell (2000) point out that this creates a virtuous cycle of disadvantage for this particular group of young people: they receive less support and hence are less likely to achieve, which, in turn, confirms schools' perception that they are less capable; hence, schools provide less support for them. As Gillborn and Youdell (2000) highlight, these institutionalised forms of racism operate through discourses of 'culture' and 'difference' rather than direct action, meaning that institutions such as schools do not actively promote this sort of behaviour but leave the complex mechanism supporting racial inequality unchallenged. Because of this, Gillborn and Youdell (2000) argue that schooling is prevalent in practices of inequality.

This means that, to tackle racial inequality, educational institutions such as schools need to engage more critically with the pervasive and complex forms that racism – and racial inequality – can take. Equally, and prob-ably even more importantly, to avoid institutionalised racism, educational institutions such as schools need to scrutinise the continuous and numer-ous policy changes more critically to ensure they are not contributing to already-existing elitism. As Gillborn and Youdell's (2000: 222) state:

> [T]he wider education system, policy makers, headteachers and teach-ers are currently remarkably busy remaking and reinforcing inequal-ity. . . (albeit that they are frequently unaware of these particular 'fruits' of their labours). It is time that this level of activity was refocused toward the achievement of social justice.

A prominent yet very sad example of institutionalised racism is the case of Stephen Lawrence. Lawrence, a 18-year-old black British man from Plum-stead, Southeast London, was murdered in a racially motivated attack while waiting for a bus on the evening of 22 April 1993. The case became one of

Jessie Bustillos and Sandra Abegglen

the highest-profile racial killings in UK history because it was suggested during the course of the investigation that the handling of the case by the police and the Crown Prosecution Service was affected by misconceptions of 'race'. A public inquiry held in 1998 concluded that the institutions handling the case, in particular the police, were institutionally racist. One of the ways in which it was suggested the police were institutionally racist was by placing Lawrence's family under surveillance during the investigation, instead of proceeding to investigate suspects. This prompted the amendment of legislation and a transformation of the police service: its recruitment, training, practices and accountability. The name of Stephen Lawrence became a potent symbol and catalyst for change, promoting widespread re-examination of questions of (in)justice, cultural identity and continuing racism in British society.

The concept of institutionalised racism, then, not only gives important insights into people's opportunities and experiences in institutions which appear to have developed and implemented equal opportunities policies, but also offers opportunities for resistance and action. This means that the notion of institutionalised racism allows the much-needed scrutiny of racialised practices at a micro level whilst retaining a contextual understanding of wider socio-economic practices and developments. A particular strength of such an approach to racial inequality, as Preston (2007: 23, emphasis in original) points out, is 'that whiteness is treated as a *practice*, not as an identity and white privilege is *institutionally* as well as individually determined'.

Although much has been achieved in terms of racial equality through a critical analysis that goes beyond the individual, there are, as the black British scholar Stuart Hall (1993: 361) famously pointed out a few years ago, further challenges to face when thinking about re-balancing racial inequalities in a globalised world:

> 'he capacity to live with difference is, in my view, the coming question of the twenty-first century – something which affects us all, including those involved in education and schools/schooling.

This means that the discussion about the role and responsibility of schooling in regards to 'race' need to be continued to make sure educational institutions promote 'true' equality in a multicultural world. Steps Towards Racial Equality, a recent report on racial equality in the UK, the government's race disparity audit (viz. www.gov.uk/government/publications/race-disparity-audit) shows that there are still pressing issues that need to be addressed. For example, the report highlights that black Caribbean pupils still fall behind their peers, although pupils in the black ethnic group made more progress overall than the national average. This means that pupils of ethnic minority backgrounds are still disadvantaged compared to those from other backgrounds, and this not just in education but also in areas of health, employment and the criminal justice system. Because of this, some – for example, the Equality and Human Rights Commission, Great Britain's national equality body – call for a comprehensive and coherent race equality strategy to foster equal opportunities for all (viz. www.equalityhumanrights.com/en/publication-download/healing-divided-britain-need-comprehensive-race-equality-strategy).

In this context, it is argued that educational institutions such as schools can (and should) do much more than closing the gap in educational achievement but provide a much better and fairer educational experience for all. It seems, therefore, important not to dismiss issues of 'race' or, as pointed out by Gulson et al. (2016), let 'race' slip to the periphery of education policy. 'Race', as many research studies show, still matters. It is therefore timely, as Gillborn (2016b) suggests, to ask 'policy in whose interest?' There is some useful work done by critical race theory (CRT), in particular in relation to white supremacy.

> White supremacy is the unnamed political system that has made the modern world what it is today. . . . the most important political system of recent global history – the system of domination by which white people have historically ruled over and, in certain important ways, continue to rule over nonwhite people – is not seen as a political system at all. It is just taken for granted; it is the background against which other systems, which we are to see as political, are highlighted.
>
> (Mills 1997: 1–2)

Considering recent political and educational developments, it seems important to continue this work and not dismiss schools as 'neutral' territory or to glorify them as a site where social equality can easily be achieved. There are dangerous racial myths which are sustained and renewed through social arrangements, processes, behaviour and discourse. Schools and the whole education system can challenge these myths by carefully addressing the specific rights and needs of all pupils, by advocating pluralism and the riches of multiculturality and also by fighting institutional racism as well as racist frameworks of reference to ensure they are not contributing to the very same problem they are trying to solve. As David Gillborn (2016a) points out, the issues of racism, as with many other social problems, are hidden in the small print. It is therefore key for schooling to be critical of its own practices, constantly asking itself: I am racist? to eliminate race thinking or, as Ware and Back (2002) state, diminish 'white-friendly' systems and structures.

Jessie Bustillos and Sandra Abegglen

6.5 Social class: asking the right questions?

A further factor to consider when speaking about inequality in education is social class. Social class has created significant divisions in English society, yet it is often very elusive. Wider discussions around class have almost disappeared from political discourse, with politicians being more comfortable discussing problems to do with institutional racism or the gender pay gap than they are discussing issues of class. Within the study of education and academic educational research, there have been several contributions not just to help render class visible but also to help reveal how it impacts educational opportunity and educational achievement.

If we asked the simple question What is social class? we might come to traditional sociological theory to provide some answers since social class has held a prominent place in the discipline of sociology for a very long time. This long history of social class in sociology might bring you to read the works of Max Weber or Karl Marx. Sociology professors and academics might argue the existence of social class based on economic inequality arguments, lack of equality of opportunity arguments or through questioning the fairness of systems that do not acknowledge the accumulation of privilege by the few in a society. Depending on who you read, you will agree and disagree with some or all of these arguments. Whether we think of social class as straightforwardly divided into 'working class', middle class' and 'upper class' or we think it is as complex as seven different categories, as suggested by a BBC survey in 2013, the fact is that class is difficult to define. Even in recent years, many articles that can be argued to discuss dimensions of class 'often use the terms "inequality", "stratification", "family background" or specific indicators (such as education, wealth, income, or occupation) – sometimes interchangeably. As a result, considerable murkiness swirls around the empirical study of social class' (Lareau & Conley 2008: 3–4). Perhaps asking what social class is might not be the best question to pose, but rather how does social class work? And, if social class is better analysed through how it works, then what are its workings in education and systems of schooling? These are some of the questions that are posed in this section.

Staying with social class: culture, class and schooling

In spite of its complexity, we should not avoid the term 'social class', particularly since it offers an analytical angle which encompasses much of everyday social life, one without which we would struggle to provide an understanding of how inequalities continue to prevail and worsen in societies. But let's begin by thinking about how schooling might actually be reproducing social class inequalities. Many educational theorists have set themselves the task of explaining how social class could be said to work in education and schooling. If you were to investigate issues of class in education by conducting a simple library literature search, you would find that many articles refer to the theorist Pierre Bourdieu. Bourdieu was a French theorist working primarily by observing French society, particularly the culture of the middle classes. A lot of his work around class can be said to be very Francocentric; works such as *Distinction* (1984) and *The State Nobility* (1996) are difficult to apply or translate to English culture and contexts. However, this has not stopped many researchers and writers who have used Bourdieu's theory and key concepts to provide an analysis of class in education. For instance, Gunn (2005) uses some of Bourdieu's ideas to understand the rise of the middle classes in Britain in the twentieth century. Unlike other theorists, Gunn (2005) does not fully accept that the rise of the middle classes in Britain came about as a consequence of the industrial revolution in the nineteenth century and the creation of middle-class occupations. Instead, Gunn uses the concepts of 'culture' and 'cultural capital' as important elements that contributed to the rise of the middle classes. What is meant by culture in this case is not to do with what people wear and eat or the languages they speak, but rather what people do, what people regard as valuable and worthwhile in their lives, from what gives them pride to what they see as leisure. Cultural capital is regarded as a set of practices and embodiments of knowledge and legitimacy which give people a sense of belonging and permanence in particular contexts, places, institutions and everyday socialities. In Bourdieu's work, the middle classes (bourgeoisie) went through a process of establishing themselves through a distinctive culture; this culture had 'class'. This is particularly important since, at the time, the lower and working classes were constructed as having no 'class' or 'culture'. The working classes have been historically discussed as being 'uncultured' or 'uncultivated' and therefore as lacking in 'class'. This is, of course, not true, but this social construction of the working classes aided the emergence and establishment of middle-class culture:

> The bourgeoisie finds in cultivated nature and culture that has become nature the only possible principle for the legitimation of their privilege. Being unable to invoke the right of birth (which their class, through the ages, has refused the aristocracy) or nature which, according to 'democratic' ideology represents universality. . . . [T]hey can resort to cultivated nature and culture become nature, to what is sometimes called 'class', through a kind of tell-tale slip, to 'education', in the sense of a product of education which seems to owe nothing to education, to distinction, grace which is merit and merit which is grace, an unacquired merit which justifies unmerited acquisitions, that is to say, inheritance'.
> (Bourdieu 1993: 235)

Jessie Bustillos and Sandra Abegglen

Bourdieu is suggesting the culture of the middle classes becomes a kind of education which in itself owes nothing to education, but which becomes distinctive learnings, attitudes and practices. This is somehow in direct opposition to how the working classes were thought of and constructed as 'classless' and 'needing an education' to elevate them and give them a sense of culture. What Gunn (2005) is proposing is that following some of the initial thoughts by Bourdieu, and with the advent of organised systems of schooling in the UK, the middle classes in Britain have, indeed, continued to pass on their cultural genes, not just in the family but through schooling. Inherently, Gunn (2005: 58) discusses how systems of schooling have absorbed the cultural ways of the middle classes historically into their everyday practices:

> Family and education intersected in the workings of cultural capital, not only because the middle-class family represented a primary site of training but also because it allowed for early immersion in precisely those codes and competences that would later be valued in formal schooling.

This is where we find many of the arguments around social class and education: at this intersection between schooling and class privilege. Many scholars agree that school has been made and changed to reflect the privileges and images of a particular class: the middle classes. Within academic educational research, there are further claims that this has continued to contribute to the exclusion of large groups of people historically, primarily the working class, even when they seem to be included in systems of schooling that are mandatory. It is at this intersection, this critical perspective, that the following works are discussed, to provide an understanding of how class has been put to work in research and academic work around education and has permeated the world of education and schooling.

6.6 Exploring class through educational theory and research

When discussing the interrelationship between class and schooling, there is a tendency to overlook the importance of another context, the home. With changes to education in the 1940s and the introduction of the Butler Act of 1944, the tripartite system of education began, and children were allocated to secondary modern, technological schools or to the more prestigious grammar schools. The children who sat the 11+ examination and obtained high scores were sent to grammar schools, and the ones who did not were allocated to one of the other schools. With the 11+ examination, some working-class children were admitted to grammar schools, which were normally far from traditional working-class communities and very different to elementary schools, with strict uniform and behaviour codes, a more extensive curriculum and regular examinations. Many of the working-class children who went to grammar schools experienced a disconnect between home life and school life. Within the discipline of sociology, there are some important contributions to the understanding of these experiences and systems of education, not just as a social institution but as an aspect of everyday life which can be very impactful on issues of class. The work by Jackson and Marsden, *Education and the Working Class*, first published in 1962, offers some early insight into class distinctions and how the home interacted with systems of schooling. Their work is regarded as pioneering a new type of sociology of education, one which, through careful narrative, built an image of class in the home and in the school with distinctiveness and clarity, an approach which clearly rivalled the more quantitative tradition of the time. Ball (2011: 959) comments on the importance of Jackson's and Marsden's (2012) work:

> *Education and the Working Class* is about class mobility, class inequality and waste, and about what Dennis describes as a 'blockage' – selective education. In stark contrast to the sometimes pathologising focus on working-class failure in much of the contemporary sociology of education, *Education and the Working Class* works with a sample of 90 'successfully' working-class children. That is, children who passed the 11+ and went to grammar school and many of whom went on to higher education.

Jackson and Marsden portray the lives of working-class children who can be said to have been successful in education and narrate the differences the home and school thresholds brought to them every day. In their work, they offer an alternative storying of working-class children in the educational system; their stories showed the many strategies the children utilised to survive and thrive in grammar schools but also, in turn, how this exerted an influence in their everyday lives. Jackson and Marsden (2012: 117) offer a textural description of the lives of the working-class children who attended grammar schools and how the class codes of schools produced home pressures for the children:

> Few working class homes had easy provision for home study. Some children went into the front room, others retired to a bedroom, but many did their homework in the living-room/kitchen at the very centre of family activity. This immediately produced difficulties. Should the wireless be on or off? Could the younger children play noisily? Could the father stretch his legs and tell the day's tales? To ask for silence

Jessie Bustillos and Sandra Abegglen

here was to offend the life of the family, was to go against it in its natural moments of coming together, of relaxation. So many learned the early habit of working with the wireless on and the family talking, of building a cone of silence around themselves. To a certain extent this worked well. . . . [T]he family was not always untroubled at this, for the private concentration could produce an abstraction, a forgetfulness, an off-handedness that also gave offence.

Moreover, *Education and the Working Class* (2012) takes us through an empowering narrative highlighting the resourcefulness of working-class children and families, but not without understanding the huge challenges and disparities that characterised these educational pathways. It is clear from their investigations that the world of schooling occurred within a cultural code which was different from that of the working-class home. This is an important reflection to consider and seek to understand when dealing with issues of class in education: namely, that the educational system itself has historically reflected the values of the middle class, disadvantaging those who represent a different social and cultural code.

Another major issue in relation to social class in schooling is that of language. Basil Bernstein focused on differences in language and how they affect aspects of schooling. His work conceptualised school as an institution that functions through language culture (Bernstein 1971). Bernstein explored language differences as representative of distinctions of class, specifically between working-class and middle-class children. He constructed his theory around 'elaborated' and 'restricted' codes which were made consonant with working-class and middle-class children. In Bernstein's work, middle-class language codes were seen as more elaborated, descriptive and expansive whilst working-class language codes were seen as restricted in comparison to the language culture of schools. Bernstein's work explained how language is not just internal but also reflected in institutions, organising and, to a certain extent, determining outcomes in education. Schooling is therefore not seen as a neutral environment in which all language codes can be accepted and readily recognised and incorporated. Instead, Bernstein suggested that differences in language codes lead to different possibilities and, what is more, different levels of achievement in educational settings. His work has raised some critique in more recent years because of the way in which its centrality on individuals has overlooked the inherent inequalities the cultures of school seem to perpetuate. Bartlett et al. (2001: 184) summarise some of the critique and controversy provoked by their work:

The danger in the position expressed by Bernstein in relation to class, language and education was the attribution of essential qualities to the differences between working-class language and middle-class language, and the potential correlation of working-class culture with less expressive linguistic forms. The use of distinction between working-class speech as 'restricted code' and middle-class speech as 'elaborated code' became infamous as it seemed to imply a hierarchy of expressive power.

When we think about school, we tend to think of places for learning or places for advancement; the works discussed so far have presented arguments which problematise these understandings of schooling. Bowles and Gintis (1976), two American writers, provide another strand of thought to the problematisation of schooling. For them, schools' primary purpose was to hone in on the 'hidden curriculum'. With this phrase, they were attempting to describe the many ways in which school was less about instruction or learning in mathematics, the sciences or literacy and more about learning your place in society. The hidden curriculum encompassed the insidious forms of control, punishment and management that characterise schools and which are directed at organising and governing pupils' behaviours and aspirations, commanding pupils to learn to respect the institution, to conform to rules and to obey authority. Their study *Schooling in Capitalist America* was an attempt to document the systematic failure of systems of education to shift wider societal inequalities, in spite of tons of educational policy change and reforms. They saw the main aspiration taught to students at school to be the acceptance of a wage-dependent life, a life which was only attainable if students learned to refrain from resistance and contestation whilst conforming to the ruling status quo.

Stephen Ball's work has been highly important in developing a systematic analysis of education and the effects of schooling on individuals. In his works, he has developed what he calls a 'policy sociology', which seeks to develop a thorough understanding of changes and reformations to educational systems in the UK through the analysis of the effects of educational policy (Ball 2008). Ball's work has also centred on developing an understanding and theorising of how the privilege of the successful in education helps us understand the challenges and exclusions inherently faced by the disadvantaged. His work has also offered an analysis of how family strategy, developed through being successful in the system themselves and through more extensive resources, influences educational achievement, attainment and pathways (Ball 2006).

More recently, there has been an increase in educational research using the notion of habitus to make sense of class distinctions in education. Habitus is a very tricky notion to define and discuss, and although there are

Jessie Bustillos and Sandra Abegglen

many pieces of research utilising this notion, its meaning is still debated. On habitus, Turner (2013: 752) offers a useful definition:

> Those within a given class share certain modes of classification, appreciation, judgment, perception, and behaviour. Bourdieu conceptualizes this mediating process between class and individual perceptions, choices, and behaviours as habitus. In a sense, habitus is the 'collective unconscious' of those in similar positions because it provides cognitive and emotional guidelines that enable individuals to represent the world in common ways and to classify, choose, evaluate and act in a particular manner. . . . [T]he habitus creates syndromes of taste, speech dress manner and other responses.

The work by Diane Reay and Carol Vincent (2014) is one of the pieces of educational research offering an insight into various class analyses within the sociology of education, paying close attention to how the institution – more specifically, schooling – helps build and shape perspectives around class. By using Bourdieu, Reay and Vincent assert the concept of habitus as to do with how schooling embodies the dominant group's cultures as a starting position of privilege within schools. In saying this, there is also a need for recognising 'institutional habitus' (Atkinson 2013: 119). Institutional habitus is theorised as the many mediations that have value within an institution and which, in turn, are used to decide which views, codes, practices, behaviours, representations and perceptions are upheld and desirable in it. With reference to class, institutional habitus overlooks and misrecognises, mostly inadvertently, anything outside its own culture. Schooling has therefore been constructed as possessing an institutional habitus that has reflected and continues to reflect the individual and family habitus of some classes over others, making it prone to reproducing social inequality. Throughout this section, there have been various examples of how the habitus of schooling is at work within education, with a distinct culture, expectations and behaviour codes which divide and perpetuate some of the social disparities we find in our societies.

6.7 Summary

The present chapter has looked at gender, 'race' and social class as 'markers' of inequality in schooling. As pointed out at the beginning of this chapter, schooling is conceived here not only as a designated and highly regulated space through which social problems are rendered visible and addressed through various social and educational policies, but also as a 'space' where social inequalities are reproduced and even enhanced.

In this chapter we dealt with introductory issues highlighting the disparities in gender, 'race' and class, which continue to be factors of people's lived experiences and opportunities. As outlined, there are still gendered understandings of what boys and girls can and should achieve, similar to still existing understandings of 'race' and social class that determine what young people can achieve in life, not because of their abilities, but by the opportunities they are presented with and are able to access.

In this context, schooling has been constructed as necessary for the continuation of society's values and stability, but it was also suggested that schooling by accumulating society's ideals lacks the means to challenge the effects of its own workings. The increasing involvement of the government in systems of schooling, impacting and determining their funding, performance indicators, assessments and curricula, can be said to reduce schools' autonomy and capacity to respond to in-school inequalities even further.

Whether we regard schooling as an important solution to address social problems and inequalities or as part of the problem, an analysis of school inequalities needs to reflect the complexity of these environments. This chapter has attempted to articulate some of these complexities, with a particular focus on gender, 'race' and social class. Yet it is necessary to understand that a more comprehensive view would explore how inequalities intersect and interact in educational settings, rather than viewing them as occurring separately.

This is particularly true as gender, race and social class, although separated for analytical purposes in this chapter, are not separate processes; they act simultaneously and affect people in many ways. This means that lived experiences are often far more complex than this chapter suggests; hence, the experience of inequalities is far more difficult to discern and rather needs to be understood as inextricably intertwined.

However complex issues of inequality are, educational institutions continue to be an important site where inequalities are perpetuated:

> Education is not, as older social science pictured it, a mirror of social or cultural inequalities. That is all too still an image. Education systems are busy institutions. They are vibrantly involved in the production of social hierarchies. They select and exclude their own clients; they expand credentialed labour markets; they produce and disseminate particular kinds of knowledge to particular users.
>
> (Connell 1993: 27)

Key points

Education and schooling

These are important sites where social problems and social inequalities are regularly and historically addressed through prescribed inclusion policy because they are seen as sites where social equality can be achieved.

Educational research

This has shown that education and schooling reproduce many patterns of inequality and disadvantage. Whilst schooling remains one of the key ways in which a society seeks to address social issues and social problems, other solutions need to be considered to diminish social exclusions.

Gender issues in education continue to disadvantage boys' and girls' life chances as well as their everyday performance in the classroom. Issues of gender influence the world of education in various ways which lead to unequal experiences and opportunities for both boys and girls. Feminist thinking and scholarship have developed a deeper understanding of these issues and talk about gender as socially constructed and not explainable in biological terms. Gender inequalities, although always changing, are still discussed as profound and prevalent in society, and the world of education and schooling is no exception to this.

'Race' still affects what boys and girls can achieve as institutional racism continues to discriminate against particular groups of pupils, in particular those from black and ethnic minorities. Schools need to do more to promote equal opportunities and provide a fairer educational experience for all. Critical race theory, in particular in relation to white supremacy, offers useful tools to analyse social arrangements, processes, behaviours and discourses.

Social class is a concept in social sciences which allows us to analyse society. Although a term that has been explored in significant detail in educational research and sociological study, it still remains neglected in the making of educational and social policy. The overlooking of issues of class in education is discussed as problematic as education is not understood to be a 'class-less' activity. It continues, similar to other social issues, to reproduce social inequalities.

Coursework questions

Research one of the key thinkers introduced in the chapter and discuss how their work has widened the understanding around gender, 'race', or social class issues in education.

Find a recent educational study exploring gender, 'race' or social class inequalities in schools and report on its key findings, critically examining possibilities and limitations.

References

Adams, R. (2017, January) 'Black students still struggle to win places at UK universities'. *The Guardian*. www.theguardian.com/education/2017/jan/26/black-students-struggle-uk-university-places-ucas

Atkinson, D. (2013) 'From sociological fictions to social fictions: Some Bourdieusian reflections on the concepts of "Institutional Habitus" and "Family Habitus"'. In Reay, D. and Vincent, C. (eds.), *Theorizing Social Class and Education*. London: Taylor and Francis, pp. 119–136.

Ball, S. J. (2006) *Education Policy and Social Class*. London: Routledge.

Ball, S. J. (2008) *The Education Debate*. Cambridge: Polity Press.

Ball, S. J. (2011) 'Social class, families and the politics of educational advantage: The work of Dennis Marsden'. *British Journal of Sociology of Education* 32(6): 957–965.

Bartlett, S., Burton, D. and Peim, N. (2001) *Introduction to Education Studies*. London: Paul Chapman Publishing.

BBC. (2013) 'The great British class calculator: What class are you?' www.bbc.co.uk/news/magazine-22000973

Bernstein, B. (1971) *Class, Codes and Control*. London: Routledge and Kegan Paul.

Birkhead, T. (2001) *Promiscuity: An Evolutionary History of Desire*. Cambridge, MA: Harvard University Press.

Bowles, S. & Gintis, H., (1976) *Schooling in Capitalist America*, New York: Basic Books.

Bourdieu, P. (1984) *Distinction: A Social Critique of the Judgement of Taste*. London: Routledge.

Bourdieu, P. (1993) *The Field of Cultural Production*. Cambridge: Polity Press.

Bourdieu, P. (1996) *The State Nobility*. Stanford, CA: Stanford University Press.

Connell, R. W. (1993) *Schools and Social Justice*. Philadelphia, PA: Temple University Press.

Jessie Bustillos and Sandra Abegglen

Daily Mail Online. (2006) 'Boys are being failed by our schools'. Accessed: 30th October 2017. www.dailymail.co.uk/news/article-390319/Boys-failed-schools.html

Daily Mail Online. (2012) 'Why lack of male teachers could be the reason for boys fail in the classroom'. Accessed: 30th October 2017. www.dailymail.co.uk/news/article-2102759/Why-boys-failing-grade-classroom-Lack-male-teachers-reason-according-new-study.html

David, M. (2015) *The State, the Family and Education*. London: Routledge.

Francis, B. (2000) *Boys, Girls and Achievement: Addressing the Classroom Issues*. London: Routledge Falmer.

Giddens, A. and Sutton, P. (eds.) (2013) *Sociology*. London: Polity Press.

Gillborn, D. (2016a) 'Softly, softly: Genetics, intelligence and the hidden racism of the new geneism'. *Journal of Education Policy* 31(4): 365–388.

Gillborn, D. (2016b) 'Interest-divergence and the colour of cutbacks: Race, recession and the undeclared war on black children'. In Gulson, K. N., Leonard, Z. and Gillborn, D. (eds.), *The Edge of Race: Critical Examinations of Education and Race/Racism*. London and New York: Routledge, pp. 3–17.

Gillborn, D. and Youdell, D. (2000) *Rationing Education: Policy, Practice, Reform and Equity*. Philadelphia, PA: Open University Press.

Gulson, K. N., Zeus, L. and Gillborn, D. (eds.) (2016) *The Edge of Race: Critical Examinations of Education and Race/Racism*. London and New York: Routledge.

Gunderson, E. A., Ramirez, G., Levine, S. C. and Beilock, S. L. (2012) 'The role of parents and teachers in the development of gender-related math attitudes'. *Sex Roles* 66(3–4): 153–166.

Gunn, S. (2005) 'Translating Bourdieu: Cultural capital and the English middle class in historical perspective'. *The British Journal of Sociology* 56(1): 49–64.

HarperCollins. (2017) *Racial Discrimination*. www.collinsdictionary.com/dictionary/english/racial-discrimination

Jackson, B. and Marsden, D. (2012) *Education and the Working Class*. Oxon: Routledge.

Lareau, A. and Conley, D. (2008) *Social Class: How Does It Work?* New York: Russell Sage Foundation.

Marks, J. (2007) 'Grand anthropological themes'. *American Ethnologist* 34(2): 233–235.

Meighan, R. and Harber, C. (2007) *A Sociology of Educating*. London: Continuum.

Mills, C. (1997) *The Racial Contract*. Ithaca, NY: Cornell University Press.

Preston, J. (2007) *Whiteness and Class in Education*. Dordrecht: Springer.

issues of gender, 'race' and social class

Reay, D. and Vincent, C. (2014) *Theorizing Social Class in Education*. London: Taylor and Francis.

Ringrose, J. (2007) 'Successful girls? Complicating post-feminist neoliberal discourses of educational achievement and gender equality'. *Gender and Education* 19(4): 471–489.

Shapiro, J. R. and Williams, A. M. (2012) 'The role of stereotypes in undermining girls' and women's performance and interest in STEM fields'. *Sex Roles* 66(3–4): 175–183.

Skelton, C., Francis, B. and Smulyan, L. (2006) *The Sage Handbook of Gender and Education*. Thousand Oaks, CA: Sage Publications.

Smaeyers, P. and Depaepe, M. (2008) *Educational Research: The Educationalization of Social Problems*. Gent: Springer.

Spencer, S. (2005) *Gender, Work and Education in Britain in the 1950s*. Basingstoke: Palgrave Macmillan.

Trades Union Congress. (2016) *Black, Qualified and Unemployed*. London: Trades Union Congress.

Turner, J. (2013) *Theoretical Sociology: 1830 To the Present*. London: Sage Publications.

Walkerdine, V. (1988) *The Mastery of Reason: Cognitive Development and the Production of Rationality*. London: Routledge.

Ware, V. and Back, L. (2002) *Out of Whiteness: Color, Politics, and Culture*. Chicago: University of Chicago Press.

 Further reading

Gillborn, D., Rollock, N., Warmington, P. and Demack, S. (2016) *Race, Racism and Education: Inequality, Resilience, and Reform in Policy and Practice*. Birmingham: University of Birmingham.

William, H. 'Lez'. (2020) 'Schooling, education, and the reproduction of inequality: Understanding Black and minority ethnic attitudes to learning in two London schools'. *Race Ethnicity and Education*. DOI:10.1080/13613324.2020.1798386

chapter 7

Childhood and education

David Blundell

7.1 Introduction

No social group figures as consistently or frequently in the discussion of social problems as do children. This is not merely because external problems impact them and the quality of their childhood or even that children and young people are themselves often seen as problematic; it is also because children are uniquely upheld as a source of hope in the search for solutions to any number of society's problems. Furthermore, education and schools are presumed to provide the arena where it is possible to address social concerns that may or may not directly impact children. This is not only because education is implicitly considered to be about making things better but also because of the practical fact that school is where children can be found for a large portion of their time. These concerns range from questions surrounding how children's academic attainment can sustain economic viability through to remedying all manner of matters seen as challenging social cohesion or as harmful to the maintenance of order and well-being, including recent high-profile concerns about gangs, drugs and the population's health and fitness.

The revision of this chapter comes at a time when the UK is in the grip of a global COVID-19 pandemic, whose immediate effects are tragically clear. These include sudden sickening and premature death, along with systemic impacts from unprecedented regulatory measures taken to control the spread of the virus. For some, this is expected to be a short-term blip in human affairs; for others, to quote Dr David Nabarro, a senior scientist at the World Health Organization (*The Guardian* 2020b), this coronavirus may 'stalk' humankind for years to come. The medium-term impacts may be clearer to readers than they are at the time of writing, but long-term shifts in mentality surrounding the way a raft of social phenomena are viewed seem possible, albeit as yet unknown. In this chapter, in preparation for a period of reappraisal, we shall seek to examine the foundation of many of the ways we see children and appraise some of the problems of childhood as one such social phenomenon, as well as the role that education and schools play in addressing these problems. However, we shall tackle this by asking a number of important questions; these include where our ideas about children and childhood come from, why we hold these ideas, and whether the ways we think about children contribute to some of the problems we identify. Furthermore, we shall ask why it is that children and childhood have become so closely identified as means to solve society's problems and even to be a hope for human salvation. I should say from the outset that our approach will be social constructionist; this proceeds from a belief that by questioning our taken-for-granted assumptions, even about things that seem to be certain and solid, we might be able to assess whether they are, indeed, so certain or solid and therefore unchangeable. This is done not merely as an academic exercise but because it may enable us to understand some of the knotted roots of the social problems that confront us and thereby find ways to address them. But first, it will be helpful to examine how the ways in which we think about children, childhood and education might contribute, for good or ill, to these problems and shape the solutions we propose.

We may well be at a fundamental hinge-point in human affairs that will demand unfamiliar responses, but it is also important for those engaged in framing and implementing social policy to take a step back to assess any assumptions that are in play and whether these are appropriate or continue to apply. Therefore, before turning directly to COVID-19 and its impacts, it is important to explore some fundamental themes that run through and shape our thinking about children and childhood.

7.2 What do we mean by childhood, and why might this be important?

Open the newspaper or catch the television news and there will be a story about childhood. The chances are that the report will express a suspicion either that all is not quite well with the nation's children or that the experience of childhood offered by various social institutions – including families, health and social-care agencies, the media, youth and sport clubs and, not least, schooling – is not as it should be. But can we assume that when people speak about 'childhood', they all mean the same thing? The

David Blundell

vocabulary may be identical, but what if, behind the words, there are very different assumptions about what childhood is, what it should be like and crucially what is meant by a 'good childhood'?

Close examination of the many agencies catering for children and young people may help us glean some sense of what childhood means in common usage. We might look for example at nurseries, schools, colleges, Saturday-morning clubs, Sunday schools, Islamic madrassahs, Jewish cheder, children's hospitals, drama schools, play centres and holiday play schemes. Social scientists describe these places as institutions of childhood, and the length and diversity of the list is, in itself, indicative of the place childhood occupies in the social structures of a society like Britain. Amidst this diversity, what unites these institutions of childhood is that a reliance on 'working models' of what children and young people are like is central to their operation. This does not mean that they share the same working model or that each operates with a single model, but if we visited each one and asked key workers what they aim to do, how they seek to achieve this and why they operate as they do, their replies would be shaped by the assumptions, beliefs, convictions and commitments that can be traced back to these working models. Their sentences might start something like this: 'We do things this way because children need/deserve/have a right to x, y or z'. These working models for children and childhood with which each institution will be operating can be seen as what the pioneering sociologist Max Weber called 'ideal types', enabling institutions to decide what they aim to achieve and determine how they should go about doing this. The ideal types establish a shared language that workers, practitioners and users can use to direct, explain and justify the operations of the institution – in short, they will be talking about the same thing or, more colloquially, 'be on the same page'.

I remember a discussion with my students about what children should and should not be expected to do around the house, and it illustrates how working models for childhood can be informed by very different assumptions. One woman with young children argued forcefully that childhood is a short time, and so she did not expect her children to do any chores; rather, they should be allowed to play and live in the moment. This was the cause of some consternation for another student, who was adamant that children should take up their share of housework; otherwise, how would they learn to become responsible adults? Each of these mothers operated with different working models for the meaning and purposes of childhood, and these provided important principles for how their families should operate. In this discussion, each student referred to 'children' and 'childhood', but it was clear that they were operating with very different meanings for the same words; for one, childhood was a time to enjoy being a child, but for the other, childhood was about becoming an adult. This basic difference in meaning for childhood between being and becoming is not trivial and has long been the subject of debate; furthermore, it has importance in shaping our response to social problems in childhood, as we shall see.

These differences in meaning are not simply matters of personal opinion but are shaped by culturally shared ways of seeing the world. Social scientists often refer to these shared ways of seeing as 'discourses' and find this a useful way to understand how our ideas about what is and is not normal are constructed – discourses shape the meanings we share through language but also inform pictures, films, adverts and the television news. Social scientists are very interested in how discourses inform our thinking and actions and especially how they support and maintain power in relationships between people – think about how differences in professional authority are maintained by what is permitted to control and dominate discourses. Discourse is an important idea that you will encounter again and again as you learn more about social constructionism.

Another example of how differing discourses for childhood animate fierce debates comes from the New Labour government's attempts to ban the use of corporal punishment by parents. Advocates of a complete ban held that hitting a child was no different to common assault, but others drew a distinction between violent assault and what the prime minister himself described as an occasional 'a tap on the legs'. On the one hand was a discourse affirming children as people who should have the same rights as any other sorts of people and, on the other, a discourse stressing children's immaturity and distinctly different instincts and needs. Although dating from the turn of the century, the debate continues with little hope of clear resolution between what are fundamentally opposed ways of seeing human nature.

However, many social scientists and philosophers are unwilling to live with a situation like this, in which our views on such an important topic are split into what they would call a dualism. Indeed, they argue that the dualisms we frequently encounter when discussing social phenomena, including children and childhood, are not inevitable but are produced by the way in which we have been looking at those phenomena since a period in European intellectual history known as the Enlightenment.

The European Enlightenment occurred between 250 and 350 years ago, and it marks an important development in the emergence of modern European societies. Enlightenment thinkers argued that the power of reason and science would lead to the conquest of nature and the improvement of humankind. Critics have argued that, in actuality, reason and science have been used to impose European ideas and political power across the globe and gave birth to European colonialism and the industrial revolution, whose harmful environmental changes now threaten the very future of life on Earth.

David Blundell

Conventional Western approaches to understanding childhood and providing for children have their roots in the Enlightenment and frequently claim a heavy reliance on scientific methods and the rational search for truths to underpin discourses surrounding children's instinctual characteristics and the needs that accompany growth. The emphasis on instincts and needs suggests that childhood and children can be understood through what natural science tells us about their nature. In this account of childhood, children are shaped primarily by what nature provides, and they grow and develop according to powerful and universal laws that cannot be changed and should not be transgressed if they are to become balanced, healthy and responsible adults. The most notable contributor to this way of thinking about childhood is undoubtedly Jean Piaget, whose theories propose that childhood is a natural phenomenon structured by scientifically observable and universal processes of development that bring physical and cognitive growth into alignment with one another. The associated vocabulary of 'stages', 'assimilation', 'accommodation', 'schemas' and 'readiness' possesses widespread currency. This developmentalist view of childhood continues to inform and justify much institutional provision for children, especially for those in the early years of life, and its language and concepts have become so commonplace that it is difficult to speak of children in professional contexts without using the language (or discourses) it provides – it is the dominant 'working model' for childhood. The Enlightenment's emphasis on the possibility of improving humankind through reason and science impacted heavily on childhood because children seemed to offer opportunities to achieve this improvement as long as these natural laws could be identified and acted upon, with nurseries, schools and other educational institutions increasingly seen as the forum within which progress could be achieved.

Recently, social scientists have questioned the claims of universality and naturalness of much that is found in Piaget's work; encounters with children living in very different societies to those of Western Europe and North America have challenged the claims that these developmentalist accounts embody universal laws or truths about childhood. Coming from a coalition of disciplinary backgrounds, including sociology, education studies, anthropology, women's studies, social psychology and cultural studies, many social scientists assert the need to reappraise how we think about children and have been leaders in the emergence of what is described as the new or critical childhood studies. These academics do not deny the manifest differences between adults and children – most children are clearly physically, sexually and intellectually immature in comparison to adults. However, they argue that biology does not tell us what its facts mean or how we should respond to them. Rather, the ways in which biology is made meaningful are a matter of cultural interpretation. We know that many questions require us to make social, legal and moral judgements that draw on biological information but rely on cultural interpretation: for example, when does childhood end? Does childhood begin at birth? Or before? Or after? When are children morally responsible for their actions? When should child-bearing begin? And seemingly less far-reaching matters, such as should infants learn fractions? Should children use mobile phones? Should television be censored for children? What sort of clothes should children wear and not wear? Moreover, they can change markedly over time. These matters of cultural interpretation will be important in understanding social problems associated with childhood, which is why social constructionism is hailed as a promising and productive approach to seeking solutions.

Since the early 1990s, anthropologist Alison James and sociologist Alan Prout have done much to challenge our existing ways of thinking about children and childhood; they expressed the distinction between childhood as a given biological inheritance and the social constructionist position in this way:

> The immaturity of children is a biological fact of life but the ways in which this immaturity is understood and made meaningful is a fact of culture. It is these 'facts of culture' which may vary and which may be said to make of childhood a social institution. It is in this sense, therefore, that one can talk of the social construction of childhood.
>
> (Prout & James 1997: 7)

Prout and James redirected our attention away from what they saw as an unhelpful search for essential truths about childhood – which, once captured, would resolve all our questions about how childhood should be – towards an appraisal and understanding of what childhood means and the way that language, practices and institutions shape any number of childhoods as differing social realities. This also means that they are not attempting to present a better, improved or truer theory of childhood than that of Piaget and the developmentalists (or anyone else for that matter), but they are proposing that we turn our attention away from the search for essential truths and become more open to difference. Feminists have also criticised the Piaget's 'working model' for the child and childhood, suggesting that its claim to universality allows a male-centred account to dominate our thinking and excludes the female experience of growing up. Social constructionists are, therefore, alive to differences and diversity in human cultures and meanings, and they encourage us to question whether one particular, culturally located way of seeing childhood should dominate our thinking in the way it does.

David Blundell

Why is this important in a discussion of social problems in childhood? There may not be a neat answer here, but it is worth thinking about whether the social problems impacting children's lives are linked to their social positioning as children, or the quality of particular children's lives is more meaningfully linked to their identities expressed in terms of social class, ethnicity, gender, disability or sexual orientation. Prout and James's social constructionist orientation steered us away from the suggestion that the choice is clear cut; indeed, prompted by the United Nations Convention on the Rights of the Child (UNCRC) (UNICEF 1989), along with other scholars and academics in the new childhood studies, they challenged the assumption that this is a decision for us as adults alone to make. At the heart of the new childhood studies was a denial of the commonplace assumption that children represent a vulnerable, passive and incomplete form of human life in need of adult direction and guidance. Rather, it asserts children's capability and agency and, therefore, their entitlement to have their voices heard in matters that concern them – and even those that do not.

The idea of agency is drawn from sociology and has been central to what Prout and James and other authors of the new sociology of childhood have to say. Their work is keen to challenge the idea that children are simply passive beings driven by forces beyond their control – like little automatons – but are as keen to control and shape their lives as we might be. These social scientists point to the resourcefulness and resilience shown by many children, not least when roles reverse and they become family carers; furthermore, they propose that it is institutions such as school that seek to turn them into 'passive dopes' and construct agency as deviation. This is what Prout and James say in proposition 4 of 'A New Paradigm':

> Children are and must be seen as active in the construction and determination of their own social lives, the lives of those around them and of the societies in which they live. Children are not just the passive subjects of social structures and processes.
>
> (Prout & James 1997: 8)

In educational terms, this is vitally important because, as educators, we should bear in mind that children and young people do not simply learn things at school from their lessons but are learning things about education and schooling through their experience; signally, these things may not be at all what teachers intend. This may explain why it seems the main lesson too many young people learn from school is that education is too hard or too demeaning and doesn't suit who they consider themselves to be.

Therefore, we shall now turn to an examination of how education and schooling have become so closely bound up with most children's experience of childhood in Western societies.

childhood and education

7.3 Education, schooling and the construction of modern childhood

Along with the family, the most significant shaper of children's experience of their childhood in countries such as the UK is school, largely because this is the place where they spend large chunks of their young lives. The coupling of education with childhood becomes central to the worldview that emerges from the European Enlightenment, along with its emphasis on science and reason as the means for humankind to transform and improve the world. The education of the young assumes central importance in this project to improve the world, and we see Renaissance luminaries such as Erasmus and Sir Thomas More writing at length in the early sixteenth century about the proper education of both boys and girls – although the actual opportunities for female education were few. Among the seminal thinkers linking children's education to questions of freedom and social progress was the Enlightenment philosopher Jean Jacques Rousseau who, in 1762, published two books: a discussion of the education of a young boy titles *Emile, or on Education* and *The Social Contract* (see Blundell 2012 for a fuller discussion).

The growing importance attaching to the education of children through the Enlightenment and industrial revolution led to the passage of the Elementary Education Act by Gladstone's Liberal government in 1870. The 1870 Act was the first legislation making mass education of children in England and Wales possible and was followed by legislation that made school attendance compulsory in 1880. This legislation installed the commonplace assumption that school was where children should be for much of their time. Alongside the family, this development has proved the single greatest institutional influence on twentieth- and early twenty-first-century childhoods; we might, however, reflect on whether digital technologies and new patterns of social interaction – including those resultant on the global pandemic – might now challenge schooling as a normal condition for the education of children and as a primary contributor to the meaning childhood holds.

Consequent to these acts, the knowledge that the nation's children were all in the same place at the same time was accompanied by a realisation that this particular group was reachable by government, largely en masse, as they sought to introduce any number of political, social and economic policies and measures. Thus, when, in the early years of the twentieth century, we see David Lloyd George's Liberal government confronted by concerns about the poor levels of fitness amongst recruits to the British Imperial Army in the South African Wars of 1899 through 1902, along with the damning indictment of widespread poverty and malnutrition published by the philanthropist Joseph Rowntree in 1901, schools are conveniently

David Blundell

recognised as agencies for social welfare interventions. In response, Lloyd George set up an Interdepartmental Committee on Physical Deterioration, which proposed a raft of social welfare legislation with schools as the vehicle for its implementation. These included the Education (School Meals) Act of 1906; the unprepossessingly titled Education (Administrative Provisions) Act of 1907, which established the School Medical Service; and the Education (Choice of Employment) Act of 1910, which established careers guidance and advice as an entitlement. Schools and the education service thereby became uniquely charged not only with the inculcation of basic educational knowledge and skills but also with being instrumental in improving the health and welfare of children and, hence, the nation (Foley 2001).

However, schooling becomes a point where different and contradictory currents converge, and whilst it has the capacity to address the nation's pressing social problems, it seems unable to decide whether children are redeemers or in need of redemption. The sociologist Chris Jenks (2005) has suggested that, far from holding a straightforward and unified view of children, our discourses are morally ambiguous, and we frequently cannot decide whether we think of them as angels or demons. He identifies these opposing discourses with reference to the qualities and characteristics of the Greek gods Apollo and Dionysius, so, whereas the 'Apollonian child' is all things sweetness and light, the 'Dionysian child' brings us chaos and disorder. Thus, moral pessimism expressing mistrust of children who require taming is set against a romantic optimism that education can realise children's best instincts to become a transformative force for social good. Some see these moralising terms as an unhelpful contributor to debates around whether childhood is in crisis, to which topic we now turn.

7.4 Is there a crisis of childhood, and what might it be?

There is evidence that people have always looked back on their lives; felt that the world had become a harder, harsher place than it used to be; and yearned for the sort of golden age found in J.M. Barrie's Peter Pan – the boy who never grew up. However, over the last 30 years or so, there has emerged a body of opinion suggesting that something has altered in the state of childhood and the quality of the lives we offer to our children and, further, that this represents an objective shift and is not merely the product of nostalgic longing. Among the early contributors was the cultural commentator Neil Postman, who published The Disappearance of Childhood in 1983. Postman's conclusion is manifest in the book's title, and he argues that television and new cultural media have broken down the distinction between the innocent world of childhood and the secrets of adulthood, much to the detriment of childhood. In his view, television sidestepped established ways to achieve social consensus about what were and were not appropriate experiences for children so that, without apparent consultation, it represents 'a broad social decision to allow young children to be present at wars and funerals, courtships and seductions, criminal plots and cocktail parties' (Postman 1983). Postman's book catalysed an extensive and continuing debate about new media and the condition of childhood – expressed luridly in the title of Sue Palmer's *Toxic Childhood: How the Modern World Is Damaging Our Children and What We Can Do About It*, in which technology and new media are indicted, along with a raft of other toxifying influences (Palmer 2006). Similarly, Richard Louv, an American environmentalist, has found a receptive audience for his claim that a condition identified as nature-deficit disorder (NDD) is prevalent amongst urbanised children growing up without access to the affordances of wild spaces and places (Louv 2005).

Do the grounds for a crisis in childhood advanced by these authors also constitute grounds to believe that this is a social problem? Furthermore, if there is a problem, does it lie with childhood and the condition of being an immature human being per se, or is it a problem linked to other social factors, such as inequalities of class, ethnicity or gender? What might be seen as a more authoritative source of data on the condition of children and young people's lives in the UK and other countries of the economically developed world comes from a series of reports by the United Nations Children's Fund (UNICEF). In April 2013, UNICEF followed up an earlier examination of the quality of children's lives published in 2008 with a comparative overview titled 'Child Well-Being in Rich Countries' (UNICEF 2008, 2013). This report sought to assess the quality of childhood in 29 countries who are all members of the Organisation for Economic and Cultural Development (OECD); 27 of the countries were in Europe, and the remaining two were Canada and the United States of America. The evaluation was based in part on the following five statistically based dimensions: material well-being, health and safety, education, behaviours and risks, and housing and environment. Each of these five areas was given a score based on statistical data, and then the countries were ranked based on this score. In 2008 the UK propped up the league table of 21 nations; however, by 2013 it had risen to 16th overall out of 29. The logic of the league table suggests that there might be grounds for some optimism that things are improving here; however, a detailed appraisal counsels a more sober response, especially when we consider that we are thinking about children and their life chances here and not league championships. That said, the continuing position of the Netherlands as a runaway league leader gives pause for thought about what might account for such a disparity in outcome

David Blundell

between it and the UK, two ostensibly similar societies. This disparity is confirmed by what children themselves had to say when asked about 'life satisfaction' – once again, the UK found itself mid-table while the Netherlands occupied the top spot by some margin. At a finer level of detail, more than 80 percent of children in the Netherlands seem to find relationships with peers and parents 'easy', whereas in the UK, just two-thirds find both their classmates 'kind and helpful' and conversations with their fathers easy. In terms of the five categories used by the report, there are concerns expressed about continuing high levels of early pregnancy in the UK and of alcohol abuse amongst teenagers. However, being 24th in the education table is the category in which Britain seems to have performed least well.

While UNICEF produced its reports on children's well-being, the Children's Society also undertook a research programme examining the meaning of and prospects for a 'good childhood' in the UK. Their report was published in 2012 and examined how children felt about their lives under the following ten headings: family, home, money and possessions, friendships, school, health, appearance, time use, choice and autonomy, and the future. Like UNICEF, this report presented worrying findings, but it also sought to offer pointers for what might be characteristic of a good childhood and steps to achieve this. Overall, the Children's Society found that the majority (91 percent) of 8- to 15-year-old children canvassed were happy with their lives but stressed how statistics can obscure harsh realities, in that the remaining 9 percent represented around half a million children who were not. Again, education did not come out particularly well; the fact that 80 percent of children were clear that 'it was very important for them to do well in their school work' does not necessarily tell us that they enjoy school or find it rewarding; furthermore, 'around 7% of children do not feel safe at school and three-fifths of these children are unhappy with their school life as a whole'. Apart from some 'small differences' in well-being between boys and girls and for differing types of household, the research does not find any clear-cut correlation between children's well-being and social factors. However, again, the UK's large population reminds us that small percentage differences can represent large numbers of people: in this case, around a quarter of a million children who are unhappy at school. Percentages may point the way, but statistics cannot tell us what it means and feels like to be unhappy at school (The Children's Society 2012).

In 2010 an educationally focused review of childhood and children's lives was published by academic and professional contributors to the *Cambridge Primary Review*. The *Review*'s finding are more measured than some of the evidence we have examined and also interesting because the team recognised that social problems of childhood are constructed by discourses that underpin representations of ideal types and are expressed through rhetorically deployed language. The report challenged the powerful influence of some of these unhelpful discourses, stating that children they met conformed neither to the image of 'innocents in a dark and menacing world or as celebrity-obsessed couch-potatoes stirring themselves only to text their friends or invade the streets and terrorise their elders' and went on to suggest that, based on the evidence, 'the "crisis" of modern childhood has been grossly overstated' (Alexander 2010: 487). The report took a relatively unfashionable and bold step by suggesting that children's lives and well-being were not being compromised and damaged by technology, being kept indoors or unhealthy lifestyles nearly as much as by social inequality and poverty; further, schools frequently represented a vital point of anchorage in keeping children and their families' lives together.

At least two conclusions might be drawn from these conflicting positions. The first is that a large body of evidence and argument surrounds children on both sides of the argument, and there seems scant hope of immediate resolution. But, no less important, the persistence of the debate suggests that there might be something intrinsic to how childhood is seen that generates controversy and – returning to the opening sentence of this chapter – possibly explains why children figure so consistently and frequently in the discussion of social problems. A case study of the Every Child Matters programme, as without doubt the most recent large-scale institutional intervention into childhood policy, might be instructive.

7.5 Educational responses to social problems of childhood – early childhood and child poverty

A central concern for the New Labour government that swept to power in 1997 under the leadership of Tony Blair was the disturbing evidence of the year-on-year increase in child poverty that had occurred since the early 1980s. It was asserted that, in 1979, the percentage of children living in poverty in the UK stood at 12 percent; by 1997, this figure had doubled to 25 percent and appeared to be rising.

The new government set itself the (now seemingly ambitious) target of reducing child poverty to three-quarters of the 1997 level by 2005 and halving it by 2010 – as things turned out, despite a reduction of 16 percent, the target was missed in 2005, and thereafter, child poverty actually increased.

Along with measures to reduce child poverty through monetary benefits, there was concern to address identified problems in child welfare, both where it occurred in specific geographical areas and at key points in the life course of children considered at risk. In particular, government policy makers were convinced by research demonstrating the merits of investing

David Blundell

in social welfare measures targeted at the early years because drawing on a range of research findings:

> [T]he weight of evidence suggests that a child's experiences in the early years are critical in shaping outcomes not just in health, but across education and welfare throughout that individual's lifespan.
>
> (Gidley 2007: 145)

Policy makers identified the need for what are termed 'upstream interventions', tackling the roots of deprivation, ill health, poor educational outcomes and disadvantage before they imprinted themselves on a child's future life chances. This contrasted with costly, so-called heavy-end provisions that responded to the outcomes of deprivation, such as treating chronic illness or addressing the challenges of early pregnancy and criminality only once they had presented. Sure Start was a specific policy response to these concerns and, as its name suggests, targeted deprivation in the early years. Consistent with New Labour's belief in holistic responses to regeneration and renewal in deprived areas and communities, Sure Start sought to tackle deprivation by working across institutional boundaries to form inter-agency collaborative partnerships.

Early evaluation of the outcomes of Sure Start was difficult, given the long-term benefits over the life span that it aspired to as indicators of success; however, it provided a template for further development of a 'joined-up' agenda for children and their well-being. Over and above research statistics, broad and diverse areas of social concern are frequently brought into sharp focus by quite specific and emblematic events; one such was the tragic death of Victoria Climbie at the hands of her supposed carers. The government's response to Victoria's death was to set up the committee of enquiry under Lord Laming. Whether this sad and quite specific event should have been the particular spur to action is a matter of controversy for some; however, the government's response to Laming and Victoria's death went beyond matters of child protection alone and led to the comprehensive 2004 Children Act that expanded the Sure Start programme under the banner Every Child Matters.

At the heart of the 2004 act's provision was the rapid expansion and enhancement of a number of relatively new institutions and agencies for children and childhood, in particular the Children's Centre. Not since the Elementary Education Act of 1870 that paved the way for mass schooling had there been the development of a new institution for children in the UK on a comparable scale. The vision for an integrated, inter-agency approach to the education, care and well-being of young children (and also older ones) was focused on the Children's Centre as 'a one-stop shop' that, in the opinion of the National Foundation for Educational Research

childhood and education

(NFER), represented a 'quiet social revolution'. A central, iconic figure in this is an holistic construction of the child whose interests and well-being should not be split into separate fractions by structural agencies such as health, education and care that are external to it. Thus, key professionals were required to collaborate in ways rarely seen hitherto. This collaboration aimed to overcome the fragmentation in service provision and failure to share information identified in the Climbie case. The spirit of partnership extended beyond the professional staff with an expectation that management boards comprised parents and service users alongside professional interests and management.

Although undoubtedly revolutionary in its reach and scope, the principle underlying the Children's Centre is actually not that new and in so many ways echoes the work of early pioneers who stressed the link between children's learning and well-being. These include the sisters Rachel and Margaret MacMillan in South and East London around a century ago. Inspiration for the Children's Centre can be seen in their template for nursery schools, wherein the children of the poor were offered education combined with care; indeed, it can be argued that the centres represent a material bridge between the sisters' Christian socialism and the vestiges of left-wing conviction found in the New Labour project. As a generality, it is worthwhile to chart the genealogy of social institutions when appraising responses to new (and not-so-new) social problems (see Blundell 2012).

In attempting to understand the Children's Centre as a response to the social problem of child poverty and a concern to arrest poor outcomes by early intervention, I am suggesting that it is helpful to examine it as a socially constructed institution operating with an ideal type or types not only for children and childhood but also for parents and parenthood and other key actors. Further, these ideal types are informed by discourses that shape and delineate how it goes about making provision for children and, more fundamentally, confirm what proper provision should be and who should rightly offer it. These discourses find a material form not only in the professional practices and language used within the Children's Centre but also in the furniture, colour-schemes, designs, layout and finishings and, furthermore, in the curricula of diploma and degree courses designed to prepare professionals to work in these institutions. All contribute to providing what is considered appropriate for the education and care of children and also convey messages about what proper childhood and, by implication, proper parenting should be. In this sense, the Children's Centre is not only a place where education and learning take place in timetabled sessions or events but also a moral space that seeks to educate and promote learning for the widest audience through its material form and practices – we might, therefore, say that its very fabric is didactic: that is, it is delivering lessons to us about what is and what should be. This is not

David Blundell

to say, however, that the lessons they seek to teach children, parents and other users are necessarily consistent or welcomed by all or, indeed, what those working in the centres intend for their clients.

As we have seen, one of the powerful discourses at the heart of Sure Start, Every Child Matters and the Children's Centre is the idea of early 'upstream' interventions in the life of young children to prevent later pathologies. This has been viewed as an extension of the idea that poor families are caught in a vicious cycle of poverty and deprivation whereby impoverished children inevitably become impoverished parents and pass their deprivation on to their children and so on, without any real hope of breaking the cycle unless help and guidance intervene. This diagnosis appears plausible, and, in principle, intervention makes strategic sense; however, critics have expressed unease about what they see as an unwelcome and probably unworkable cultural, social and moral agenda through which this strategically plausible principle actually seeks to realise its goals. These critics (see Gidley 2007) suggest that the Children's Centre has what philosophers would call an in-built *telos*: that is, a clearly defined end point, in the form of a completed person or human subject, towards which its work is directed. Clearly, any organisation or agency must be directed by goals; however, critics argue that it is unacceptable when those goals impose standards of behaviour and value on people either without consulting them or without reference to and appropriate respect for their social or cultural circumstances. They suggest that the children's policy agenda can be seen as more about meeting the needs and interests of the state through the production of children as liberal citizens who are 'set free of the state, autonomous but required to act responsibly towards themselves and others − for example eating healthily, not smoking, and parenting well'. Furthermore, the *telos* or 'normative model of successful parenting promoted by initiatives like Sure Start closely tallies with the values of white middle-class parents, which implicitly suggests that parents from other backgrounds by definition need intervention' (Gidley 2007: 150). These critics worry that what can be seen as a measure providing help and support is actually underlaid by an assumption that it is the poor and their impoverished social habits that are the problem. Indeed, for them, the institutional affordances of the Children's Centre may mask a much older judgement that it is impoverished families who are to blame for their children's poverty, and the Children's Centre's mission is to offer redemption from their self-imposed shortcomings. That said, it would be unfair and offensive to infer that shortcomings in institutional ethos are shared by those who work within them or that they do not work assiduously to mitigate negative social deterministic institutional practices; how workers navigate these mismatches can be a fruitful field of enquiry for students of childhood institutions.

childhood and education

In the years since New Labour was voted out of office in 2010, responses to the economic crash of 2008 have justified severe austerity measures applied to budgets across the public sector and social policy realm. This has led to a rolling back of the quiet social revolution identified by NFER and included the closure of many Children's Centres. These piecemeal reductions in service provision have arguably made championing and upholding the spirit in Every Child Matters harder to sustain, and the landscape is marked by its fragmentation. Childcare is understood more as economic necessity to release workers than social good, and time spent in school or other institutions by children has increased and intensified what, in 2002, the sociologist Berry Mayall was already calling the scholarisation of childhood.

7.6 Summary

In this chapter we have explored some social problems of childhood, along with historical policy responses to these problems. Along the way, we have questioned whether many of these problems can be 'ring-fenced' as solely belonging to childhood, or they are particular manifestations of wider social phenomena. As social scientists, we have adopted a social constructionist approach that is concerned with understanding the ways in which we make sense of childhood and the meanings we ascribe to it. We have adopted this approach because it is argued that powerful ideas about human nature find expression in what social scientists refer to as discourses, and these discourses shape and inform the institutions that we build for children to live, learn and grow in. These institutions can be made from bricks and mortar and other materials – such as schools and nurseries – but many social scientists think about institutions in a broader and, at times, less apparently tangible form. So institutions can also be the language and concepts we expect to use about children, or they can be the 'ideal forms' (that Weber talks about), around which rules and routines are designed to regulate and direct their lives. Almost certainly, we have all experienced the way that institutions like school shape our experience of childhood: for example, what we wear, when we must be in one place rather than another, how we address others, how we walk up and down stairs and what we do when bells are rung. However, we have seen that the discourses informing these institutions are frequently ambiguous or dualistic, and we do not seem to be able to decide or agree on what we think and should do with any clarity. Should children work for their upkeep or be protected from adult cares? Should children be reasoned with when they are naughty or punished physically? Is children's nature fundamentally 'Apollonian' (sweetness and light/innocent and virtuous) or 'Dionysian' (chaotic and disordered/sinful and needing to be tamed)? Should

David Blundell

childhood be about preparation for adulthood (a process of becoming) or about living in the moment (a state of being in its own right)? In an obvious sense, these dualisms make it difficult to frame policy responses with confidence; furthermore, we inhabit societies that are increasingly characterised by diversity in traditions, values, beliefs and practices, and this challenges the conviction that there are singular truths to determine and follow. Social constructionism tells us that human societies make what they regard as reality but also, by implication, that any particular social reality might be different. Furthermore, as Prout and James suggested, this all seems to presume that children lack active agency and do not construct views of their own about their lives – how often do we ask children what they think? Social constructionism could be very useful as we face an increasingly uncertain future.

What could not be foreseen amongst this philosophical and policy landscape was the sudden emergence of COVID-19 and the global pandemic that has accompanied it. On the one hand, there are those who invest great hope in technology and the potential of a vaccine to put the world back on track while, on the other, there are warnings that the virus will not go away so readily, and life, not least for children (Child in the City 2020b), may never again be as it was.

Although it is not yet clear what the medium-term impacts of the coronavirus pandemic will be, let alone the long-term consequences, it is clear that the immediate effects have frequently re-emphasised familiar debates and pre-existing concerns about the social problems across the social policy arena. As a grimly stark example, data on incidence of death has emphasised immediate and glaring disparities in life expectancy linked to poverty and also revealed the structural inequalities experienced by minority ethnic citizens within a society that continues to exhibit institutionalised racism. Statistics published by the ONS demonstrated that death rates amongst members of black, Asian and minority ethnic (BAME) communities were around four times higher than for those identified as white-British and even higher amongst health professionals from these communities. Additionally, the circumstances of lockdown have provoked fierce discussion surrounding the meaning of essential and non-essential workers under conditions where well-being and even survival are on the line. These have been accompanied by intensified discussion around particular long-standing social issues and their associated problems, including children's growth and environmental determinants of health, childcare, risk and insecurity in employment, family housing quality and the suitability of accommodation and children's safety under conditions in which domestic violence and abuse prevail.

Schooling has not been marginal in the debates surrounding short- and longer-term policy responses. For example, arguments surrounding the

childhood and education   127 practicalities of reopening schools following lockdown have reprised questions about the purpose of schooling and its relation to family life and supporting parental employment. For many teachers and educators, the particular interest in opening up for the youngest pupils emphasised the extent to which schooling is shaped by the needs of the wider economy and their translation onto parents facing insecure employment; as corollary, questions have revolved around how the safety of children and their families should be balanced against the economic interests of the country (Blundell 2020b). Although focused on the immediate issue of the pandemic, the schooling debate also revives pre-existing arguments surrounding the nature and purpose of the curriculum, beneath which particular constructions of childhood and ideals concerning children's lives seem to lurk. For example, some critics have framed their arguments by reference to educational benefits that seem to accompany delaying formal school entry, citing high-performing jurisdictions like Finland as the paradigmatic case. Similarly, there has been explicit advocacy for play to return to the heart of the curriculum because of its potential to align learning and therapeutic experiences as locked-down children return to school (*The Guardian* 2020a). The advocates argue that an overly skills-based and instrumentally driven curriculum needs to be re-imagined with children's mental health and well-being at its core; these methods that would certainly find favour with historical progressive educators, such as Froebel, the MacMillans, Montessori and Steiner, along with child psychoanalysts and therapists advocating the ideas of Donald Winnicott et al, (see also Burns et al. 2019 for a case study of adventure play).

Uncertainty about the longevity of COVID-19 also impacted discussions about schools and their institutional arrangements in the immediate context of a return to schooling. The immediate challenges of remodelling existing buildings to allow low-risk pupil circulation and physical distancing in classroom and other spaces and facilitate regular hygiene and sanitisation practices may present challenges to ways that space and time are allocated and apportioned within the material footprint of the school but also might promote opportunities to expand the learning space beyond it. Processes described as 'segmentation' could spell the end of mass class groups as pupils' time and space are rationed; for example, so-called vertical grouping practices – challenging strict division of children by date of birth and championed by Plowden (CACE 1967) and progressive educators (see Bott et al. 1969: 142–143) – which have been practiced during the height of the pandemic to accommodate children of key workers may have utility in future arrangements.

The pandemic has forced adoption of technological possibilities to create a virtual learning halo space whose potential has hitherto been under-realised, so a reordering of where, when and with whom learning occurs may result – ironic that whilst social distancing separates us from what is local, adoption of technology readily brings the far distant into our immediate ambit. Advocates of environmental education have long championed its potential to reorder and revive the curriculum in productive ways. Weaving screen time into the rich contextual possibilities found in environmental education can not only facilitate flexible management of where and when learning happens but also promote enriching encounters with differences that may be rooted in localised experience but reach out to other learners across all scales (Blundell 2020a). However, it should be recognised that the pandemic has also revealed the extent to which technological means are not equitably shared by children and their families, so affording access to hardware and networks surely warrants adoption as a human right. That said, the lockdown has also emphasised how important time in school and space away from home can be for some children; the provision of nutritious meals, access to technology for those without it at home and precious time to learn and play, as well as removal from dangerous circumstances, can be transformative and should not be overlooked by an overly romantic rush to de-school.

With a nod towards the earlier discussion in this chapter, whilst many claims about what children do and do not want have been made, in actuality, there have been few opportunities for children to express their views about living with COVID-19 and how they see their futures. Contradictions abound as, on the one hand, this adult-led discourse claims that children have very clear views on a range of topics, yet on the other, they are not invited and may not to be trusted to speak for themselves. Others, notably the Association of Play Industries (API 2020), have gone further and pointed out the almost complete silence about children and their need for safe play space in the UK government's strategy document entitled 'Our Plan to Rebuild' (HMSO 2020). That said, the picture is different in Scotland where a Lockdown Lowdown survey recorded children's concerns about the pandemic and feelings about the future (www.youthlinkscotland. org/media/4486/lockdown-lowdown-final-report.pdf), and UNICEF have undertaken imaginative surveys using video diaries compiled by children across the world (Child in the City 2020a). Despite the apparent invisibility of children in the crisis response, one of the few silver linings to the dark cloud of COVID-19 has been tangible improvements in environmental quality that have driven home messages about how damaging urban spaces can be for young people's health. Cities are where many of our most vulnerable and overlooked children live and where safe play space can be in short demand (Blundell 2020a). Dramatic reductions in road traffic, including the abandonment of the school run as schools close and the lockdown is enforced, have demonstrated how improvements in the health of children's developing lungs and others with significant respiratory conditions might be achieved. Additionally, the absence of continual traffic streams has opened up neighbourhood spaces for play. Thus, the enforced conditions of the pandemic have provided material examples of the sorts of measures long advocated by those seeking change and brought tangible pressures for the reformulation of policy in ways that do not merely work for children but also with them (Child in the City 2020b).

Acknowledging children as legitimate agents, whether in matters directly concerning them or not, has implications far beyond merely widening the circle of consultation. Because of children's status within modern childhood, championing their entitlement to be heard challenges the presumed primacy of certain privileged forms of reason along with the idea that circles can be drawn around who is and is not included. This has far-reaching implications for others deemed to be outside the hallowed circle. If there is any good to come from these dark, painfully distressing times, it may lie in their potential to effect a change in prevailing mentalities. As the 'globalised order' fails, a re-evaluation of the way humans imagine, think and talk about, as well as interact with, each other and the rest of the planet may be the outcome. As a final reflection, there is some irony that, as the 150th anniversary of the passage of the 1870 Elementary Education Act comes around, empowering children may lead to a significant unravelling of the Victorian factory schooling system it created.

 Key points

Children are subject to social problems and are also seen as problematic. Further, childhood is seen as a time when social problems can be addressed through what are described as 'upstream interventions' that can not only change society and an individual's life chances but also, in the process, save expenditure on rectifying social ills later. Education and schooling frequently occupy a pivotal position in addressing social problems, not just because of children's youthfulness but also because nineteenth-century public schooling brought so many children within immediate reach.

The quality of contemporary childhood is the focus of a series of panics about children's lives

Are these problems of childhood per se, or do they have roots in broader social problems, such as poverty, changes in social structures and working lives or new media and communications? Does

David Blundell

childhood as a category based on biological immaturity mean we overlook other sociological variables, such as gender, class, ethnicity, disability and sexuality and their influence in forming young people's lives and identities?

Social constructionism may help us. This is because it turns our attention away from universal and essential truths about children and childhood – that is, truths that are constant for all people at all times and in all places – towards the way societies and cultures construct shared social realities. These social realities are informed and structured by discourses that mediate powerful ideas. Conflicts may occur when different social realities collide, but this can also lead to change and constructive adaptation – in short, social constructionism suggests that things do not have to be the way they are and can be different.

COVID-19

Although unexpected and sudden, COVID-19 has intensified existing inequalities as well as provoking arguments and policy responses that draw on existing debates and long-standing controversies. The COVID-19 pandemic has tested the durability of many of the working assumptions surrounding the ways society and economy work. Whilst the long-term effects are not clear, what has been learned can revive and re-energise demands for change that begins with a genuinely inclusive rethinking of childhood and acknowledgement of the contribution children are entitled to make.

 Coursework questions

Should children play a part in solving social problems and creating the world of the future? Explain your thinking.

Should our policy address child poverty or poverty per se?

Has childhood become more or less problematic? Explain your answer with reference to the part schooling has played in bringing this about.

Critics of the Children's Centres and the children's agenda said that they sought to impose middle-class values and expectations on children and their families. How do you think professionals working within these settings should respond to this criticism?

References

Alexander, R. (ed.) (2010) *Children, Their World, Their Education: Final Report and Recommendations of the Cambridge Primary Review*. London: Routledge.

Association of Play Industries. (2020) 'Play "completely overlooked" in UK lockdown exit strategy'. Accessed: 26th May 2020. www.childinthecity.org/2020/05/13/outdoor-play-completely-overlooked-in-uk-lockdown-exit-strategy/?utm_source=newsletter&utm_medium=email&utm_campaign=Newsletter%20week%202020–20

Blundell, D. (2012) *Education and Constructions of Childhood*. London and New York: Continuum.

Blundell, D. (2020a) 'Education, urbanisation and the case of "The Child in the City'". In Simon, C. and Downes, G. (eds.), *Sociology for Education Studies: Twenty-first Century Approaches*. London: Routledge.

Blundell, D. (2020b) 'Elementary education and child labour: From economic to ecological histories of modern childhood'. In Bustillos Morales, J. A. and Abegglen, S. (eds.), *Understanding Education and Economics: Key Debates and Critical Perspectives*. London: Routledge.

Bott, R., Davies, M. P., Glynne-Jones, M. L., Hitchfield, E. M., Johnson, J. E. L. and Tamburrini, J. R. (1969) *Fundamentals in the First School*. Oxford: Blackwell.

Burns, T., Abegglen, S. and Blundell, D. (2019) 'Adventure play in 70s East London - Parts 1, 2, 3'. Accessed: 22nd May 2020. www.childinthecity.org/2019/02/11/adventure-play-in-70s-east-london-p1/

CACE. (1967) *Children and Their Primary Schools – The Plowden Report*. London: HMSO.

Child in the City. (2020a) 'Our lives during COVID19: Kids tell their stories'. Accessed: 29th May 2020. www.childinthecity.org/2020/05/27/our-lives-during-covid-19-kids-tell-their-stories/?utm_source=newsletter&utm_medium=email&utm_campaign=Newsletter%20week%202020–22

Child in the City. (2020b) 'COVID-19 could become a lasting crisis for children'. Accessed: 26th May 2020. www.childinthecity.org/2020/05/14/covid-19-could-become-a-lasting-crisis-for-children/?utm_source=newsletter&utm_medium=email&utm_campaign=Newsletter%20week%202020–20

The Children's Society. (2012) 'The good childhood report'. Accessed: 24th July 2013. www.childrenssociety.org.uk

Foley, P. (2001) 'The development of child health and welfare services in England (1900–1948)'. In Foley, P. et al. (eds.), *Children in Society: Contemporary Theory, Policy and Practice*. Basingstoke: Palgrave Macmillan, pp. 6–20.

Gidley, B. (2007) 'Sure start: An upstream approach to reducing health inequalities'. In Scriven, A. and Garman, S. (eds.), *Public Health: Social Context and Action*. London: McGraw-Hill.

The Guardian. (2020a) 'Prioritise play when schools reopen say mental health experts'. Accessed: 27th May 2020. www.theguardian.com/education/2020/may/07/prioritise-play-when-schools-reopen-say-mental-health-experts-coronavirus-lockdown

The Guardian. (2020b) 'Trump advisers doubt swift reopening as WHO official says virus will "stalk human race"'. Accessed: 26th May 2020. www.theguardian.com/us-news/2020/apr/12/trump-fauci-hahn-reopening-who-virus-stalk-human-race

HMSO. (2020) 'Our plan to rebuild: The UK Government's COVID-19 recovery strategy'. https://www.gov.uk/government/publications/our-plan-to-rebuild-the-uk-governments-covid-19-recovery-strategy/our-plan-to-rebuild-the-uk-governments-covid-19-recovery-strategy

Jenks, C. (2005) *Childhood* (2nd ed.). London: Routledge.

Louv, R. (2005) *Last Child in the Woods: Nature Deficit Disorder and What We Can Do About It*. New York: Algonquin Books of Chapel Hill.

Palmer, S. (2006) *Toxic Childhood: How the Modern World Is Damaging Our Children and What We Can Do About It*. London: Orion.

Postman, N. (1983) *The Disappearance of Childhood*. London: W. H. Allen.

Prout, A. and James, A. (1997) 'A new paradigm for the sociology of childhood? Provenance, promise and problems'. In James, A. and Prout, A. (eds.), *Constructing and Reconstructing Childhood*. London: Routledge.

UNICEF. (2008) 'Child poverty in perspective: A comprehensive assessment of the lives and well-being of children and adolescents in the economically advanced nations'. Accessed: 27th May 2020. www.UNICEF-irc.org/publications/pdf/rc7_eng.pdf

UNICEF. (2013) 'Child well-being in rich countries: A comparative overview'. In *Innocenti Report Card 11*. Florence: UNICEF.

United Nations Convention on the Rights of the Child. (1989) Accessed: 27th May 2020. www.UNICEF.org/crc/

 Further reading

Blundell, D. (2012) *Education and Constructions of Childhood*. London: Bloomsbury.

Bustillos Morales, J. A. and Abegglen, S. (2020) *Understanding Education and Economics: Key Debates and Critical Perspectives*. London: Routledge.

Chapter 8

Precarious work, the new 'gig economy' and unemployment

Brian McDonough

8.1 Introduction: work, patterns of employment and social identities

Work is central to the ways in which people live their lives. The sorts of work we do, where we work and how much we get paid are all crucial in determining other aspects of the way we live. For example, the quantity and quality of goods we can afford are often determined by the kinds of paid work we carry out. For most people, work takes up more time than any other social activity. Most of us must work to earn a living or rely on pensions and other benefits that are often a redistribution of taxes collected from other people's employed work. Work also provides a measure of social worth and status. We are often categorised, assessed, ranked and rewarded on what we do for work. Work can dictate the sort of housing area we can afford to live in; whether we live in social housing; the kind of house or flat we live in; and what sort of car we own, should we have one, as well as determining the sorts of other goods we are able to afford depending on our income. But our job and work status not only affect our income and possessions but also impact our way of living more broadly. They influence the sorts of people we meet, the friends we have and the social activities we engage in, many of which continue over the course of our lives. Historically, work has always been tied up with a person's social identity. People have associated their occupation with who they are: for example, naming themselves after their work – consider the surnames Mason, Butcher and Baker, which all began as descriptions of occupations people once did. However, work today is fundamentally changing. 'Only one generation ago, most workers could expect to be full-time employees in secure full-time jobs, working for just one or two companies over the course of their careers' (Mulcahy 2016: 3). That generation could build a career with consistent income, as well as a range of entitlements and fringe benefits – from holiday entitlements to retirement packages. But today emerges a new generation, for whom stable employment is not always available, and a world where we can no longer speak of one single work identity but where we must use the plural – work identities. The new generation of workers must be multiskilled and adaptable to several types of paid work over their lifetime. Employers, conscious of the 'baggage' (the taxes, holidays, sick pay and retirement contributions) that comes with employing full-time workers, are more inclined than ever before to make use of temporary, part-time or self-employed staff wherever possible. With fierce market competition, many companies save costs by eliminating full-time workers using redundancies, downsizing and company reorganisation.

As patterns of employment change, our relationship to work and our work identities change too. We no longer have stable and reliable employers who will look after us until the day we retire. Instead, we are reliant on what has become known as 'precarious work' (Standing 2015: 2), denoting 'non-standard' and 'insecure' forms of employment (McDonough 2017: 97). Understanding the precariousness of employment in the UK and elsewhere involves evaluating its 'instability, lack of protection, insecurity and social or economic vulnerability' (EC 2004: 47). From fast food restaurant workers to hospital nurses and university lecturers, precarious workers are in every sector of society. Within the remit of precarious work, a new and very different type of workforce and economic environment has emerged, nicknamed the 'gig economy'. We tend to think about 'gigs' performed by musicians, comedians and other live performers. They turn up for one night only – paid for just a few hours. Well, today, the term *gig* is now applied to other workers too. Consulting and contractor arrangements, freelancing and on-demand work through media technology platforms are all part of the 'gig economy' and all subject to temporary work, often with an uncertain future. The 'gig economy' has facilitated new services and created millions of jobs. But it also passes significant risk and responsibility from large organisations and employers to the workers who make the 'gig economy' possible (Woodcock & Graham 2020). It is for this reason that, when we discuss social problems at work, we include the emergence of the new 'gig economy' alongside the wider problems of precarious work and unemployment.

This chapter discusses the 'gig economy', precarious work and unemployment with several underlying assumptions. First, the chapter addresses the way in which work is socially constructed in our society. We live in a society which puts the emphasis of getting a job, being in employment and providing for oneself and ones' family as individualistic. Despite the societal and structural factors affecting individuals' lives, there is an assumption that those who are poor, are experiencing in-work poverty, have precarious forms of employment or are unemployed just need to try harder. We shall discuss such underlying discourses which illuminate our understandings of work by referring to the notion of the 'work ethic', offering alternative ways of viewing 'work' sociologically. Following from this discussion, we shall look at precarious work and the gig economy, outlining the ways in which 'working harder' does little to help people escape from some of the social inequalities attached to this kind of lifestyle. The chapter will also explore the pros and cons of the gig economy, not least why companies and some workers reap benefits of a changing world of work. We shall then examine unemployment as a social problem, this time highlighting the way in which unemployment is socially constructed. We shall consider different 'constructs' of unemployment from a range of perspectives, but first, it will be useful to discuss the issue of work in more detail, not least because our understanding of what work is can determine the meaning of work and non-work and the varying definitions and understandings of precarious work and unemployment.

8.2 Defining work

If we intend to investigate work activities, then we must first decide what we mean by work. One way of understanding work is to define it in terms of task-based activities for which people are paid by an employer, client or customer. However, this definition fails to recognise work which is unpaid but still contributes significantly to the functioning of society. For example, voluntary work contributes to the sustenance of Britain in a range of ways. Unpaid charity fundraisers, community workers and others who altruistically give up their time to help others are rendered invisible when a narrow definition of work is used. So, too, are youth work-experience 'employees', who can get paid nothing for carrying out the same work as formal members of staff. This definition of work as 'paid employment' is made even more problematic if we consider that many of the activities people do within employment are also carried out by people who are technically not

Brian McDonough

employed. Care workers employed by the health-care service and private care homes are paid and recognised as 'real' workers because they are employed, but those people in Britain who work as carers for their elderly or impaired parents or partners do not get the same recognition. During the 2015 to 2016 financial year, 8 percent of the UK's private household population were 'informal carers' for someone (of whom nearly two-thirds were women), according to survey data from the Department for Work and Pensions (ONSb 2020). These people are often not seen as workers, despite the fact that the activities in which they are engaged are the same as those provided by full-time paid employees.

As feminist sociologists have pointed out, domestic chores like washing, ironing, cooking, child-minding and many other tasks all exist both as paid and unpaid labour, yet within political discourse, the former is more usually considered 'real' work and so is more valued than unpaid labour (Grint & Nixon 2015). Women's work in the home, in particular, is often made invisible in this way; as Oakley (1974) and others have argued, domestic work and childcare come to be seen as lacking in value and are unrecognised when considering work as only paid employment. Feminists since the 1970s have challenged the traditional conceptual boundaries of work and non-work, when criticising the taken-for-granted assumption that work undertaken in the private sphere of the home is not real work. Yet without the enormous volume of domestic labour carried out by women, the formal economy of wages and salaries would cease to function. Feminists have argued that the allocation historically of domestic labour to women, along with responsibilities for sustaining the social network of the family, are aspects of the ways in which power is organised and deployed in society so that the 'relations of ruling' (Smith 1987) are organised in the interests of men.

Since the 1990s, the proportion of households headed by single parents has increased. The Office for National Statistics reported that there were nearly 2 million lone parents with dependent children in the UK in 2015, a figure which has grown steadily but significantly from 1.6 million in 1996 (ONS 2020a). Most of these parents are women, although some are men. For single parents who wish to attend courses and join work-experience schemes or take part-time or full-time paid employment, the difficulties of juggling economic activity with childcare responsibilities can be particularly severe. For many women who balance childcare with precarious (insecure and unstable) forms of employment, the 'work' (sheer labour effort) they put into their activities can be doubly exploitative – poor pay and lack of entitlements at work and no pay at all for the childcare carried out.

And so, the term *work* appears easy to define, but when we consider the specific ways in which 'work' is constructed, the picture is more complex. What counts as work depends on the specific social circumstances under which activities are undertaken and, importantly, how these circumstances and activities are interpreted by those involved (Grint & Nixon 2015). This problem with defining work has called for a re-evaluation of what is meant by the term. For example, Glucksmann (2007) argues for an understanding of work as the 'total social organisation of labour'. This definition is more inclusive and recognises the labour carried out which is unpaid but of value and importance to the British economy and society overall. But, whilst this alternative definition of work may be more adequate sociologically, we still may need to recognise that the ways in which work is currently defined within national consciousness and political discourse reflect in part the relations of power within society as it is. So, for example, if domestic work or childcare is regarded as 'real' work or 'leisure' or something else, then it is because we are constructing our activities through a particular kind of viewpoint or discourse. As Grint and Nixon (2015) say, the discourse of work is provided by symbolic representations through which meanings and social interests are constructed, mediated and deployed. To put it simply, the meaning of work is created, challenged, altered and sustained through contending discourses, and these are embedded in particular social relations.

8.3 Work, the 'work ethic' and inclusion in paid work

As we have seen, there are several competing discourses that constitute the way in which people think about work. One discourse centres on the idea that paid work is dependent on what individuals do to find employment and the efforts they make to work hard. Perhaps those in part-time work and the unemployed just need to 'try harder' to find a full-time job. However, these 'choices' are outside of the remit of most individuals when full-time jobs are in short supply or when their circumstances (e.g. disability, age or care responsibilities) limit their ability to choose a suitable full-time position, assuming a full-time post is something desired. This assumption about 'trying harder' connects to a discourse of the 'work ethic', in which individuals must take responsibility for finding paid work and doing so with a hard-working ethos. The 'work ethic' provides a narrative with which we go about our everyday lives and feeds into the meritocratic idea that our success is determined by our raw talent and hard work. The discourse of the 'work ethic' also feeds into the notion of inclusion as participation in paid work (Levitas 2005). This is not only evident in common-sense assumptions amongst the British public and the British media but is also core to legislative policies in Britain. Social policy in Britain has been preoccupied with the idea of inclusion in the labour market, and the importance of paid employment has dominated British politics for many years,

Brian McDonough

in conjunction with the important conception of the 'work ethic'. As the nineteenth-century sociologist Max Weber (1864–1920) showed, the idea that work in itself constitutes a value has its historical origin in particular parts of Europe following the period of the Reformation and extending into the eighteenth century (see Weber 2010). The consequence is that in our culture, we polarise a notion of the 'work ethic' with laziness, which we condemn.

This discourse of the 'work ethic' and inclusion as participation in paid work has been evident in UK politics and policies since the 1990s and is still present in the ethos of the government led by Prime Minister Boris Johnson today. Twenty years ago, it was evident in the thinking behind Gordon Brown's New Deal scheme (introduced in 1998 and renamed the Flexible New Deal in 2009), with its emphasis on 'making work pay' (Levitas 2005). The same logic was used to justify the 'benefits cap' in 2013, limiting the amount of support a person could receive (a max of £20,000, or £23,000 in London). Behind the policy change was the idea that it would 'always pay to work' – except it failed to recognise that not everyone is able to take on paid employment due to circumstances such as poor health or caring responsibilities. Such policies have been aimed at increasing labour market participation among specific groups including the young, the long-term unemployed, people with disabilities and lone parents and amending the benefits system so that people could not be better off on benefits than in paid work. This aspiration has been continued in the Universal Credit system today, designed to simplify the benefits system and to incentivise paid work by replacing and combining pre-existing benefits for working-age people (Employment and Support Allowance, Child Tax Credit, Working Tax Credit, Housing Benefit and Income Support). Critics argue that the Universal Credit system punishes and stigmatises people who are unable to work through no fault of their own. This was best illustrated in the Ken Loach movie *I, Daniel Blake* (2017), based on a 59-year-old joiner who is sent from 'pillar to post' to find a new job when he is made redundant from his long-term job. The emphasis and enormous pressure the state applies to getting people into paid work is encapsulated by the 'fit for work' tests carried out at homes and in job centres. Blake had suffered a heart attack, but because he could walk 50 metres and was able to raise one arm to his shirt pocket, he was declared ready for employment. He eventually died of ill health brought on by stress. The film depicts a cruel welfare system that vilifies people for not having a job.

And so the 'work ethic' reinforces the idea that everyone of working age should be in paid work rather than dependent on the state. This concern for limiting the role of the state goes back to the emergence of neoliberalism as developed by the Thatcher government from 1979, which sought to reverse a trend in the development of what they critically referred to as the 'nanny state', a form of political approach also developed by Ronald Reagan in the USA. These policies aimed at getting people into work have been accompanied by a moral importance of paid work. Because of the emphasis on paid work, working families are perceived as morally more worthy than others, with those not in paid work as morally inferior.

There are many strains and contradictions in these policies. In political discourse, there is often an emphasis on the importance of parenting and of community, but these can be in some tension with an overriding emphasis on paid work. In fact, both these aspects of society depend on unpaid labour. If, for example, two lone parents look after their own young children, they are deemed not to be working, but if they register as child minders and swap children for 35 hours a week, they will be defined as working.

Whilst feminists have challenged the terms in which we think about the value and productivity of domestic labour and, in the case of Smith (1987), the other activities which women often undertake in ensuring the sustenance of the so-called private sphere, which enables the activity which occurs in the world of paid work, a Marxist tradition has often provided the theoretical context to develop a critique of the concept of 'work' in capitalism. For Marxists, the ways in which work is defined within political discourse, as well as the symbolic significance of the 'work ethic', can only be grasped if we locate our analysis in the context of the class relations of capitalism. For Marx, the key contradiction in capitalist society lies in the class relationship between a ruling class, the bourgeoisie, and a class whose labour is exploited by them, the proletariat. In his early writings such as the *Economic and Philosophical Manuscripts* of 1844, Marx developed the concept of alienation to characterise the damage done to people forced to work within the constraints of a capitalist economy in which they were distanced from their own creativity, from other workers and from the product of their labour. For Marx, the 'species being' of humans calls for them to be free to engage in conscious, practical, creative activity. The critical traditions which are the inheritors of Marx's critical analysis have continued to emphasise that capitalism is an economic and social system which distances people from fulfilling activity by turning work into something that has to be done in order to survive because capitalism is organised to pursue and accumulate profit rather than to benefit the mass of members of society.

Writers such as the French social philosopher Andre Gorz (1923–2007) have sought to apply aspects of this Marxist analysis to contemporary capitalist societies. In a critique of work relations within capitalism, *Reclaiming Work: Beyond a Wage-Based Society*, Andre Gorz (1999) argues that capitalism has socially constructed the idea of work and what it represents. It has created a discourse which sees work as paid employment and does not recognise the 'real work' that many people carry out. Gorz argues that

Brian McDonough

we must learn to see work differently: no longer as something we have or do not have, but as what we do. Drawing on Rifkin's (1995) book *The End of Work*, Gorz argues for an end to work which is peculiar to industrial capitalism:

> the work we are referring to when we say 'she doesn't work' of a woman who devotes her time to bringing up her own children, but 'she works' of one who gives even some small part of her time to bringing up other people's children in a play group or nursery school.
>
> (1999: 2)

Later, Gorz (2010) wrote *The Immaterial: Knowledge, Values and Capital* to critique the 'knowledge economy' – an economy in which growth depends on the quality, quantity and accessibility of information, rather than the means of production. Instead of buying and selling material goods, this economy exploits knowledge by privatising it and claiming ownership through private licences and copyright. Gorz (2010) calls for a true knowledge economy, based on zero-cost exchange and pooled resources, enabling the creation of knowledge to be treated as humanity's common property.

Overall, Gorz (2010) argues for a conception of 'real work' that encompasses the broad creative scope of human activity and is not limited to what we do when 'at work'. He further argues that society should cease exploiting workers for their labour, whether this is in terms of the production of goods and services or the production of knowledge (i.e. the knowledge economy) and instead value what people contribute to the society in which they live. Gorz (1999) argues that socially, we must move beyond the constraints and exploitation of the wage relation and move beyond the wage-based society in order to achieve a system in which there is a decent livelihood and decent life for all. Like many other analysts of work, he argues for a universal basic income.

8.4 Precarious work, recognition of real work and universal basic income

In recent years, there has been global interest by academics, politicians, policy makers and community activists in developing new policy provisions which completely reinvent peoples' relationship to work. The aim has been to recognise all work, not just paid work, and to recompense those who do not occupy standard full-time jobs. Perhaps the most popular is universal basic income: 'a regular cash income paid to all on an individual basis, without means test or work requirement' (McDonough & Bustillos Morales 2020: 3). Some have referred to this as a 'universal dividend', 'citizen's wage', or 'existence income' (see Van Parijs & Vanderborght 2019). Many critics believe that a basic income paid from the state to every member of society is far too ambitious since it is grossly expensive and will bankrupt society. But with advanced taxation systems already in place, especially in countries like the UK, the means of paying for a basic income are arguably already in place. Most advocates of a basic income believe it is affordable and would offer a safety net to overcome some of the social problems we face in capitalist society: uncertainty, insecurity, poverty and a whole host of related social inequalities. A UBI gained popularity during the coronavirus crisis of 2020 since it offered a way of relieving those who were in 'lockdown' and could not work and as a way of compensating all those who were made unemployed during the consequential economic crash. Some sociologists have argued that a UBI could be a way out of 'coronavirus poverty' (McDonough 2020: 2), providing an immediate and constant source of income for everyone affected by the crisis of the most recent pandemic.

One key benefit to a universal basic income is that it offers a solution to precarious employment. Precarious employment results from the kind of global economics we call neoliberalism. This is rooted in a model known as 'laissez-faire' economics, meaning 'let the market rip' (or do 'as it pleases'). Labour markets are opened up through deregulation; peoples' labour becomes commodified, bought and sold (or hired and fired) depending on the strength of the market. With lax labour laws, or ones which intentionally promote 'flexibility' for companies to employ workers using poor contractual conditions, organisations get away with maximising profits at the expense of precarious employment for workers. The Marxist-influenced economist Guy Standing (2015) defined this new class of global workers as 'the precariat' (precarious proletariat) to denote the commonly insecure and unstable employment conditions workers from around the world and from all kinds of occupations and industries were experiencing. Standing (2015: 51) explains that even human labour has become commodified so that work activities can be 'offshored (within firms) or "outsourced" (to partner firms or others)' to other places and countries. This fragments the labour process – for instance, careers become disrupted when workers never know if their jobs will be replaced by cheaper labour from abroad.

A universal basic income helps protect precarious workers who are subject to insecure, unprotected and poorly paid working conditions because it offers a regular cash income that supplements earnings. But it also means that workers are less reliant upon their employers and are therefore less likely to be exploited – forced to work unsociable hours or to work on poorly paid terms under poor conditions. A universal basic income also helps reconceptualise the notion of 'work'. As Gorz (1999) and other advocates of a basic income (Standing 2017; Van Parijs & Vanderborght 2019) have pointed out, capitalist society has for a long time understood 'work' as merely earning a wage. Standing (2017: 23) says that a universal basic income can help to reduce the binary thinking that exists between 'work' and 'non-work' – work which is unpaid is unrecognised and invisible in society. Those who are doing important unpaid work in society, such as caring for the young, old or disabled or volunteering to help others in their local community, can receive recognition and are compensated, to some extent, at least, through a regular cash income.

One of the fundamental discussions around universal basic income is the idea of 'freedom'. Liberal democratic societies like the UK supposedly offer many freedoms, like the right to food, drink and shelter – or even the right to work. But capitalism encroaches on our freedom when the wages we are paid are not enough to live 'normal', decent lives. For example, the rise of in-work poverty in Britain means that there are individuals who work yet are trapped below the poverty line. An estimated 7.4 million Britons are classed as being in in-work poverty, according to the New Policy Institute (NPI 2016). A universal basic income has the potential to provide freedom from poverty and freedom from exploitative employers and can also 'provide the freedom to care for children or the very old or disabled without living below the poverty line' (McDonough & Bustillos Morales 2020: 27). A good example is the freedom to own a property. All capitalist societies allow people the freedom to purchase their own homes. In truth, however, many financial and social inequalities linked to social class, occupation and income prevent people from doing so. Unfortunately, with the rise of in-work poverty in the UK, having a job does not give people the freedom to live 'ordinary' lives without suffering from hardship, impoverishment or destitution. Perhaps a universal basic income can provide a vital safety net, helping all citizens be free from poverty, using a regular cash transfer directly to the bank accounts of all in society.

8.5 The new 'gig economy'

The gig economy is seen as one of the most recent examples of 'atypical' or 'non-standard' forms of work and refers to 'the parcelled nature of the small tasks or jobs (the "gigs") that individuals are contracted to carry out by companies (often platforms) adopting this model of service provision' (Tassinari & Maccarrone 2020: 1). Using internet technology, gig economy companies adopt online platforms to operate, acting as intermediaries of labour supply. Examples include the ride-share company Uber and food delivery services such as Deliveroo and Uber Eats. These companies have come under considerable criticism from workers, unions and labour movements. They represent some of the worst aspects of the gig economy because of the exploitative relationship between the organisation and workers. For example, using delivery platforms, companies like Deliveroo can access a flexible labour force without the need for management responsibilities. All labour costs are minimised because couriers are hired as 'independent or para-subordinate contractors' (Tassinari & Maccarrone 2020: 2) and, as such, have no right to minimum wage, paid holidays or sick leave. Because of the contractual arrangement, workers have few, if any, protections from dismissal. Whilst platforms promote working-time flexibility as key advantage, in reality, many couriers must sign up for shifts in advance (Tassinari & Maccarrone 2020: 2), making it much more like a routine job (but without the benefits). Most food delivery platforms switch from hourly wages to payment by the job. For those who cannot keep up with the speed at which they must deliver, wages are reduced, sometimes below what would normally be considered 'the minimum wage'. Even worse than that, quiet periods mean that workers simply do not get paid since there's no job to do. The gig economy can be likened to exploitative dock work or the mining industry from the past. Instead of queuing up on a dock or mining site, workers queue in line on a website or platform app, only to find there's 'no work today'.

The gig economy has reorganised work 'by transforming our labour market of jobs into a labour market of work' (Mulcahy 2016: 12). In many respects, the gig economy has brought about many benefits to companies, enabling them to cut costs by working more efficiently – tending to small tasks or jobs as they are required. The gig economy has been considered positive for many workers too (Kessler 2019; Mulcahy 2018); for instance, by 'disaggregating work from a job, workers can realise levels of autonomy, flexibility, and control that have been traditionally unavailable to employees' (Mulcahy 2016: 12). Delivery drivers, dog walkers and errand runners can receive notifications on their smartphones when a job becomes available and 'choose to either accept or reject it' (Kessler 2019: 2). Some self-employed graphic designers pick which jobs they would like to do and which clients they would like to 'work' for – working flexibly and enhancing their own portfolios to meet their own ends. Some companies break down work into small tasks that take only minutes and pay relatively little, like transcribing audio tapes or 'stuffing-envelopes'. Whilst these jobs are monotonous and often low paid, they do enable workers to work from home, allowing the flexibility to care for children or older relatives whilst making an income. Many workers of the new gig economy generation find the idea of being tied to one employer tiresome and overbearing. Those most successful in the gig economy have started new businesses, restructured their finances, planned their own time off and created lives which are arguably 'more engaging, satisfying, and better aligned with their priorities' (Mulcahy 2016: 2).

Brian McDonough

As this chapter shows, there are both pros and cons to the new gig economy. The new gig economy bends the rules of working arrangements, operating within legal grey areas where workers are left without safety nets. Companies, small and large, can use online platforms to access large workforces across different districts and continents. Whilst the rise of such organisations and models of working can bolster economic growth, they also create a raft of social problems and issues related to precarious work, technology and exploitation.

8.6 Defining and measuring unemployment

It is extremely difficult to compare rates of unemployment over time in any one country or between countries. This is because governments frequently alter the way unemployment is measured, often for political reasons. For example, between 1979 and 1989, Conservative governments in the UK changed the way unemployment was measured 30 times, and virtually every one had the effect of reducing unemployment figures (Edgell & Granter 2019). Today, most countries are adopting a definition of unemployment held by the International Labour Organisation (ILO), a specialist UN agency. They classify people as unemployed if they are without a job, actively seeking employment and available to work. But some governments define unemployment by those who are registered as unemployed and in receipt of unemployment-related state benefits. It is not surprising, then, that these two rates of unemployment are very different, given that they measure different things. The ILO measure 'typically produces a higher level of unemployment rates than the "claimant count"' (Edgell 2019: 175).

These differing measures of unemployment tell us that the unemployment rate is a product of the decisions taken in relation to how to define unemployment. In other words, what is measured is not unproblematic but is a phenomenon constructed through social and political decisions about definitions. For example, in November 1982, those who were not eligible for benefits were excluded from unemployment figures in Britain. And in March 1983, men over the age of 60 who were claiming long-term supplementary benefit (now called income support) were no longer required to sign on and so were no longer recorded as unemployed.

Although we will want, as sociologists, to attend to official statistics relating to employment rates, we will need to bear in mind that these figures do need to be treated with great caution. As a student of the social sciences, you will become familiar with the ways in which statistics are put together in particular ways and for particular purposes. (Indeed, the argument that statistics are socially constructed is a theme that runs throughout this book.)

Debate about unemployment is often intensely political. For example, in the 1980s, when unemployment was at its peak in Britain, Lord Young, then the employment secretary, and Jeffrey Archer, the novelist and former vice chair of the Conservative Party, claimed publicly that up to one million people were included in the unemployment statistics who should not be because they were working and claiming benefits illegally or were not genuinely looking for work. This view was decisively rejected by politicians of the left, who saw this claim as an attempt to justify a Conservative strategy to use unemployment as a tool to deal with an economic crisis. Sociologists usually argue that official unemployment statistics have underestimated the amount of unemployment rather than exaggerating it. However, the main point to take from this section is this: unemployment is something that is measured in particular ways by particular groups of people and for particular reasons – often politically motivated. No unemployment statistic can be taken as a purely 'objective' figure but must always be understood in relation to the way it has been produced and, arguably, the purposes it may serve.

8.7. The social construction of unemployment

There has recently been an intensification in the discourse which depicts the unemployed as lazy or idle individuals who are disinclined to work. A particular public discourse presented by the media tells us that the 'unemployed' are welfare dependents sponging off the state, using the taxes of others to pay for their widescreen TVs and mobile smartphones. Tabloid newspapers such as *The Sun*, for example, have consistently reported on 'the benefit scroungers' of Britain, calling for them to be stopped. This is a construction of the unemployed which typifies them as 'scroungers' who have become a drain on society. They manipulate the system to receive support, taking from society but giving nothing back. This perception of the unemployed is sensationalised by newspaper tabloids, consistently discussed in public and political debate and used as clear justification for reducing welfare benefits by political parties. For example, Prime Minister David Cameron declared in 2013 that the benefits bill was 'sky-rocketing' while 'generations languish on the dole and dependency'. In the same year, Chancellor George Osborne also added:

> [W]here is the fairness . . . for the shift-worker, leaving home in the dark hours of the early morning, who looks up at the closed blinds of their next-door neighbour sleeping off a life on benefits?
> (Ian Mulheirn, *New Statesman* 15 March 2013)

The question raised by Osborne is imbued with a number of assumptions. One is that the population can be divided between those who work and

Brian McDonough

those who receive benefits. Another is that people on benefits are parasitic. However, many people who receive benefits are, in fact, also legally employed. Also of interest is some research which was carried out by the Department for Work and Pensions (March 2013), looking at the benefit histories of dole recipients. Their findings undermine the view that our welfare system is full of people taking advantage of a 'something for nothing' deal. The analysis looks at the benefit claims history of people who made a claim for unemployment benefit in 2010–2011, going back four years prior to their latest claim. In a sample group of 32- and 33-year-olds who claimed jobseeker's allowance (JSA) in 2010–2011, 40 percent had not made a claim before in that period, 63 percent had spent no more than six months of the previous four years on JSA, and almost four out of five claimants had spent at least three-quarters of the past four years off the 'dole'. On the basis of these data, the idea that claimants are universally 'trapped' in a 'dependency culture' is hard to defend.

The assertion that the unemployed are 'sleeping off a life on benefits' also implies that life 'on the dole' is enjoyable or even luxurious. But for those living below the poverty line, life is often anything but enjoyable. In practice, it's difficult to find families in which no member has ever worked, let alone generations of people on the 'dole'.

There is therefore a particular social construction of the unemployed that often structures common-sense perceptions and, according to critics of the government, has been employed as a political cover for policies aimed at cuts to welfare benefits. It could be argued that this social construction operates as an ideology in a Marxist sense – that is, that it obscures the economic and social relations which give rise to high rates of unemployment by blaming the unemployed themselves. The conclusion which can be taken from the research findings by the Department of Work and Pensions pulls in a different direction: most people who claim unemployment benefits each year spend at least three-quarters of their time in work. And for 40 percent of claimants, the claiming of JSA is not part of a lifestyle choice since they have no recent history of having done so before. Only a small minority of adults, 11 percent of claimants in 2010–2011, had a history of spending more than half of recent years on the dole.

We have also seen in recent years some changes in the sorts of work contracts available to people as employees. Full-time jobs with permanent contracts and strong pension arrangements have become less available, and more people are self-employed or employed on the basis of short-term contracts, which do not offer the same job security as was available to people employed in earlier generations. The Labour Force Survey in 2012 reported that more than 250,000 people were on zero-hours contracts (0.8 percent of the total workforce) – contracts which do not offer a guarantee of any hours or times for work but under the terms of which would-be employees commit to being available or 'on call' to work for organisations as and when required. However, the reported figures for zero-hours contracts are probably understated, given that many respondents in the survey may be unaware of their contractual arrangements or may not recognise the term 'zero-hours contract' at all. These shifting work relations feed into, and serve to decrease, unemployment statistics.

For those relatively small groups of people who are long-term unemployed, there are a number of structural issues as well as many other social problems identified in this book which might underlie why certain groups remain unemployed. For example, it may be that the local or national economies have failed and caused long-term high unemployment or factors relating to disadvantages in the education system or neighbourhoods where gang and anti-social behaviour have become alternative sub-cultures. All these structural and cultural issues play a part in people's lives and can constrain the opportunity for some people to find employment. Some of these structural issues are examined more closely in the following section.

8.8 Structural issues: gender, ethnicity and social class

As we have seen, there is a common perception that unemployment is a problem which stems from the choices made by individuals. Some of us are keen to find jobs and work, whilst others are lazy, work-shy and/or incapable of finding ourselves work. But if unemployment depended upon the free will and independent choices of individuals, then we would not expect to find social patterns among groups in the population based on such things as gender, ethnicity and social class.

In relation to gender, for example, official figures show consistently higher rates of unemployment for men than for women, with the unemployment rate for men sometimes two and a half times that of women. In explaining these figures, however, we need to recognise that married women are sometimes ineligible for benefits and do not show up as being registered unemployed. (Refer back to Section 4.4 on measuring unemployment.) In fact, where partners are cohabiting, entitlements to state support are often affected. Despite rates of unemployment being higher for men than women, it must be noted also that women are more likely than men to occupy part-time employment, and many of these jobs are low-paid and low-status work (Edgell & Granter 2019). Also note that this impacts the gender pay gap, with men earning on average significantly more than women in nearly all sectors of work. Nevertheless, these differences in unemployment rates between men and women are gendered differences and therefore structural, not simply a matter of an individual's personal decision to work.

Brian McDonough

Another structural factor that impacts unemployment is social class. The conception of class within sociology is complex, but here we will take it to refer broadly to occupation. As we have seen in the earlier section, the occupations available to people and the contracts which govern them change over time. Research shows that 'lower' social classes are generally more likely to experience unemployment than other social classes. Table 8.1a shows figures for unemployment by occupation between January 2016 and March 2018.

If you place your finger on the table and shift it across from left to right, you will notice a range of different figures for different occupational groups. Those occupations starting from the left tend to be those occupied by the 'higher' social classes (managers and senior officials, professionals and those with jobs requiring technical skills). These are followed by the middle sections (administrative, secretarial and skilled occupations). Those on the right (sales and customer services, machine operatives and elementary occupations) tend to have occupations typically defined predominantly as working class. If you run your finger downwards in any one occupational-type group, you will see a consistency with the level of unemployment. This itself shows that different sectors are subject to certain levels of unemployment. Let's take two occupational groups and compare them. For those in 'professional occupations', the Labour Force Survey counted 89,000 unemployed between January and March 2018. But for those who occupy 'elementary occupations' the number is two and a half times as many, with 232,000 unemployed in the same year. Given the consistency of these figures over several years, we can say that those who occupy 'professional occupations' are less likely to suffer the effects of unemployment than those who occupy the 'elementary occupations'. What is apparent and most important is this: the differences in unemployment are structural differences to do with societal factors that impact the opportunities for certain groups of people (in this case, certain occupational groups/social classes) to be employed and cannot be simply a matter of choices made by individuals. The structural barriers determined by one's social class have led some sociologists to describe it as 'the class ceiling' (see Friedman & Laurison 2019).

Evidence concerning ethnicity and unemployment also shows clear variations, with black, Asian and minority ethnic (BAME) groups suffering from much higher rates of unemployment than those of the ethnic majority. The Labour Force Survey carried out in 2018 found that just 4 percent of white people were unemployed compared with 7 percent of all other ethnic groups combined (Labour Force Survey 2018). Ethnic minorities can find employment particularly difficult when faced with racist prejudice before they even enter the workplace. In 2013 there was an employment tribunal over race discrimination. A man claimed that Virgin Atlantic had

Brian McDonough

Table 8.1 Unemployed by occupation of last job (up to March 2018)

	Unemployed (in thousands) by occupation of last job (Standard Occupational Classification SOC 2010)								
	Managers, directors & senior officials	Professional occupations	Associate professional & technical	Administrative & secretarial	Skilled trades	Caring, leisure & other services	Sales & customer services	Process, plant & machine operatives	Elementary occupations
Jan-Mar 2016	50	89	116	109	100	118	178	88	309
Apr-Jun 2016	53	85	109	96	93	130	145	73	313
Jul-Sep 2016	57	105	108	107	79	124	151	80	283
Oct-Dec 2016	51	110	96	96	79	109	150	70	268
Jan-Mar 2017	51	103	108	105	90	108	155	82	253
Apr-Jun 2017	46	102	114	99	85	95	159	84	240
Jul-Sep 2017	50	106	99	89	82	101	153	63	217
Oct-Dec 2017	48	90	98	95	76	105	143	70	215
Jan-Mar 2018	49	89	91	115	94	105	133	71	232

Source: Labour Force Survey (accessed March 2020) Office for National Statistics

discriminated against him on the grounds of race when it rejected his job application, allegedly because of his African name. The man was a British citizen with a degree in international relations and was shocked to find he had not been interviewed for a job in a Swansea call centre working for Virgin's organisation. Suspicious that it could be due to his foreign-sounding name, he reapplied with a typically British name and was invited several times to attend an interview. 'There was an enormous difference in the way I was treated when I used a British name', he said (*The Guardian* 2013). This experience is not unprecedented. Stories from applicants and recruiters suggest that prejudice and discrimination are still commonplace. The racist attitudes towards job seekers serves only to worsen unemployment for ethnic minority groups.

8.9 The consequences of unemployment

There are several consequences of being unemployed. Some unemployed people miss out on a number of opportunities, not least because they are not earning a wage or salary. For example, long-term unemployed people are often unable to sustain friendships, social contacts and networks; they have less control than the employed over their social environment to achieve external goals, lack financial security and can suffer from low self-esteem and social status. The consequences of unemployment are different depending on the social and cultural aspects of those unemployed. In this section we shall take a look at the consequences of unemployment by way of age, gender and social class.

For younger people about to enter the labour market, the financial needs are very different from those of prime-age males and females who may have families to support. Young people and school leavers are a social group who suffer considerably from unemployment. They are more unlikely to find a job during a recession and do not always qualify for unemployment benefits, which are typically based on being in work for a given period of time (Edgell & Granter 2019). To make matters worse, long spells of unemployment for young people can result in permanent scars on their curriculum vitae, and future employers are unlikely to give jobs to young people with histories of long-term unemployment.

Unemployment for the middle-aged can also cause severe health and social problems, and people in their 50s can find it difficult to be redeployed since employers are typically reluctant to recruit older workers (Edgell & Granter 2019). This happens despite the Employment Equality Regulations (2006) legislation, which makes it illegal for employers to discriminate on the basis of age (ageism). On top of this, long-term unemployment can result in low self-esteem, poor health and depression (Edgell & Granter 2019). Unemployment also relates to marital status, with single men more likely to be unemployed than married men (Grint & Nixon 2015). This, however, is probably related to a number of inter-related factors: married men are probably more inclined to retain their employment status with families to support, and women are arguably more likely to seek marital relationships with men who have a 'steady' and secure employment history. Also, employers may prefer married men because they are deemed to be more constrained by the domestic commitments. When a married man becomes unemployed, however, this can result in marital discord – minor quarrels between married couples can increase in situations of deprivation and intensified by unemployment (Edgell & Granter 2019). In all, however, marriage appears to stabilise employment for men (Grint & Nixon 2015).

Unemployment can affect various social classes differently. The working class are said to suffer more from the financial consequences and a lack of financial savings and are more likely to take the next job on offer than those of the middle class. And for many of the working classes in areas of high unemployment, the problem is exacerbated by the fact that unemployment becomes more of a social condition than an individual problem. Despite the mass numbers and mass experience of unemployment, the problem is still experienced individually – people blame themselves for not being able to find work.

This individualising of what is fundamentally a social problem is what Wright Mills (2000) brought attention to in his book *The Sociological Imagination*. He argued that the public issue of social structure becomes perceived as the personal troubles of a milieu (Wright Mills 2000). Social problems are experienced as personal problems since the issue is pulled away from the social structure and relocated with the apparent personal failings of the individual (Grint & Nixon 2015). Where unemployment is caused by redundancy, there is still widespread belief among future employers that those individuals may have lost their jobs because of their work records, and so employer hostility increases the longer the person remains unemployed. And despite some arguing that the unemployed should lower their demands and seek work of any kind, few employers are prepared to take on unemployed workers who do this because they assume that the person must be desperate and therefore have no real interest in the job (Grint & Nixon 2015).

8.10 Unemployment, social problems and crime

One of the many social problems associated with unemployment is crime. Emile Durkheim (1858–1917) argued that, actually, from the point of view of sociology, crime is normal. Not only is it a characteristic of all societies in the sense that all societies impose boundaries on permissible behaviour

Brian McDonough

and negatively sanction behaviour which is deviant from the norm, but also, in doing so, societies reaffirm their own moral substance. Durkheim (1979) also developed the concept of anomie to refer to the idea that in modern societies traditional norms and values become undermined; there is a disjunction between societal organisation and societal morality. Anomie exists when there are no clear standards to guide behaviour in particular aspects of social life, particularly when the norms and values in society break down due to the rapid pace of social change. In Durkheim's time, he saw a problem in that a morality based on a taken-for-granted traditional social hierarchy was out of kilter with occupational developments related to the more complex division of labour of industrial society, which called for a more meritocratic morality.

In the twentieth century, Robert Merton developed a useful perspective for understanding the relationship between unemployment and crime in his 'strain theory'. Merton (1957) developed this theory drawing on the conception of anomie developed by Durkheim and argued that in American society, not everyone can realise the dominant dream of material success. When legitimate opportunities to achieve success are blocked, some people – whom Merton called 'innovators' – develop illegitimate means to acquire societally approved goals such as nice houses and big cars. People may engage in illegal activity, such as buying stolen goods or taking something which does not belong to them. People might avoid paying taxes from cash-in-hand work carried out or tell lies to the government to maximise state benefits. Significantly, people may engage in black market economic activity such as drug- or people-trafficking. Merton also identifies a category of 'rebels' who both reject the socially approved means and ends and seek to overthrow the capitalist system itself, developing a vision of a society that transcends capitalism and the goals it deploys.

Merton thereby explained that it is possible for culturally prescribed goals to overcome and completely dominate consideration of culturally prescribed means. In his words, 'there may develop a very heavy, at times virtually exclusive, stress upon the value of particular goals, involving comparatively little concern with the institutionally prescribed means of striving toward these goals' (Merton 1957: 132). According to Merton, society and social institutions place a greater emphasis on cultural goals than on institutional or legitimate means to achieve them. When these goals (i.e. 'making money') are so emphasised that they get far more attention than the institutionalised means (i.e. going to work) to achieve them, the result is anomie and criminality. The unavailability of work and rising unemployment levels can therefore lead to various criminal activities.

One example we can examine here is the London riots in 2011. The media tended to report the unrest in terms of a kind of irrational, meaningless and pointless kind of deviance. The home secretary and later prime minister, Theresa May, talked about 'sheer criminality'. However, as social scientists, we will want to consider whether the concepts Durkheim and Merton have developed can be of use here. Whilst there was much speculation in the media that the rioting was caused by 'gangs', data collected at the time suggested that gangs were not the main source of the rioting. It may be, however, that the riots expressed the problem of anomie as developed by Durkheim – a problem of lack of moral consensus rooted in the disjunction between society's values and the recent economic crisis – or that they could, in part, be explained through Merton's conception of innovation, in which people employ illegitimate means to acquire goods they could not otherwise have. The phenomenon of the riots is complex in part because people gave a variety of accounts of their motivations and experiences of involvement.

8.11 Summary

We began the chapter by looking at work and the various ways in which work is changing: from traditional and stable careers to precarious forms of work and the new gig economy. We said that the definition of work as paid employment is problematic because large numbers of people in Britain carry out work which is unpaid, yet this activity is still valuable to the functioning and economic stability of British society. Charity workers, carers and those who look after children or carry out domestic duties all arguably carry out 'real' work, whether this is paid or not. What counts as work, it was argued, depends on the specific social circumstances under which such activities are undertaken and, importantly, how these circumstances and activities are interpreted by those involved. Grint and Nixon (2015) argue that there is a discourse of work provided by symbolic representations through which meanings and social interests are constructed, mediated and deployed. Some types of activities take on those characteristics appropriated by the given discourse (such as making food in a café), whilst others do not (such as cooking at home).

In the next section of this chapter, we discussed work and the 'work ethic'. We said that the work ethic was part of a particular discourse which has dominated British politics for many years. Social policy in Britain has been preoccupied with the idea of inclusion in the labour market. Politicians have created policies which are directed at getting people into work. But we saw that this preoccupation with paid work inherently puts a higher value on working families and assumes that they are morally more worthy than others. Gorz (1999, 2010) argues that capitalism has socially constructed the idea of work and what it represents, and in order to rescue and sustain 'real work', we must recognise that real work is no longer what we do when 'at work'. This has led many politicians, activists and policymakers

Brian McDonough

to rethink our relationship to work by calling for a universal basic income. Such a policy would provide a regular, no-strings-attached income to all citizens, providing more freedom to work on their own terms (McDonough & Bustillos Morales 2020). Such a policy would offer a solution to some of the most vulnerable and marginalised in society – millions of British people who, for example, are carers, single parents and/or precarious workers who would benefit from a regular cash income. The section on universal basic income also showed how such a policy could overcome economic crises such as the coronavirus pandemic.

The rest of this chapter looked at unemployment. Just as the definition and organisation of work is socially constructed, so, too, unemployment can be seen as a product of particular ways in which it is defined and measured. We showed evidence of this by the unevenly dispersed rates of unemployment between different social groups, such as middle class and working class, ethnic minorities and the white population, and different age groups.

We said that measuring unemployment is difficult because it is extremely difficult to compare rates of unemployment over time in any one country or between countries. We said that this was because governments frequently alter the way unemployment is measured, often for political reasons. Because of this, rates of employment can be very different, depending upon how they are measured.

We also argued in this chapter that there has been a recent underlying discourse which depicts the unemployed as lazy individuals who are disinclined to work. We discussed a particular public discourse presented by the media that tells us that the 'unemployed' are welfare dependents sponging off the state, using the taxes of others to pay for their widescreen TVs and mobile smartphones. We said that this is a construction of the unemployed which typifies them as 'scroungers' who have become a drain on society. This perception of the unemployed has permeated common-sense knowledge. It is fed into public and political debate, often sensationalised by newspaper tabloids and can be deployed as justification for reducing welfare benefits by political parties. But we gave a perspective on this which avoided common-sense assumptions and the sensationalism of newspaper tabloids. Instead, we looked at research that showed that the so-called dependency culture of welfare recipients is a myth.

We also paid attention to the changing patterns of work and work contracts. Many newly created jobs are part time and often pay only the legally minimum wage. This has led some sociologists to refer to a portion of the workforce as the 'precariat' – a section of the workforce whose employment is insecure, casualised and has poor promotion and career development opportunities. The idea of the unemployed as lazy and unwilling to work sits uneasily with this reconfiguration of work relations.

precarious work and the 'gig economy'

Overall, this chapter has laid out a range of social problems connected to work, including precarious and 'gig' work, and unemployment. Some of these problems are placed on individual shoulders, with ideas of the 'work ethic' used as justification for certain groups of people to be blamed for their own misfortune. Precarious working and unemployment are not social problems that arise from individual decision making but are related to structural factors in our society and can only be resolved through new government legislation and policy making.

 Key points

Defining work

This is problematic as we cannot define work as merely paid employment. For example, people who look after elderly relatives might carry out the exact same work as paid carers working within a nursing home. Similarly, employed cleaners get paid for work, yet women who look after children and carry out domestic responsibilities are said to be 'out of work'. This has called for a reconsideration of work and to consider the total social organisation of work.

The 'work ethic'

There is a discourse of inclusion in the labour market. This discourse provides us with assumptions and expectations that everybody in society should work (with the exception of the very young, old or ill). Those of us who participate in paid work are 'working', whilst those of us who are not in paid employment are deemed 'out of work'. The 'work ethic' is tied into social policy in Britain – for example, benefits or allowances which encourage people to enter paid employment. But the 'work ethic' is focused on paid work and not on all other work that is of equal importance to the smooth running of society.

Precarious work and the 'gig economy'

Non-standard, insecure and atypical work is referred to as 'precarious' work. It can often rely on the use of poor-quality contracts of employment, such as 'zero-hours' contracts. Precarious or 'gig' workers often do not have paid holiday entitlements, life insurance, employer pension contributions, maternity and paternity leave and a whole host of other benefits that workers on full-time and 'standardised' contracts have. Precarious and 'gig' work is a direct result of a neoliberal economy in which the market is allowed to dictate who has work and who does not.

Brian McDonough

Measuring unemployment

There is great difficulty in comparing rates of unemployment over time in any one country or between countries. This is because unemployment is measured differently by different people, often for political reasons. For example, the ILO measure typically produces a higher level of unemployment than the claimant count (Edgell & Granter 2019). These differing measures of unemployment tell us that unemployment is a product of the social because it is both defined and measured by it.

The social construction of unemployment

Political and public discourse views unemployment as a social problem stemming from lazy and work-shy individuals. A particular public discourse presented by the media discloses the 'unemployed' as idle, lazy individuals who 'sponge' off the state. They are welfare dependents using the taxes of others to pay for their widescreen TVs and mobile smartphones. This is a construction of the unemployed which typifies them as 'scroungers' who have become a drain on society.

Unemployment in the UK is often constructed as an individual issue, not a social problem

Public discourse views unemployment as the responsibility of the individual. If a person cannot get a job, they are deemed to have not taken up all opportunities available to them. But unemployment is intrinsically related to social structures which operate outside any individuals' decision to get a job or not. Structural factors include age, ethnicity, social class and gender, as well the economic conditions (such as available jobs) and locations in which people are born.

 Coursework questions

What are key problems with precarious work?
The new gig economy is good for workers since it provides flexibility and autonomy. Discuss.
To what extent is unemployment an individual issue, and to what extent is it the consequence of structural inequalities?
What are the main social problems associated with unemployment?

precarious work and the 'gig economy'

References

Durkheim, E. (1979) *Suicide: A Study in Sociology*. New York: The Free Press.

Edgell, S. and Granter, E. (2019) *The Sociology of Work: Continuity and Change in Paid and Unpaid Work*. London: Sage Publications.

European Commission Research. (2004) 'Precarious employment in Europe: Comparative study of labour market related risks in flexible economies'. *ESOPE*. Accessed: 23rd January 2020. http://cordis.europa.eu/pub/citizens/docs/kina21250ens_final_esope.pdf

Friedman, S. and Laurison, D. (2019) *The Class Ceiling: Why It Pays To Be Privileged*. Bristol: Polity Press.

Glucksmann, M. (2007) 'Why "Work"? Gender and the "Total Social Organisation of Labour"'. *Gender Work and Organization* 2 (2): 63–75.

Gorz, A. (1999) *Reclaiming Work*. Cambridge: Polity Press.

Gorz, A. (2010) *The Immaterial: Knowledge, Value and Capital*. Cambridge: Polity Press.

Grint, K. and Nixon, D. (2015) *The Sociology of Work*. Cambridge: Polity Press.

The Guardian. (2013, April 11) 'Can anonymous CVs help beat recruitment discrimination?' https://www.theguardian.com/money/work-blog/2013/apr/11/can-anonymous-cvs-help-beat-job-discrimination

Kessler, S. (2019) *Gigged: The Gig Economy, the End of the Job and the Future of Work*. New York: Macmillan.

Labour Force Survey. (2018) Accessed: 23rd January 2020. www.ethnicity-facts-figures.service.gov.uk/work-pay-and-benefits/unemployment-and-economic-inactivity/unemployment/latest

Levitas, R. (2005) *The Inclusive Society? Social Exclusion and New Labour*. Basingstoke: Palgrave Macmillan.

Merton, R. (1957) *Social Theory and Social Structure*. New York: The Free Press.

Mulcahy, D. (2016) *The Gig Economy: The Complete Guide to Getting Better Work, Taking More Time Off, and Financing the Life You Want!* New York: Harper Collins.

Mulheirn, I. (2013, March 15) 'The myth of the "Welfare Scrounger"'. *New Statesmen*. https://www.newstatesman.com/politics/2013/03/myth-welfare-scrounger

New Policy Institute (NPI). (2016) 'In work poverty: What it is, what it isn't, why it matters'. www.npi.org.uk/blog/income-and-poverty/work-poverty-what-it-what-it-isnt-why-it-matters/

Oakley, A. (1974) *Housewife: High Value – Low Cost*. London: Penguin.

Office for National Statistics (ONS). (2020a) 'Lone parent families data'. Accessed: 23rd January 2020. www.ons.gov.uk/peoplepopulationand

Brian McDonough

community/birthsdeathsandmarriages/families/adhocs/006183lonepar
entfamiliesintheukbycountry1996to2015

Office for National Statistics (ONS). (2020b) 'Unpaid carers provide social care worth £57 billion'. Accessed: 23rd January 2020. www.ons.gov.uk/ peoplepopulationandcommunity/healthandsocialcare/healthandlife expectancies/articles/unpaidcarersprovidesocialcareworth57billion/ 2017-07-10

Smith, D. (1987) *The Everyday World as Problematic: A Feminist Sociology.* Boston, MA: Northeastern University Press.

Standing, G. (2015) *The Precariat: The New Dangerous Class.* London: Bloomsbury Publishing Plc.

Standing, G. (2017) *Basic Income.* London: Penguin.

Tassinari, A. and Maccarrone, V. (2020) 'Riders on the storm: Workplace solidarity among gig economy couriers in Italy and the UK'. *Work, Employment and Society.* https://doi.org/10.1177/0950017019862954

Van Parijs, P. and Vanderborght, Y. (2019) *Basic Income: A Radical Proposal for a Free Society and a Sane Economy.* Harvard: Harvard University Press.

Weber, M. (2010) *The Protestant Ethic and the Spirit of Capitalism.* Blacksburg, VA: Wilder Publications.

Woodcock, J. and Graham, M. (2020) *The Gig Economy: A Critical Introduction.* Bristol: Polity Press.

Wright-Mills, C. (2000) *The Sociological Imagination.* Oxford: Oxford University Press.

 Further reading

McDonough, B. (2017) 'Precarious work and unemployment in Europe'. In Isaacs, S. (ed.), *European Social Problems.* London: Routledge.

McDonough, B. (2020) 'Coronavirus poverty, precarious work the need for a universal basic income'. *Discover Society.* https://discoversociety. org/2020/03/26/coronavirus-poverty-precarious-work-and-the-need-for-a-universal-basic-income/

McDonough, B. and Bustillos Morales, J. (2020) *Universal Basic Income.* London: Routledge.

chapter 9

Poverty

Stuart Isaacs

9.1 Introduction

The poor, it is often said, will always be with us. In a purely empirical sense, this is true. In a market economy, there will be income gaps between people according to their earnings. If we use household income to measure poverty, then there will always be a percentage of people at the bottom of the economic scale: those earning less than average. In the late nineteenth century, when socially concerned individuals became interested in trying to map poverty in Britain, this was the measure that they used. It is perhaps the most obvious, 'common-sense' approach. But, as we shall see, it isn't the only way of measuring and defining poverty. In many ways, it is also quite limited. However, considering household income is a good starting place. Seebohm Rowntree (1871–1954) was among the most well-known of the late-nineteenth-century social surveyors who first sought to systematically measure poverty. He used the idea of a poverty line.

In 1899 Rowntree conducted his famous study on the conditions of working people in York. He argued that there ought to be a basic minimum level of income provided by the state that allowed for subsistence living. This he initially took to be what people needed to provide themselves with food and shelter in order to survive. However, in his later, interwar studies of poverty, he revised this to include a broader range of consumer goods and emphasised the idea of an 'acceptable standard of living'. Beveridge used a calculation of subsistence level to set social security income in the 1940s. But he was criticised for not taking account of the need to give people support beyond Rowntree's earlier, very basic measure.

The poverty line measure that Rowntree devised and that was used in the first modern social security system is set at a level of income below which a household ought not to fall. If a family fell below the pounds, shillings and pence required for subsistence living, then it was considered to be below the poverty line and, therefore, poor. The poverty line was meant to provide a clear indicator to government about where state support was required. The early social surveyors believed that the idea of the poverty line would be a powerful weapon to provoke action from the state. They wanted to show that the use of empirical social scientific methods could highlight urgent social problems and point government in the right policy directions.

The notion of a poverty line, based on what is judged to be an adequate budget for people to live on, is a measure that government still uses extensively. The Household Below Average Income (HBAI) is the standard measure that the Department of Work and Pensions (DWP) employs for all social security payments. The poverty line is set at 60 percent of the median average income. In other words, to qualify for most of the income-related benefits that people receive from the state, households have to be at least 40 percent below average income. This is a very tidy, transparent way for government to measure and define poverty. By looking at these figures, we can also get a general idea of who is poor in the UK today. For example, in 2018–2019, the DWP's figures showed that 20 percent of households in the UK were HBAI households, after housing costs were taken into account (www.gov.uk/government/statistics/households-below-average-income-199495-to-201819).

There are many other demographic indicators that we can find out about by using the HBAI measure. We can see whether the poor are married/cohabiting or single people, lone-parent families, from particular minority ethnic groups and so on. This helps build up a useful understanding of the social groups that might most often fall into income poverty. Yet, although it is a useful tool for social scientists and even more so for governments, who like clear, standardised measures, this does not give us the whole picture. Simply drawing upon quantitative data to analyse poverty is not enough. We would always need more and more data to fill the gaps. For example, the figures given here do not indicate whether there have been increases in income for those above or well above average earnings. We would need further statistics to inform us whether the gap between rich and poor has been growing or shrinking. Furthermore, as the HBAI is based on average income, if household incomes for the country as a whole fall, the poverty line will be set at a lower income amount too. That would artificially remove some households from being officially poor, even though their incomes would not have changed. In the end, however thorough our research, collecting statistics and data will never give us the social insight into poverty that we seek.

9.2 The social construction of poverty

The solely empirical and 'common-sense' approach to defining and measuring poverty based around income is narrow and limited. To get a fuller understanding of poverty in the UK using quantitative methods would require a wide range of indicators, including historical shifts, the gap between rich and poor (and, indeed, across various occupational levels) and the cost of living. Even then, quantitative evidence alone could not capture the social and cultural dimension of poverty: what has been understood as relative poverty in the past and, more recently, what we take to be social exclusion. But before looking at UK poverty in this more qualitative manner, there is another aspect of poverty not captured by the poverty line approach. That is, of course, the social construction of poverty.

Perceptions, assumptions and normative judgements about the poor have always permeated debates about poverty. Public discussions around issues that affect the poor, in particular those concerning social security benefits, are intertwined with discourses that seek to determine the characteristics of poor families in specific ways. Many of these are moral critiques of the poor: that they are lazy, work-shy welfare dependents, happy to sponge off the taxes of 'decent, hard-working families'. This is a construction of the poor that can be traced back at least to the Victorian Poor Laws. The Victorian state's response to poverty, and one that has been common ever since, was to offer those prepared to work a small, means-tested relief of poverty, rather than a sustained wage or income. While the Victorian Poor Laws provided some cash relief to poor families, the centrepiece was the quintessential self-help institution, the workhouse. The social message from the state was clear. Poverty was the responsibility of the individual. If someone was not prepared to work, even for the most rudimentary subsistence relief, they did not deserve help.

The workhouses may be long gone, but the values that they represent still remain. There is a still a strongly held view that if the state provides a basic minimum relief of poverty, individuals must show a willingness to work. The linking of poverty, welfare and work is a discourse which is reinforced in government policy. The well-known quote that follows is a good summary of this position.

> 'I have a problem, I'll get a grant'. 'I'm homeless, the government must house me'. They're casting their problem on society. And you know, there is no such thing as society. There are individual men and women, and there are families. And no government can do anything except through people, and people must look to themselves first.
>
> (Margaret Thatcher, 31 October 1987, *Woman's Own* magazine interview)

Stuart Isaacs

This type of construction of the poor as taking 'something for nothing' and being a drain on society's resources is a moralised and individualised approach to poverty. Often, such statements are tied to a view of our society which maintains that there is no longer poverty in the UK. Go to any large social housing estate and you will find HD TVs, it is argued. People have Sky and Virgin cable packages. And those on benefits are carrying around smartphones and tablets. This sort of moralised individualist approach to poverty feeds off people's limited personal experiences and anecdotal evidence. It focuses on the emotive, sensational issues that are the stuff of newspaper headlines and TV reports designed to create newsworthy stories. It is not based on social research or sociological analysis. It ignores the underlying social institutions and structures that give rise to inequalities that are the causes of poverty. These are particular and diverse: a range of factors that come together to limit people's opportunities and life chances. It might be poor housing which undermines educational achievement; racist attitudes; assumptions about children on free school meals; lack of awareness of disability; local or national economies that have failed, causing long-term high unemployment; or poor neighbourhoods where gang and anti-social behaviour have become alternative subcultures. All these institutional and structural issues as well as many other social problems identified in this book might underlie poverty.

In order to say something meaningful about the diverse group whom we may consider to be poor, we need to act as social scientists, investigate the social research, look at the arguments put out by authors who have studied these problems and try to set aside common-sense opinions based on limited experience.

One of the first things that the social research tells us is that poor people tend to work harder than anyone else. Polly Toynbee (2003) documents this well in her turn-of-the-millennium study, *Hard Work*. In this book she presents quantitative and qualitative evidence to suggest that the poor work longer and harder now than they did 40 years ago. Comparing the wages of some of the lowest-paid workers, she illustrates how the poor have seen their wages rise more slowly than the rest of the population. For example, hospital porters (a typical minimum wage occupation) have seen their wages drop in real terms since the 1970s. Not only incomes but also working conditions have got worse. This includes many thousands of low-paid workers in the public sector. This is particularly true for those working for privatised or contracted-out agencies that provide welfare services. According to Toynbee, people working in these jobs have very little in the way of security or rights. Many people on the lowest incomes (a disproportionate number of whom are from minority ethnic communities) have to put together two or even three jobs in one day to generate enough money to live. This is particularly true for women, including women who are lone parents. They have to juggle childcare with jobs that have unsocial hours and no career prospects that give them little sense of self-worth. Toynbee concludes that, far from being lazy or work shy, the poor work longer and in tougher working conditions than most. Toynbee's study does not stand alone. There is a substantive body of social research that you can investigate that indicates that the social construction of the poor as work shy does not match the social experience of many. O'Hara (2014) shows this in her study of poverty in Britain following the Conservative and Liberal Democrat coalition government coming to power in 2010.

Another way to think about this is to look at income maintenance. Alongside the view that the poor are lazy often sits the related argument that the poor are usually unemployed people who live a life of comfort on benefit payments. Indeed, the very language that is deployed suggests that 'welfare' or 'benefits' in themselves are giveaways by the state to the 'undeserving poor'. Some readers might have noticed that I have previously been using the term *social security*. This is how cash-based income support has also been understood, as a form of social protection that is needed by those who qualify for it. However, increasingly, the use of the terms *benefit* and *welfare* have come to replace *social security* and *social protection*. This language is ideologically loaded. Whereas 'security' and 'protection' sound like claims that social citizens might reasonably make on the state, claiming 'cash benefits' or 'welfare' implies using other people's taxes for you own unearned income. Increasingly, those reliant on the state for additional income to live face being seen as welfare spongers. As well as having to cope with poverty, they also have to take the blame for their poverty. The idea that there ought to be some form of social security to protect vulnerable people from the risks of the market economy and the insecurities of the labour market seems to be withering away. There is, then, a construction of the poor as welfare dependents and the architects of their own circumstances through their unwillingness to work. However, despite these views being common currency, the way that income maintenance has developed since the 1980s would suggest that this is unlikely to be universally true. From the New Right Conservatives under Margaret Thatcher through New Labour to the Coalition and subsequent Conservative governments, there has been a policy trend to ensure that the vast majority of people receiving social security benefits are actually working (www.ifs.org.uk/uploads/WP201912.pdf).

Furthermore, fewer than 1 percent of benefits are claimed illegally, and much more benefits actually go underpaid (www.bbc.co.uk/news/election-2017-39980793).

This suggests that the system is not open to wide abuse. If the social construction of the poor as lazy and not wanting to work is so easily dismissed by social research, why then is it so prevalent? One of the reasons

Stuart Isaacs

might be the invisibility of the poor. Cheap clothes stores, new and second hand, as well as cheap technology, might disguise the visible sense of poverty that was so discernible in the Victorian age. The poor are not in rags or sleeping in large numbers on the streets of our cities. The poor on the whole may not be starving, although according to the Child Poverty Action Group, a sizable minority do go hungry. The poor look like you and me. Except that when they go home, they may live in sub-standard housing or temporary, insecure accommodation. They may struggle to pay for public transport or for nutritious fresh food or a mobile phone to communicate with people. The poor today, many of whom are elderly, will be scared to put the heating on in case it costs too much. They count every penny. This is how around 20 percent of the population of the UK live.

Another reason the poor might be constructed negatively may have something to do with politics and ideology. Ha-Joon Chang (2010) suggests that since the early 1980s, the neoliberal, free-market discourse has dominated the way that we think about poverty. He argues that reflecting upon social problems begins with the assumption that individuals have total control over their own lives and destinies, regardless of their personal circumstances and background. Celebrities, successful businesspeople, sports stars, Hollywood actors and so on deserve their wealth because they have worked for it. The implication is that the poor are poor because they haven't. This takes away from structural inequalities such as historically deprived neighbourhoods, where many have inappropriate, insecure housing; lack of localised investment in jobs and people; and educational underachievement because of insufficient household resources or knowledge, as well as disadvantages because of discrimination based on ethnicity, gender, sexuality or disability. In a way, Chang points to a remarkable turnaround in the way that the rich and the poor are perceived in our society. To return to the nineteenth century, even though the poor were constituted in many respects as undeserving, there was also a similar view of the very rich. They were often portrayed in newspapers and satirical pamphlets as greedy individuals feeding off the hard work of others. Yet the term 'the idle rich' has almost disappeared from popular discussions about the distribution of wealth in the UK. In a consumer society where material wealth is often prized as a mark of success in itself – regardless of the achievement – the poor have suffered just as the very wealthy have benefited. For example, although the UK recessions from 2010 were the consequences of decisions and policies made by the global financial industries under weakly regulated structures, it was the poor who got the blame and welfare spending that was cut.

As we have seen, blaming the poor for being poor ignores the underlying causes of poverty, which are institutional and structural. Individual circumstances will be particular and may, indeed, involve responsibility on the part of that person. But thinking through the issues as social scientists, looking at the research, the evidence and the arguments, it is wrong to suggest that the poor are work shy and undeserving. To understand further how we might best articulate the circumstances of poverty in the UK, the next section of this chapter will look at poverty in the context of social exclusion. This theoretical approach suits our social constructionist methodology. It also offers an alternative to the useful but limited income-based, poverty line tradition as a way of defining and measuring poverty.

9.3 Social exclusion

If we situate our understanding of poverty within the context of social exclusion, we are able to compile a set of broad issues that affect the poor. Unlike the poverty line tradition, using a theory of social exclusion enables us to think about circumstances beyond the distribution of wealth and income. The theory of social exclusion also shares many of the characteristics of the social-constructivist methodological framework we are trying to develop. When we apply social exclusion to poverty, we are drawing upon quantitative evidence but also making judgements about the kinds of people we might argue are in this category. In other words, determining how social exclusion affects those on low incomes involves 'making a case', articulating our values about social justice as to why a social group deserves to be the focus for policy solutions. Social scientists disagree about the definition and use of this theory; there is a large body of literature concerned with the theoretical debates alone. Nevertheless, it is possible to work through a basic understanding.

One way of explaining the social exclusion perspective is to see it as originating in the debate about relative poverty. In 1979 Peter Townsend (1980) published a landmark study titled *Poverty in the UK*. In this text he argued that poverty ought to be understood in terms of relative deprivation, rather than just in terms of income. To cut a very long study short, Townsend argued that there is a social-cultural dimension to poverty. In order to understand the real impact of poverty on people's lives, a methodology was needed that took account of changing living standards, affluence and people's expectations. With an army of researchers, Townsend set about asking a large sample of the UK's population to list the sort of consumer goods as well as activities that they thought they ought to have access to in order to have a decent standard of living. This being the 1970s, people mentioned central heating, a TV, a home phone, a car, at least one holiday a year and so on. The methodological details of the study and its findings are complicated and can be read in Townsend's book. For our purposes, the interest of this study is that it indicated that without access to three or more of the listed consumables or activities, people could be deemed 'relatively poor'. In other words, they fell (and possibly felt) out-side a social norm as defined by the majority of the population. They were not able to participate in what might be considered an average lifestyle. This may well have had its underlying cause in a lack of income, but its effects were that people were 'excluded' from a perceived normal way of life. Although Townsend and his researchers would not have used the term 'social exclusion', his study was important in pushing us towards this idea.

The notion of relative poverty gets us some way to understanding the notion of social exclusion as a way of constructing poverty. But social exclusion as a concept goes further than Townsend's relative poverty model. In a strange way, it is in the work of the American libertarian social scientist Charles Murray, whose perspective is directly opposite that of Townsend, that we find the next development. Murray is notorious for suggesting that intelligence and genetics underlie individual achievement. However, we must remember that he did also acknowledge that social factors had a part to play too. In his study of the underclass, he maintained that as well as poverty being determined by genetic heritage and IQ, there are also historical, social and cultural factors at play. Murray argued that people living in poverty become welfare dependents. Over the years this devel-oped into a way of life, a norm that was passed on from generation to gen-eration. Although his methodological assumptions construct an argument that individualises poverty and ignores many of the institutional and struc-tural issues considered here, his conclusions are ones that also fuelled the development of the notion of social exclusion. Writing in the 1980s and 1990s, Murray argued that the key to removing these generations of poor families from their poverty cycle is to empower them to take charge of their own lives. In other words, to integrate them into mainstream society so that they feel that they are socially included. This might most successfully be done, he suggested, through the education system and employment.

9.4 New Labour and social exclusion

New Labour came to power in 1997 with the explicit aim of tackling social exclusion. One of the first things that it did in government was to estab-lish the Social Exclusion Unit. This oversaw the introduction of policies designed to challenge social exclusion through every government depart-ment. It also regulated and monitored local authorities to do the same. Targets were set at national and local levels to bring about a wholesale and fundamental programme to socially include groups identified as socially excluded. The centrepiece of these policies was a work-based training scheme known as the New Deal. This was Labour's welfare-to-work initia-tive, paid for by a windfall tax on the previously privatised utilities. Between 1997 and 1999, £5.2 billion was raised in this way and spent on the New

Deal in its early phases. New Deals were targeted at social groups that consisted of a disproportionate number of people likely to face the difficulties associated with social exclusion. So there was a New Deal for Young People, a New Deal for Lone Parents, the over-50s, the disabled and even for musicians! The sole aim of the New Deal was to get people into work. Most of the jobs were low paid. The argument was that any job was better than no job at all. This was because it provided a foundation that could lead to long-term employment opportunities. The assumption behind this was that people would become work shy if they remained on 'welfare'.

In this way New Labour both expressed a desire to aid those who were identified as socially excluded and reinforced the individualised perception of the poor as having developed a lifestyle in which the work ethic had been lost. During its time in office New Labour believed that paid employment was the golden route to social inclusion. If people had a job, then they would have a stake in society. There was an assumption here, too, that disregarded structural inequalities, a belief that the labour market functioned according to merit, regardless of age, gender, ethnicity, sexuality, disability or any other form of social identification. Finally, there was probably the most fundamental assumption of all underlying this strategy: jobs would always be available. It was simply up to individuals to take the responsibility to go and get one. Oddly, then, New Labour displayed sensitivity to constructing poverty around the broad and sophisticated definition of social exclusion, yet it did so within a market-led, individualist framework.

New Labour initiated other areas of state intervention designed to complement the New Deal. The introduction of the minimum wage and the tax credit system gave real cash benefits to people to make them better off in work. There was also help with childcare for lone parents and low-income families, through tax credits, vouchers and increased state nursery places. There was help in education through Sure Start and Connexions. The Academy programme was also designed to help children in poor neighbourhoods have well-resourced state-of-the-art facilities at school. In this respect, New Labour did try to address poverty by increasing cash benefits for the low paid and removing some of the institutional and structural barriers to work, particularly for lone parents and women.

So how successful were New Labour's rather ideologically mixed-up set of policies? Evaluations of the New Deal have indicated that there were initial moderate successes. Higher employment rates were achieved for most targeted groups through the New Deal. However, in the medium term, the success was more limited. The economic downturn from 2009 through 2010 played its part in undermining the New Deal. But so, too, did the poor quality of jobs on offer. This was particularly true of the New Deal for Young People (NDYP) (2002). The National Audit Office, reporting on the data of the NDYP in 2002, stated that a worrying aspect of the scheme was that 30 percent of young people had dropped out of it. It claimed that the NDYP had bred a resistance to work among these young people. They had not only left their New Deal jobs but had also dropped out of the benefit system altogether. Their destination was 'unknown'. It seems that although government may have assumed that low-paid jobs with few career prospects were better than no jobs at all, these young people disagreed and voted with their feet. This may well have been because the jobs that were created were perceived as 'dead end'. The New Deal places were also often forced on young people, under the threat of having their benefits cut. The use of the 'stick' of sanctions as well as the 'carrot' of paid employment was a very crude way of implementing a policy around the notion of social exclusion. As is so often the case, central government policy designed around a 'one-size-fits-all' solution did not work. Evidence suggests that the over-50s were more receptive to New Deal opportunities and had a different attitude to work. But young people, we can speculate, were more sceptical about being exploited. In the end, by ignoring the needs and views of young people, the NDYP had unintended outcomes. New Labour hoped to induct young adults into a work ethic. It constructed the problem along the lines of a work-shy youth. However, the issue for young people was not being work shy but needing to feel as if the jobs they were being offered gave them genuine opportunities. Offering a low-paid job with little substantive training and no prospects was not enough to make them feel socially included. A programme such as the NDYP would have had to make a substantive, long-term and material difference to their lives in order to give them a sense of belonging.

New Labour used the language of social exclusion to address poverty. However, ultimately, its policies were tied to an individualised construction of the poor as needing to be pushed into work, of whatever quality. Once given this 'opportunity', individuals had to take the responsibility to make the best of it. The emphasis on job creation relied not only on the belief in the power of individuals to change their own lives but also on the misguided view that paid employment was the key to alleviating poverty. A report in 2012 by the Institute of Fiscal Studies (IFS), sponsored by the Joseph Rowntree Foundation, concluded that improvements in education and employment under New Labour did little to prevent poverty in the long term. Although this might go against a 'common-sense' approach – that would assume there was a link between being in paid employment and getting out of poverty – this is not what the social research indicates. The IFS study illustrates that insecure and low-paid jobs do not resolve issues of poverty. Employment remains sporadic in these cases and does not necessarily make a poor household better off.

To its credit, the gains that New Labour did make in combatting poverty came not with the New Deal or the social exclusion strategy but through the more direct, benefit-related redistributive policies around the issue of child poverty. New Labour targeted the reduction of child poverty by 50 percent between 1998–1999 and 2010–2011. By the redistribution of wealth through the benefit and tax credit system, a third of households coming under this category were removed from poverty by 2002. By 2010–2011, 1.1 million families were removed from poverty, a figure arrived at by using the HBAI measure (although that is before housing costs). This was 600,000 households short of New Labour's target. However, during its time in office, on average, New Labour's benefit changes made children from poor families £77 per week better off. This was a significant increase in resources for those households, even though the gap between rich and poor expanded at the same time. The moderate success of these income-related policies seems to suggest that, although social exclusion as a definition and measure of poverty is more sophisticated than either a poverty line or relative poverty measure, in terms of what government can effectively do, good, old-fashioned redistribution of wealth has a more immediate effect. This is not to say we ought to dismiss theories of social exclusion as a way of understanding poverty. However, the New Labour period suggests that if this theory were to be applied in practical policy terms, it would need a much more considered approach.

An important aspect of this would be more localised sets of policies that engaged with the views and needs of the people that were targeted, as the case of the NDYP showed. 'Top-down' policies set around national and universalist criteria have not proved to be effective. The other important lesson of the New Deal is that sustainable jobs with the potential for good career opportunities would have to be at the heart of any welfare-to-work programme. The prospect of policies designed to combat poverty being based around a theory of social exclusion that reflects the sophistication and nuance of that approach seems remote.

The social construction of the poor as welfare dependents and work shy has continued since New Labour, under the Coalition and Conservative governments. The Coalition scrapped the New Deal and in 2008 began their austerity economics. Most significantly, this meant cuts to welfare benefits through the implementation of austerity measures such as Universal Credit. Any of the lessons learned or tiny steps forward made by New Labour were set in reverse. This is despite successive governments signing up to new targets to combat child poverty by 2020, set by the outgoing Labour government. Sadly, these child poverty targets have not been met, and there is evidence to suggest things have gone in reverse (https://cpag. org.uk/sites/default/files/files/Austerity%20Generation%20FINAL.pdf).

Stuart Isaacs

9.5 Homelessness

One of the perennial social problems associated with poverty is homelessness. Just as it is said that the poor will always be with us, a similar pessimism pervades this issue. If you were asked to think of an image of the homeless, you might find yourself remembering someone you have seen in the street: a dirty, smelly old bloke lying drunk on the pavement. Or a desperate-looking young person, sitting on a high street with a sad-looking dog next to them, begging for money. While many people may have experienced seeing these types of people and have different reflections on the validity of their claims to be homeless, these experiences are far from the reality of what homelessness means to the vast majority who are actually in that position.

Rooflessness, or rough sleeping, is only a very small part of the social problem of homelessness. For example, estimates of the number of people who sleep rough in England are very sketchy. They range from 1,600 to 3,000. The figures vary because these are a very difficult group to keep track of. While some rough sleepers have regular places where they stay, most have erratic lifestyles. In addition, although those who sleep rough in a city might have a fairly ritualised and structured lifestyle, many rough sleepers live in rural areas and are harder to pin down. There are also particular personal problems that rough sleepers tend to suffer from that distinguish them from most other homeless people. Rough sleepers are often drug addicts or alcoholics. They may have mental health problems too. In a sense, the fact that rough sleepers are on the streets is not primarily a problem of not having a home, but it is a condition brought about by much more deeply rooted personal issues. For this reason, it is more appropriate, in terms of looking at social problems, to focus this final section of the chapter on the majority who are homeless. In 2019 there were 280,000 people who were officially recognised as homeless and on local authority waiting lists in England (note, not the UK as a whole), according to Shelter. (Shelter 2019) These people are officially recognised as homeless because they do not have a permanent, secure and appropriate home to live in. However, as we shall see, those who are 'officially homeless' in this way (qualifying for social housing under the terms of a local authority's rules of 'priority need') account for some but not all who fit this definition.

Poverty and social exclusion often underlie homelessness. But there are other causes that also need to be discussed. These may or may not have an association with poverty. The first of these is demographic changes. If we take London as an example, its population has grown by over 20 percent since the mid-1990s, hitting new highs in successive years from 2018 through 2020 (9.3 million population). This growth has been due to an increasing older population and internal domestic and external foreign migration to the capital, as well as increased fertility. Such trends put pressure on public services like hospitals and schools as well as housing. However, on their own, these demographic trends are long-term changes that government can plan for. It is not unusual for a city to grow in this manner over the course of a few decades. London has the scope to expand and absorb a larger population, given the right planning.

The political will to make provision, including for demographic change, is the link to the second main cause of homelessness. This is government policy. Since the 1980s, there has been a sustained decline in the number of social houses being built. This affects people on low incomes, who subsequently struggle to afford a home. The right-to-buy policies from the era of Margaret Thatcher onwards are symbolic of this deliberately chosen policy direction.

Under the Conservative government of Margaret Thatcher, people were encouraged to buy their own homes. Local authority housing was said to be of poor quality and badly managed and helped to sustain a 'nanny state', making people dependent on 'welfare'. It was, therefore, a political decision to decrease investment in social housing and sell off existing stock through the right-to-buy scheme. This allowed council house tenants to buy the property that they had rented from the council at hugely discounted rates. For families, some of them on low incomes, this gave them a chance to own their own home for the very first time. Or at least to buy it and sell it on quickly at a very healthy profit. But although this may have given some families the chance to have the sort of investment that they could never have otherwise dreamed of, it took hundreds of thousands of state-subsidised homes permanently away from the public sector. This housing was never replaced.

The direction of government policy ever since has been to remove housing stock owned and controlled by local authorities into the private sector, largely to housing associations. The social housing that has been left under local authority control has largely been less desirable homes on large estates. At the same time as state-subsidised housing has diminished and been residualised, rents have gone up.

These policy decisions through successive governments have led to the death of council housing in the UK. Their legacy is a housing shortage that seems almost impossible to ever see being manageable. As a result of social housing being in short supply, the private rented sector has also seen prices rise. This again affects the poor, who are more likely to be without secure, permanent and appropriate housing. In other words, many families and single people living on low incomes may have a roof over their heads, but they can still be classified as homeless.

The final cause of homelessness to think about is a number of individual circumstances that can be grouped together. These include personal

Stuart Isaacs

circumstances such as no longer being able to stay with family or friends. This could be due to emotional tensions or simply changing circumstances, such as the friend moving away. Relationship breakdown is another common cause of homelessness. So, too, are mortgage arrears and loss of tenancy. These latter two may relate to individual circumstances, but they are likely to also have a general, underlying social cause. In fact, potentially, all these individual factors that social scientists have consistently recorded as significant could have a relationship to poverty. For example, one of the most common reasons for relationship breakdowns is problems over household finances. Demographic change, government policy and individual circumstances can all be said to be causes of homelessness. However, as we have seen, although individuals will have particular, personal issues, there often are structural factors affecting these. The most common is to do with low income. This is borne out by the fact that those groups which are identified as officially poor (HBAI) or have been targeted as more likely to be socially excluded are also the most vulnerable to homelessness. Increasingly, the homeless population is made up of elderly people on low incomes, young people who have struggled to find jobs and victims (mostly women) of domestic violence and harassment. Asylum seekers are also increasingly homeless, often ending up as rough sleepers as they have no familial support or friendship networks.

Of the causes given here, it is government policy that might be said to be the factor that we have most control over. It may come as a surprise, then, that attention to homelessness as an issue of welfare came very late in the day. Given that the modern Beveridge welfare state was established in the mid-1940s, it wasn't until 1977 that we had the first attempt at a coherent national strategy to deal with homelessness. If we situate homelessness as an aspect of government housing policy, then it is not hard to see why this might be. Except for exceptional periods after the First and Second World Wars, all governments have been reluctant to engage in costly, state-led house-building programs. Rather, UK governments have prioritised home ownership. A private and privatised model of housing is the cultural and political tradition in the UK. Given the preference of political decision makers to prioritise homeownership, it is no wonder that the homeless were off the mainstream welfare radar for so long.

It wasn't until the 1960s that pressure really built up, external to government, for something to be done about homelessness. The 1960s were a boom time in Britain. This period has often been labelled 'the affluent society'. There were full employment, good wages and a growing economy. Young people had money in their pockets for the first time, and a youth culture developed around their styles and music. This was the time of 'swinging London' and the Beatles and a sense that the class barriers were down. Everyone had money. Britain was becoming a truly modern, meritocratic society. Part of this affluence was the affordability of consumer goods, particularly TVs. This brought entertainment into people's living rooms. But it also brought facts that they had perhaps previously not known. One evening in November 1966, millions of people sat down to watch a programme called *Cathy Come Home*. It told the story of a young woman living with her family who is let down by the welfare state and in the end loses her husband, her child and her home. Thousands of people rang the BBC to offer the now-homeless Cathy a place to stay. They were touched by how easy it seemed for an ordinary young woman to become homeless. But this wasn't a documentary; it was a drama. The awareness that this was a fictionalised account that was symbolically telling the story of what was happening to thousands of people in the UK's affluent society made the issue even more pressing. The programme provoked debates in Parliament and huge support for the newly set up homeless charities of Crisis and Shelter. It was the momentum from this TV programme that just over ten years later finally saw the first statutory provisions for the homeless.

The Housing (Homeless Persons) Act 1977 introduced criteria that meant that all local authorities had a duty to house people who came under a new category of 'priority need'. On the one hand, this was a step forward in the recognition that people on low incomes were struggling to find secure, permanent, affordable homes. However, at the same time, it set clear limits on those whom local authorities could help. This is understandable, given the huge demand for state-subsidised housing. There had to be boundaries. However, 'priority need' constructed categories of the 'deserving poor' and 'undeserving poor' in a way that we have seen is part of the discourse of poverty in the UK.

The main people who were deemed to be 'deserving' were homeless women with children and women who were pregnant; people who were vulnerable due to age, mental illness or disability; and those who had lost their homes due to natural disasters. It was single people, particularly men, who were excluded from 'priority need'. They were deemed 'undeserving', following the British tradition that able-bodied individuals ought to take responsibility for their lives and find work. It was not until 1996 that an amendment was made to the 1977 act to include victims of domestic violence under 'priority need', thereby making them 'deserving'. New Labour's Homeless Act 2002 also extended this category to care leavers under 21 and 16- and 17-year-olds. Unfortunately, no extra resources were put in place for local authorities to cope with these newly discovered 'deserving' groups.

The use of 'priority need' is understandable as a pragmatic solution to manage high demand. Yet it also has an ideological and political aspect. In a rudimentary way, it makes it possible for government to lower the homelessness figures by sticking to the official statistics based on those accepted by local authorities. Perhaps more importantly, it has also constituted an

Stuart Isaacs

artificial difference among the homeless between those accepted as 'priority need' and those who are not. Campaigning organisations have tried to address this by constructing the idea of the 'hidden homeless'. These are the people who are not officially recognised as homeless but are no less homeless for all that. They are made up of single people as well as those who are deemed to have made themselves 'intentionally homeless'. It also includes, according to Shelter, over one million children who are living in poverty. These children might be living in conditions that are not considered to come under the legislation and qualify them for a place on the housing waiting list, but their circumstances are still such that they do not have a secure, affordable and appropriate home. For example, families living in overcrowded conditions. This might seem a trivial issue, but for many people, estimated at around half a million, it is a serious problem. It might mean school children not having a space for homework or study, which undermines their education; teenagers not able to have any privacy; or young children having to sleep with their parents.

Sofa surfing is another predicament of the 'hidden homeless'. This is an increasingly common experience for many young people. Unable to remain with parents, perhaps because of arguments or overcrowding, they skip from one friend's sofa to another. Single people on low incomes who may not have work or who experience sporadic employment have very little chance of securing a permanent affordable home. Private rents have increased as social housing has declined. And house prices are way out of reach.

The lack of resources given to local authorities by central government means that even for those they do accept, they do not have enough social housing to place them in. These families likely will be forced to live in unsuitable bed-and-breakfast accommodation, sometimes with waits of many years before they secure a permanent home. The lack of sufficient funding means that local authorities have to implement 'strict eligibility' rules. In other words, if you turn up at a housing office to register as homeless, it will attempt to get rid of you. In particular, it will try to find out if you have become intentionally homeless. Intentionality can be broadly interpreted under the legislation. So if you have not been able to afford your rent and are being evicted, perhaps because you lost your job through no fault of your own, this is generally classified as you making yourself intentionally homeless! This reflects the situation that social housing in the UK has now become a minimal provision.

9.6 Summary

We began the chapter by looking at the poverty line as a way of defining and measuring poverty. This approach, developed by the early social surveyors, uses quantitative data to highlight statistical and demographic information. This is a useful tool for relating general trends and telling us which social groups are most affected by having low incomes. However, it is a limited measure as it does not highlight other aspects of poverty: namely, its social construction and the broader context of social exclusion. That said, for governments, the use of a base-line measure of average household income is very useful. It allows the state to apply a universal measure to legitimate claims for income maintenance. It also facilitates national policy making under the assumption that the circumstances of the poor are similar. The introduction of Universal Credit by the Coalition government is a good example of this.

The social construction of poverty was the next aspect of poverty that was explored. It was argued that poverty is not a neutral, value-free social condition that is capable of being captured by statistics. This is because there are moralising discourses that have developed that construct how we think of the poor in particular value-laden ways. One of the most powerful social constructions of poverty has at its centre the view that the poor are lazy, work-shy individuals who are happy to live off the luxury of state benefits, paid for by the taxes of 'decent, hard-working families'. In this way the problem of poverty is not understood as a social problem, with underlying institutional and structural causes, but, rather, a moral lack of responsibility on the part of individuals. Such a perception can symbolically be traced back to the ethos of the workhouse, which distinguished between the 'deserving poor' (who were willing to work) and the 'undeserving poor' (who were unwilling to accept low-pay conditions). The individualised moral construction of the poor in this manner ignores the structural issues that may have led to poverty. These might include issues of discrimination around ethnicity, disability, gender or class as well as a lack of educational opportunity, poor housing, unemployment, issues to do with adult or childcare and ill-health. Furthermore, in the work of Polly Toynbee, we saw that, in fact, the poor are hard at work. Most households that rely on benefits have at least one person in work. The poor often work longer hours and in worse conditions than most people.

The social research that has been looked at reflects a view of poverty that has little relation to the notion of the poor as lazy and work-shy welfare dependents. It was maintained that the reason this perception remains a powerful one is the ideological dominance of neoliberal, free-market ideas: that is, the view accepted by the major political parties that private sector–led enterprises will always be the best means of distributing wealth. The state's role is merely as a regulator of market conditions. This is where the idea springs from that if an individual works hard they will 'get on'. But, as we have seen, the poor do work hard but remain tied to low-income jobs.

Stuart Isaacs

A theory of social exclusion was investigated as an alternative means of defining, measuring and constructing poverty. The development of this idea was traced from Townsend's socio-cultural argument about relative poverty to Charles Murray's analysis of the underclass. Using the broader notion of social exclusion, issues of poverty were deemed to go beyond matters of income and even further than the comparative cultural dimension of relative poverty measures. Rather, social exclusion highlights some of the underlying institutional and structural factors associated with poverty. These include educational underachievement, a lack of job-relevant training and skills and disadvantages around communication and transport, as well as possible issues of poor housing and health. It can be seen that these issues correspond with the types of social problems and structural issues indicated in the social research. This becomes even clearer when considering the social groups revealed by studies of social exclusion: lone parents, young people, people with a disability, the elderly with low incomes and black and minority ethnic groups.

New Labour's application of social exclusion when in government was examined to see at how it was applied in practice. It was argued that New Labour narrowed its commitment to social inclusion around paid employment. This was because it did not move away from the discourse of the poor that constituted them as lazy and work shy. New Labour's acceptance of neoliberal assumptions about the role of the free market and enterprise undermined its social exclusion strategies. These involved rather punitive measures against those who did not accept a welfare-to-work place. The New Deal for Young People was analysed in this respect. This highlighted that by not taking account of the views of the socially excluded groups that were being targeted, New Labour failed to appreciate how its welfare-to-work scheme would be received. For many young people, it was coercive: a way of getting them to work in no-hope jobs for very little wages. Consequently, the policy had the opposite effect to the one that was intended by creating a resistance to low-paid work.

The area of policy where New Labour did make a difference to poverty was through increasing cash benefits to poor families. This saw their incomes rise in real terms. It was maintained that this wasn't evidence that social exclusion as a theory could not be applied in practice but, rather, that it would not work in a universalist manner or by being imposed from the top down without a genuine engagement with its intended target groups. Furthermore, unless the individualistic, moralising discourse about the poor was disregarded, policy would never begin to approach the institutional structural issues underlying poverty.

Homelessness was given as a final example of the long-lasting legacy of this discourse. Not only did emphasis on homelessness by government develop rather late in the twentieth century, but when it did become a concern of the state, there was yet another construction of the 'deserving' and 'undeserving' poor embedded in it. Seen in the context of UK housing policy, homelessness and the need for affordable, state-subsidised social housing have been undermined by the privileging of home ownership. It was argued that this was particularly promoted by political decisions made from the 1980s, notably the right to buy. The emphasis on homeownership has resulted in the decline of social housing. Thought about another way, there is nothing inevitable about wide-scale homelessness. It is the result of political decisions that have kept people in poverty rather than alleviated it.

 Key points

Defining poverty by using only a measure of household income is limited

To understand poverty fully, we need to have a method that incorporates statistical and demographic trends and an analysis of normative debates and allows for the examination of the structural causes of poverty. Investigating the social construction of poverty and looking at the broader features associated with social exclusion equips us to do this.

Poverty in the UK is often constructed as an individual issue, not a social problem

Political discourse and successive government policy decisions situate poverty as the responsibility of the individual. If a person is poor, they are deemed not to have taken their educational opportunities or not been willing to work. This is a morally loaded constitution of the poor as lazy and work shy. It is often associated with the view that the benefit system perpetuates a lack of moral responsibility. Welfare is understood not as necessary social security for vulnerable people, but as an easy ride of cash benefits that encourages a workless lifestyle. This perspective is often tied to an underlying ideology that takes the free market as an equitable and meritocratic distributor of wealth and life chances.

Social research continually indicates that the poor work hard and that cash-based social security is essential to tackling poverty

All the main official and academic statistical indicators available highlight the fact that the poor want to work and that most of them do work. The vast majority of benefits are given to the 'in-work' poor.

Stuart Isaacs

There is no social research to suggest that any group identified as socially excluded are unwilling to work. These people just want to be able to access jobs that can give them meaningful occupations and the potential to improve their social circumstances. Welfare initiatives by New Labour that increased cash payments to those in child poverty made a real impact on the lives of these families. Conversely, the introduction of Universal Credit is likely to take away the gains that many low-incomes families saw during the early part of this century.

Social exclusion in theory and its application in practice were very different

There is a wide and complex academic debate about the meaning and application of social exclusion. Discussions centre on the need for consultation and voluntary participation by targeted groups, as well as on social justice. However, when New Labour attempted to apply social exclusion to policy, it did so in an authoritarian and reductionist manner. Work was taken as the main route to social inclusion. The jobs created under the New Deal were predominantly low paid, without any career prospects. This led to a large degree of resistance, especially among young people.

Homelessness is a feature of poverty that successive governments have ignored

If we are looking for an example of the way that individualised moral discourses and the orthodoxy of neoliberal ideas have affected policy decisions, then the issue of homelessness is a prime one. There has been a continual reluctance by governments to fully fund state-subsidised housing, to the extent that the state has all but removed itself from this area of collective welfare responsibility. Homelessness is in large part the result of political decisions. Political leaders have failed to seriously address one of the most important welfare issues associated with poverty.

 Coursework questions

Is social exclusion a useful way of measuring, defining and understanding poverty?
Can a notion of social exclusion work in policy practice?

To what extent is poverty an issue of individual responsibility? To what extent is it a consequence of social institutions (like the welfare system and government policies) and/or social structures (like social class divisions)?

What are the main social problems associated with homelessness?

References

Chang, H.-J. (2010) *23 Things They Don't Tell You About Capitalism*. London: Penguin.

The New Deal for Young People. (2002, February 28) 'The new deal for young people'. National Audit Office report, HC 639.

O'Hara, K. (2014) *Austerity Bites: A Journey to the Sharp End of Cuts in Britain*. Bristol: Policy Press.

Shelter (2019) 'This is England: A picture of homelessness in 2019'. https://england.shelter.org.uk/professional_resources/policy_and_research/policy_library/policy_library_folder/this_is_england_a_picture_of_homelessness_in_2019

Townsend, P. (1980) *Poverty in the United Kingdom: A Survey of Household Resources and Standards of Living*. London: Penguin.

Toynbee, P. (2003) *Hard Work*. London: Bloomsbury.

 Further reading

McClenaghan, M. (2020) *No Fixed Abode*. London: Picador.

McGarvey, D. (2018) *Poverty Safari*. London: Picador.

Stuart Isaacs

chapter 10

Researching social problems

Anne Foley

10.1 Introduction

Research is central to life at university, and it is important to learn the basics early in your studies to get off to a good start. Essentially, research is the systematic investigation into phenomena with the aim of establishing facts and reaching new conclusions. There are many different levels of research which this chapter will not describe in any depth as numerous excellent guides to research in general are published every year. A number of these are listed in the 'Further reading' section at the end of this chapter. The role of research in the area of social problems is to attempt to understand the assumptions surrounding social problems, to describe the issues, to look for causal relationships between particular factors and to begin to outline a more thorough explanation of the construction of social problems. Having done this, the research can lead towards if not solutions, then a more comprehensive appreciation of why and how social problems emerge into the public sphere and how government and other agencies respond.

10.2 Primary and secondary research

Primary research involves the researcher directly collecting original data by methods such as interviews, surveys, questionnaires and focus groups. Before carrying out primary research, the researcher will usually have done some secondary research into their topic by carrying out a literature review. A literature review is an appraisal of published works in a topic area and the scope of the review is dependent on the extent of the enquiry being carried out. The literature review informs and supports the research.

To carry out a rigorous literature review, it is necessary to develop the ability to plan and execute effective literature searches. Undergraduate students may be required to carry out a limited amount of primary research during their studies, but typically, secondary research in the form of literature searches for essays and literature reviews is more common. For essays and other coursework, regardless of the scope, students need to carry out literature searches to identify literature that will inform and underpin their analysis of an issue and provide evidence for claims and arguments. This chapter focuses on the skills and knowledge necessary to carry out effective literature searches, as well as outlining the range of literature students are likely to encounter during their studies.

10.3 Introduction to literature types and uses

Success in assessments and study develops from critical interaction with a wide range of literature. To begin this process, it is necessary to become familiar with the types of literature available in, and appropriate to, academic contexts.

The literature is made up of a broad range of material, available either in print or online, written by individuals and/or groups. The literature can be divided into two general areas: academic (also called scholarly literature) and non-academic, which comprises popular literature and trade or professional literature. The main sources of literature are:

Books: textbooks, readers, monographs
Journal articles
Conference papers
Grey literature: reports, white papers, policy documentation
News media

Academic books are not all the same; they have various features and purposes, depending on the category to which they belong. This section will help identify the characteristics and intended uses of different types of books.

Textbooks

Textbooks provide a comprehensive overview of a subject and are written for student readers. They are useful for those unfamiliar with a specific subject or topic and provide introductions to key theories and context. As the purpose of textbooks is mainly introductory, and they are therefore

Anne Foley

general in nature, they are best used as launchpads for more in-depth study. Textbooks contain comprehensive reading lists and references to original works in topic areas. Example: Giddens, A. (2017) *Sociology*. 8th edn. Cambridge: Polity Press.

Readers/handbooks

These provide an in-depth view of a subject and are the work of several authors. They provide different perspectives on topics and are essential for critical examination of these topics. Handbooks are compiled by an editor or editors, who choose the handbook's content. Editors may or may not contribute chapters but always provide an introduction. Example: Greve, B. (2020) *Routledge Handbook of the Welfare State*. London: Routledge.

Subject-specific and general reference books

Reference books are used for precise information such as the correct spelling and meaning of a word, the exact meaning of a phrase within a specific discipline or synonyms (alternative words) and similar words. Examples:

Language dictionaries (e.g. *Oxford English Dictionary*)
Subject-specific dictionaries (e.g. *Dictionary of Social Policy* or *Dictionary of Sociology*)
Thesauri (e.g. *The Oxford Thesaurus*)

In the study of social problems, other reference books may be useful; these include directories, which give details of organisations and people. An example of a directory is the *DWP Public Bodies Directory* published by the UK Department of Work and Pensions (DWP), which gives details of public bodies sponsored by the DWP. Also, public groups publish directories and/or handbooks. For example, *Welfare Benefits and Tax Credits Handbook*, produced annually by the Child Poverty Action Group.

Monographs

In an academic context, the word *monograph* usually refers to a scholarly work that covers a single topic in depth, usually reporting the findings of primary research carried out by the author. Monographs are written mainly for an audience of academics and postgraduates, and, as their focus is typically narrow, they may be of limited use to undergraduate students. However, monographs are generally excellent for a thorough exploration of a topic.

Grey literature

The term *grey literature* refers to published and unpublished research and reports not controlled by commercial publishing groups. Grey literature is produced by governments, commercial and public organisations and private individuals and can be in print or electronic format. Significant sources of grey literature in the area of social problems are government documents and research reports produced by public organisations such as the Joseph Rowntree Foundation (www.jrf.org.uk).

Conference papers and proceedings

Conference papers are produced by researchers from, amongst other sources, university research institutes, advocacy groups and professional organisations and detail the findings of specific research carried out by that researcher or group. At conferences, researchers present papers detailing their research findings, and these may then be published either as individual papers in journals or in volumes. The volumes of collected papers are called conference proceedings and may be available on the website of the producing organisation. Conference papers may be published in journals or written up as monographs.

News media

Newspapers and other news media can be very useful but are not academic literature. The advantages of using newspapers for information when researching social problems are many; for example, you could compare how different types of newspapers (tabloid and broadsheet or those considered right wing or left wing) report on issues such as single mothers, poverty and youth crime. You may notice a sometimes-subtle, sometimes-blatant difference between the positions taken on these topics by different newspapers. Also, newspapers can provide a good historical overview of a particular issue. Most universities provide access to news databases, such as NexisUK, which can be searched for articles in a topic area.

Journals

These are a key resource for students and researchers; learning how to locate and use articles from journals in your subject area is a skill best learned early in your studies. From experience, I am aware that many students find journals difficult to understand, to find and to use. The prominence given to journals in this chapter reflects this. The advantages of using journals articles in your research are the following:

> They contain up-to-date information and debate on current topics in your subject area.

They contain specialised information that may not be available elsewhere.
They describe research by experts in your subject area.
Many academic journal articles are peer-reviewed before publication. This means that the articles in them have a guarantee of quality as they have been scrutinised and approved by other experts in the subject area.
The works cited in articles are a useful source of further relevant information.

10.4 How journals are organised

A journal, also referred to as a periodical or serial, is a publication produced on a continuing basis. New issues maybe published monthly, quarterly, or bi-annually. The non-academic equivalent to a journal is a magazine, such as *The New Statesman*. The titles of journals, for example *Critical Social Policy*, usually give a good indication of the general focus of the subject matter to be found in the articles within. As they are published on a regular basis, journals have volume and issue numbers to help identify and locate them. The volume number usually covers a specific year (e.g. 2021 may be Volume 45), and the issue number refers to a specific instalment of the journal within that volume (i.e. Issue 1 or 2 or 3 etc.), depending on how many times per year the journal is published. Sometimes, the month of publication is used instead of an issue number. This information is key to locating specific articles.

There are two main types of journal:

Academic journals (also called scholarly journals) usually contain research articles written by subject specialists, scholarly commentary and critical evaluation of issues by experts – articles written in academic style. Most academic articles are peer reviewed, which means they have been evaluated by independent subject experts. Examples: *Critical Social Policy* and *Sociology: a Journal of the British Sociological Association*.

Trade or professional journals usually contain news articles and commentary on current issues. Articles are written in everyday language; they have practical information and often a 'jobs' section. Examples: *Sociology Review, Children and Young People Now.*

Each issue of a journal contains several articles written by subject experts, researchers or practitioners within the subject area. The title *British Journal of Sociology*, for example, indicates that this journal contains articles relating to all aspects of sociology. The title *British Journal of Sociology of Education* indicates that this journal contains articles within the sub-topic of education in sociology. Not all journals, as you can see from the examples here, have the word *journal* in the title.

There are three main types of articles:

In commentary/debate articles, an author may describe or evaluate a piece of legislation relating to a specific social group or critically examine and comment on several pieces of previous research.

In primary (or empirical) research, the author(s) have carried out first-hand research – for example, interviewing a group of young men about gang membership – and are presenting, describing, evaluating and drawing conclusions from their research.

In review articles, the author summarises, synthesises and draws conclusions from the published works of other authors.

The typical layout of a journal article reporting research looks something like the example here, but not all are laid out in this exact way.

Title: indicating/describing the subject covered in the article.

Author(s): name(s) and, often, their credentials/qualifications and place of work/affiliation.

Abstract: a summary of the article describing the article's purpose, research method (where relevant), findings and conclusions.

Keywords: words used to describe the main topics within the article. These are used for various reasons (e.g. when scanning for relevance of the article to your own studies or to help retrieve the article from an online database).

Introduction: sets the scene; describes what the article is about and what problem/issue is being addressed in the article.

Section heading: a detailed statement of the problem/issue being addressed. The title of the heading should indicate the specific sub-topic being described in that section.

Literature review: details literature related to the issue being addressed and how it informs the current work. Not all articles have a separate literature view section, but most research articles do.

Research methodology and/or method: if the article is describing research, this section describes the methodology and/or method applied to the research. It may also highlight key theories (such as feminism or multiculturalism) that are used in the paper.

Findings: if the article is describing research, this section details the results of the research.

Conclusion/discussion/recommendations: summarises the conclusions drawn from the research (if a research article); discusses the

Anne Foley

implications of the research findings for the topic area and may recommend further research.

References: an alphabetical list, by author, of the sources (e.g. books, journal articles, reports and statistics) referred to (cited) in the article.

10.5 Evaluating journal articles

This is a guide to a basic critical evaluation of a journal article. When evaluating an article, the main questions are as follows:

Is the article relevant to the topic you are researching? Is the content of the article reliable?

To answer these questions, examine the article, asking the following questions:

What is the main issue being discussed? Is this issue significant/relevant to the topic you are researching? The abstract and/or keywords will usually provide enough evidence to help you decide.

Is the article related to the UK (geographical context)? This is of significance to many courses in the social sciences as government policy and practice issues are country specific. However, if you are doing a comparison between the UK and another country, you will obviously need articles relating to that country. The abstract, keywords and references made in the main content of the article will indicate the geographical context.

Does the author provide their credentials (authority)? Do these credentials indicate that this author has the expertise or experience to write on this topic? This can be established either alongside the author's name, under the title of the article or in the main content of the article.

What are the major concepts discussed in the article? Is the article dealing in depth with issues relating to the topic you are researching? Also, you may need to establish the theoretical standpoint or approach of the author – such as critical, feminist, Marxist – or a combination of theoretical standpoints. Sometimes the author will state their theoretical standpoint, but often this is implicit in the text.

What are the important facts presented in the article? To quickly establish this, look at the conclusion, as this is where the facts and findings are summarised.

Can you verify the facts presented by the author in the article? A scholarly/academic article will have citations within the text, used to provide evidence of claims made, and a reference list providing the full details of the sources of these citations.

What conclusion does the author come to about the main issue? Do these conclusions match your own views on the issue (or those of other authors whose works you have read)? If not, are the arguments good enough to make you reconsider your own views? If not, can you find evidence from other articles or sources to support your views? Do they make a more persuasive argument and, if so, why?

What are the arguments presented as evidence of, or supporting, the conclusions drawn at the end of the article? Do the facts presented by the author support the arguments? A good scholarly article will present the evidence in a clear, systematic manner, laying out each issue and describing exactly how the evidence proves the claim the author is making in the conclusion. Sometimes the author's conclusion is that the research has not provided clear evidence to support an issue and recommends that further research is necessary.

Does the author use emotional words or phrases, or is the article written in a neutral manner? A good academic/scholarly article should not use emotional terminology or words in order to influence the reader into accepting the author's views. An argument written in a neutral, emotionless manner, presenting evidence for claims made, is a key element of a good academic article.

10.6 How to recognise a journal article reference (Harvard referencing style)

Figure 10.1 is an example of a journal article reference. It is important that you recognise the journal title as this is what you will need to search your library catalogue.

Journal articles references can be easily distinguished from book references as book references do not have a volume or issue Number. There is

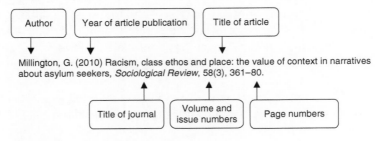

Figure 10.1 Journal article reference

Anne Foley

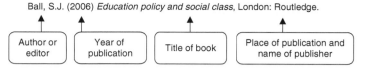

Ball, S.J. (2006) *Education policy and social class*, London: Routledge.

| Author or editor | Year of publication | Title of book | Place of publication and name of publisher |

Figure 10.2 Book reference

no place of publication or name of publisher in a journal article reference, as there is in a book reference. Figure 10.2 is a book reference.

Finding a journal article via a library catalogue

The key to finding a journal article is first to locate the journal title. The process is similar to finding a chapter in a book; when you need to find a particular chapter in a book, you search for the book's title first, not the chapter. First search for the journal title; when you have located that, then find the year the article was published, then the volume number, then the issue number, then the page numbers. When you have familiarised yourself with how a journal reference is laid out (see Figure 10.1), finding an article is easy. Most library catalogues have a specific area for journal searches.

Most journals are available online, usually accessible via your library catalogue, with a username and password. Databases, in this context, are searchable collections of journal articles; enter keywords or phrases into database search boxes to retrieve articles related to your topic. Some databases are subject specific; PsyARTICLES, for example, is a database of scholarly literature in the field of psychology. Some databases are multidisciplinary; Academic Search Complete, for example, is a database of scholarly literature in the social sciences, humanities and sciences. Databases are searched using keywords or phrases, rather than sentences. Extract the keywords and phrases from your topic and use these to retrieve articles from a variety of journals. No single database will have the full text of every article published on a topic. Some databases, such as the International Bibliography of the Social Sciences (IBSS) will provide no full-text access but are invaluable for locating information about published articles. These are known as indexing and abstracting databases or services.

10.7 Government documents: green papers, white papers, bills and Acts of Parliament

Government documents are a key resource in the study of social problems, and most are available online, on government websites. When researching homelessness in the UK, for example, it is important to be familiar with legislation related to statutory homelessness, such as the 1996 Housing Act and the Homelessness Act 2002. The text of these documents and all other UK legislation are available on the website legislation.gov.uk. During the process of enacting an Act of Parliament, green papers, white papers and bills are produced by the government. Green papers are the first step, with the intention of setting out the government's objectives in a particular area, and the public are invited to comment on these. 'Quality & Choice: Decent Homes for All (2000)' is an example of a green paper. The next step is the white paper, a more detailed document, which incorporates comments and further research and is more detailed. 'Building Britain's Recovery: Achieving Full Employment (2009)' is an example of a white paper detailing the UK government's plan to tackle unemployment. The next step is the bill. Bills are discussed in the House of Lords and the House of Commons, and a vote is taken on whether to pass these. When a bill is passed, it becomes an Act of Parliament. In the Queen's speech of December 2019, several new bills were announced; these included the Withdrawal Agreement Bill for leaving the European Union.

10.8 Statistical data

Statistical data are a key resource in the study and research of social problems. The Office for National Statistics (ONS) is the main source of data relating to the population of the UK in areas such as health, education, ethnicity, housing, families, household spending and unemployment. A census is carried out in the UK every ten years (the next one will be in 2021), during which every home receives a questionnaire; the responses are collated by the ONS, and results are published online. In addition to census data, the ONS publish statistics on crime, business and the economy, transport and more. This data is used to inform policy making at a national and local level. Use the data available on the ONS website to support your arguments in essays and other coursework. When using statistics, ensure that you understand exactly what is being examined and what claims are being made in relation to the data.

10.9 Primary and secondary sources

Primary sources are contemporaneous accounts of events, written by people who witnessed the events. Some examples of primary sources are diaries, interviews, speeches, personal journals, photographs, film recordings and biographies. Secondary sources are less easy to define than primary sources; essentially, secondary sources make use of existing data, and many books and journal articles are often interpretations of primary data. The data was collected by somebody other than the author, who collects and interprets the data for his or her own purpose. Some examples of secondary sources are textbooks, journal articles, encyclopaedias, histories and reviews.

10.10 Reading at university

The main tasks at university are reading, researching and writing. Writing critically about a topic requires an understanding of the topic, which does not come from lectures or seminars alone. A report on research carried out at the University of Huddersfield (Stone et al. 2012) showed that students who borrowed the most books and accessed the most online resources got higher grades. Of course, it is not enough to just borrow a book or log in to an online journal or e-book; the literature has to be read critically in order to be useful. Reading at university is an acquired skill, and there are many good books and websites available to help students develop reading skills. Most universities provide study skills guides and classes or workshops; check out your university website or ask your librarian for information on these. Though the amount of reading at university can seem daunting, learning reading techniques will make the task much more manageable and maybe even allow some time for a social life.

10.11 Researching social problems: planning and carrying out a literature search

The task of researching for essays or other coursework can be approached in a systematic manner, whatever the subject or scope.

Developing a search strategy is arguably the most important part of any literature search. A well-considered search strategy saves time and returns the best available results. Keep the question 'What do I need to know?' in mind when planning and reading and review your search strategy regularly. Ask yourself what the key themes are and note down the answers. If you are unsure of any aspect of an assessment, ask your tutor. As you progress through your research, it is easy to lose focus and thus get diverted from your original goals. Review your progress regularly and return to your themes when reviewing any literature you find in your research. Ask yourself if the literature helps answer the question and serves as evidence to support an argument you want to make.

The first task in a good literature search is to carry out a thorough analysis of your topic.

➢ Extract the keywords and/or key phrases and consider alternative words or phrases (synonyms) associated with these. You will use these words and phrases, rather than sentences, when doing your literature search.
➢ Next, consider whether any of these need a specific definition. For example, the topics of homelessness and poverty are not clear-cut issues. Are you researching rough sleeping, those who live in hostels, those who sofa surf etc.? How will you define poverty?

- ➢ Are you focusing on a particular age range in the population?
- ➢ What geographical area are you focusing on? Do you want to find literature relating to the whole of the UK, to England only, to a city such as London only or to a borough within the city?
- ➢ What is your theoretical standpoint or approach (e.g. social constructionist, feminist, Marxist)?
- ➢ What do you already know about this topic? Did you attend a lecture and/or seminar on the topic? Have you got notes from these? Have you got a recommended reading list from your tutor?

When you have completed your initial topic definition, you should then turn your attention to a consideration of the resources you will use in your research. It is helpful to consider these in the manner laid out in Table 10.1, with resources available via your library in one column and web resources in the other.

Table 10.1 Planning a search strategy: resources

Library resources	Web resources
Books/e-books: Most academic libraries now have key texts, at least, available as e-books. This has generally been accelerated since the Covid pandemic.	**Google Advanced Search**: for reports from organisations, government documents etc. Use **site/domain search** to limit results to specific websites.
Databases: to find several journal articles on your topic, from various academic journals. For example: • **Academic Search Complete** • **IBSS** • **Sociological Research Online**	**Google Scholar**: for summaries of journal articles and books. Also possible to set up links to your university library collections and get direct access to full text, where available.
Individual journals in your subject area, such as: • *Journal of Social Policy* • *Race & Class* • *British Journal of Sociology* • *Critical Social Policy*	**Office for National S**tatistics: for national or regional statistics. The **Neighbourhood Statistics** section is useful for local data. **Zanran** Numerical Data: for reports and other documents containing numerical data in your topic area.
WorldCat Or a local version of this or other federated discovery tool.	**Relevant Websites**: e.g. • Joseph Rowntree Foundation • Shelter • ESRC • UK Social Policy Association

Anne Foley

Search techniques

Using search techniques can save time and ensure that searches retrieve relevant results.

Phrase search is a useful technique when you want to retrieve literature containing a specific phrase. Using quotation marks at the beginning and end of a phrase, such as "hidden homeless" or "social problems", ensures that the words are retrieved adjacent to each other, exactly as you entered them.

With Boolean searching, you can broaden or narrow a search using the Boolean operators *AND*, *OR* and *NOT*. For example, if you are searching for literature on the topic 'homelessness amongst young people in England' but want to limit your results to literature relating to the 'hidden homeless', Boolean searching can help you retrieve more relevant results.

Using *AND* limits the search; the results will have both phrases.
Example: "young people" AND "hidden homeless"
Using *OR* expands the search. This search will retrieve literature related to surfing therefore more results:
Example: "young people" AND "hidden homeless" OR "sofa surfing"
Using *NOT* allows you to eliminate results that you are not interested in.
Example: "young people" AND "sofa surfing" NOT "rough sleeping"
Using a symbol at the end of a word stem will retrieve all variants of the word. This is called truncation.
Example: **educat*** will retrieve the words *educate, education, educational, educator* etc.
Using a wildcard is similar to truncation, but only one letter is replaced. The most common symbol used in truncation is **?**, but **!** is also used.
Example: organi?ation will retrieve examples of both spellings of this word: *organization* and *organisation*.
Nesting is an effective way to limit results by using brackets (parentheses).
Example: (hidden homeless OR sofa surfing) AND "young people"
The phrases in brackets will be searched for first, and the Boolean *OR* is generally used.

10.12 Using search engines and reliable websites for research

A search engine is a piece of software used to search the World Wide Web (www). Google is the most popular search engine but not the only one; other examples are Bing, Alta Vista and Yahoo (directory search).

Meta-search engines bring together the top results from other search engines; some examples of these are WebCrawler, MetaCrawler and Dogpile. Google has some very useful features for students, such as Google Scholar, Google Advanced Search and Google Books.

> Google Scholar can be a good way to begin your research and to find journal articles, books and other academic literature in your topic area. It does not usually provide full-text articles, however, just abstracts or summaries of articles. However, it may be possible to set up links to your university library collections and get direct access to full text, where available. If not, when you find a journal article abstract that looks relevant, search your university's library catalogue for the journal. If the library subscribes, you may be able to access the whole article. The same applies to books found on Google Scholar and Google Books.
>
> Google Books searches only for books and often provides a preview of sections of these. Use the search techniques listed earlier to refine searches.
>
> Google Advanced Search allows for more refined searching of the web. This is crucial as not all web sites provide reliable information. One of the most useful functions on Google Advanced Search is the site or domain search, which searches specific sites only. When looking for government documents, which can be difficult, searching the domain. gov.uk limits results to UK government websites only. Similarly, use. nhs.uk for health information or, if you want to find documents from a local authority – for example, the London Borough of Tower Hamlets – use towerhamlets. gov.uk. Advanced Search also has the ability to limit searches to specific date ranges, countries, reading levels, and file types.

Using the main Google search can be useful for research also but be aware that not all websites are reliable or relevant to university-level studies. Tutors take a dim view of student work that references random websites. Instead of randomly searching Google for information on a topic, get to know the reliable subject websites and use these; often your tutors will list these along with the recommended reading for a subject.

10.13 Managing the literature search

When undertaking a literature search, it is a good idea to begin to keep records of searches undertaken from the outset. Use a table or worksheet like Table 10.2, listing the keywords and phrases you have used and the resources (databases, journals, books etc.) you have searched. This will save time and help you stay focused on the search topic.

Anne Foley

Table 10.2 Managing the literature search

Date	Keyword(s)/ phrases	Academic Search Complete	Sociological Research Online	IBSS	Dawsonera e-book database	Critical Social Policy	Google Scholar
21/03/2013	"Youth crime" AND "gangs"			X	X		X
23/03/2013	"youth justice" AND inequalities OR discrimination	X	X		X	X	

It is a good idea to begin taking note of references as soon as you identify the relevant literature. It is easy to lose this vital information, and this may result in charges of plagiarism if you paraphrase or quote directly from the literature without attribution. There are many ways of doing this, ranging from using reference management software such as End Note or RefWorks to simply noting the details on a Word document. Check with your tutor or librarian for information about the software available to you. When saving downloaded articles or reports, it is a good idea to organise these in folders and files – perhaps a separate file for each section of an essay. Additionally, always use the same naming format when saving downloaded items; use author's name and date, for example. Organising your literature in this way will ensure that you can find things easily when writing up your work, and you won't waste time saving duplicate copies.

10.14 Plagiarism and referencing

Many students new to university are concerned that their tutors will not approve of using citations and references in their coursework as it looks like they have no original ideas. This is not the case; citing the work of authors and using this as evidence to strengthen your own arguments is considered the best practice for students and researchers. Read a journal article or a subject handbook for evidence of how citations and references are abundantly used in the work of scholarly authors. Authors do this to acknowledge the work of others, work that has helped to inform their own work.

By not referring to the literature you have used and not using citations when you have quoted or paraphrased from the literature, you are committing plagiarism. Plagiarism can be avoided by learning how to reference and cite correctly in written coursework. Plagiarism is commonly defined as deliberately or accidentally taking someone else's work or ideas and passing them off as your own. Plagiarism is taken very seriously by academic institutions, and penalties for those who plagiarise range, depending on the seriousness of the offence, from expulsion to being required to re-submit assessed work. Plagiarism takes many forms; some common examples are:

- Copying the work of another student.
- Copying and pasting from websites.
- Paraphrasing from a source without providing a citation.
- Incorrect information in references.
- Not using quotation marks when quoting from a source.
- Changing some words from the work of another and presenting the result as your own work.

10.15 Collusion

Collusion is the unauthorised presentation of the work of another student, in whole or in part, for formal assessment. Students are very often required to work together in small groups, frequently to prepare presentations for assessment. These are authorised collaborative assessments and, as such, are not collusion. However, when students work together on a piece of individual coursework and then submit identical work, in whole or in part, then they are considered guilty of collusion. Working with other students, such as in study groups, is a very effective way to learn, but formally assessed coursework submitted must be the work of the individual student. Deliberately submitting somebody else's work or allowing somebody else to submit your work is collusion, and penalties for this are usually the same as penalties for plagiarism.

10.16 What are referencing and citation?

Referencing is the practice of acknowledging the sources you have referred to in your coursework. There are several different styles of referencing, but the Harvard system of referencing is generally used in the social sciences, except for psychology. In the UK, most universities have their own referencing guides. If you are unsure about which specific guide is recommended, check with your course leader. Harvard referencing has two parts: the reference list and in-text citations.

Citations are abbreviated details of sources you have used in your essays and are used within the text of the essays. If you have quoted, paraphrased or referred to the work of another person in your written work, you must cite the work you have referred to. Full details of the work are then placed in

Anne Foley

your references list at the end of your work. Your recommended referencing guide should have details of the exact format required for in-text citations.

Many students new to university find referencing confusing and begin to wonder if they should reference almost every sentence they write in essays. Obviously, this doesn't make sense as a certain amount of every essay will comprise what is known as common knowledge. Common knowledge could be described as facts known to a large number of people: facts that are easily accessible. To help clarify whether what you are writing is common knowledge or not, ask yourself if you were aware of the fact(s) before you started your studies. For example, the fact that Britain is a welfare state does not need to be referenced in an essay as this is a generally known fact. If, however, a student writes in detail about the foundations of the British welfare state, the student would have had to carry out some research relating to this era. Details about the reforms put in place by the Liberal Party in the early 1900s and descriptions of some of the Acts of Parliament from this era, such as the Children Act 1908, would therefore come from literature the student had read, and this literature would need to be referenced.

10.17 Your academic librarian

Almost all UK universities have subject specialist librarians whose role is to support students with their information and research needs. Wise students get to know their librarian early in their studies. Your subject librarian will support your studies by recommending resources for your essay topics and showing you how to search library resources such as the library catalogue, databases and journals. They can advise on referencing issues and on devising search strategies for literature searches. As well as offering individual support to students, teaching classes in the use of library resources and purchasing the books and journals on your reading lists, academic librarians create online guides for students in their subject areas. These subject guides are usually available on the library web pages and list key library and web resources in various subject areas.

10.18 Digital literacy and information literacy

Both digital literacy and information literacy are essential attributes for study, research, work and life-long learning. Information literacy involves knowing how to find, evaluate, use, manage and communicate information. Digital literacy involves finding, organising, managing and communicating information by means of digital technology. This chapter has outlined the skills and knowledge necessary to become information literate, and these skills can be transferred and used to plan any essay or other task requiring information gathering. Digital literacy encompasses the attributes of information literacy and also the ability to use digital communication tools and to carry out tasks in a digital environment. It is important to learn how to effectively use all the ICT tools you come across in your studies, including your VLE, to be aware of how you are representing yourself on social media sites and to communicate effectively and appropriately using digital technology.

References

Stone, G., Pattern, D. and Ramsden, B. (2012) 'Library impact data project'. *SCONUL Focus 54*, [Online] 25–28. www.sconul.ac.uk/sites/default/files/documents/8_0.pdf

 Further reading

Bryman, A. (2015) *Social Research Methods* (5th ed.). Oxford: Oxford University Press.

Burns, T. and Sinfield, S. (2016) *Essential Study Skills: The Complete Guide to Success at University* (4th ed.). London: Sage Publications.

Cottrell, S. (2019) *The Study Skills Handbook* (5th ed.). Basingstoke: Palgrave Macmillan.

Some useful websites for studying and researching social problems in the UK

British Youth Council: www.byc.org.uk/

Centre for Research in Social Policy, Loughborough University: www.lboro.ac.uk/research/crsp/

Child Poverty Action Group: www.cpag.org.uk/

Office for National Statistics: www.ons.gov.uk/ons/index.html

Refugee Council: www.refugeecouncil.org.uk/

Shelter: www.shelter.org.uk/

Zanran Numerical Data Search: www.zanran.com

Some useful websites for study and research skills

Learn Higher: Resources for students: http://learnhigher.ac.uk/home.html

Safari: The Open University: www.open.ac.uk/safari/

Social Research Methods: www.socialresearchmethods.net/

Index

Note: Page numbers in bold indicate a table on the corresponding page.